In this volume . . .

GET RID OF YOUR unattractive and inefficient closet doors by replacing them with modern bifolds. The whole closet becomes immediately accessible. See the article on page 770.

BUILD THIS CONNECTICUT shelf clock from the plans starting on page 750. The styling is authentic, the construction is clearly detailed and very simple, and the cost is low.

ABE LINCOLN was a handyman, and while living in New Salem he wove a new splint seat for this chair. Make the chair, then splint it yourself. See plans on page 650.

Look what you'll find in other volumes!

DESKS GALORE! Take your choice of these novel home offices. There's the "wall-hugger" (far right) that takes little floor space; the "in-a-chest office" (above right) that unfolds for your use; and the "split level" (right) that offers all kinds of room. See page 935 of Vol. 6.

HERE ARE MORE DECK IDEAS that can add charm to your home. The article in Vol. 6, page 920, shows details on building benches and rails, floor construction, deck patterns, and methods of attaching a deck to your house.

YOU CAN COLOR concrete. Make your patio and garden walks any color—or colors—you wish. See the article that starts on page 840 of Vol. 6.

BUILD A DECK to gain more room. It's one of the least expensive ways to extend your living space, and adds a great new dimension to outdoor living. The plans on page 914 of Vol. 6 show you all the construction details you need to know to add a "room" outdoors.

IF THE FOYER of your home looks a little drab, you can perk it up easily and quite inexpensively by remodeling the door and adding an archway made of translucent panels and hardboard precut in a filigree pattern. The article is in Vol. 8, page 1148.

YOU CAN MIX color into concrete before you pour it; you can dust it onto the surface after the concrete is poured, then trowel it smooth; or you can paint or stain the concrete after it has set. Your choice depends upon your project. See page 840 of Vol. 6.

BUILD A WINE RACK that suitably complements your selection of fine wines. In the article on page 3070 of Vol. 20, you'll find plans for this attractive counter rack as well as a charming hardwood rack and a lustrous rack made of plexiglass.

HERE'S A KNOCKOUT that will enhance any kitchen—a canister set that's a miniature version of old-time grocery bins. See the article on page 1594 of Vol. 10.

THIS BEAUTIFUL VACATION HOME would make a fine headquarters for anyone's holidays. You'll find a selection of other unique vacation homes, from an inexpensive "supercamp" to an updated A-frame, in the article on page 3010 of Vol. 19.

MORE AND MORE SMALL ENGINES are used in yard and garden tools. These portable power plants can save backbreaking labor, but also can be cantankerous. See the definitive article on small-engine servicing, with check-out lists, starting on page 1128 of Vol. 8.

BACKPACKING is a fine sport—but only if you're in shape. The same is true of virtually every other sport. On page 1158 of Vol. 8, you'll find specific exercises to discipline your body for backpacking, for canoeing, for climbing and for other sports.

ICE FISHING offers special rewards to the dedicated fisherman. In an article in Vol. 10 on page 1521, you'll find two quick projects for ice fishermen.

Popular Mechanics

do-it-yourself encyclopedia

in 20 volumes

a complete how-to guide for the homeowner, the hobbyist—
and anyone who enjoys working with mind and hands!

All about:

home maintenance
home-improvement projects
wall paneling
burglary and fire protection
furniture projects
finishing and refinishing furniture
outdoor living
home remodeling
solutions to home problems
challenging woodworking projects
hobbies and handicrafts
model making
weekend projects
workshop shortcuts and techniques
hand-tool skills
power-tool know-how
shop-made tools
car repairs
car maintenance
appliance repair
boating
hunting
fishing
camping
photography projects
radio, TV and electronics know-how
clever hints and tips
projects just for fun

volume 5

ISBN 0-87851-070-2
Library of Congress Catalog Number 77 84920

MANUFACTURED IN THE UNITED STATES OF AMERICA

contents

VOLUME 5

Outdoor furniture that's simply elegant

By PENELOPE ANGELL

■ THESE aluminum-and-canvas chairs can help you get ready for summer entertaining and relaxing. You can make them from ¾-in. Reynolds Do-It-Yourself Aluminum tubing with 90° elbow and T-butt connectors, available at hardware and building supply dealers.

Tools you need are minimal: steel tape measure, masking tape, large square, drill, hammer, screwdriver, hacksaw or tubing cutter, parallel clamp, center punch and Pop riveter.

SEE ALSO
Decks . . . Garden shelters . . . Gazebos . . . Grills . . . Kitchens, outdoor . . . Outdoor tables . . . Patios . . . Picnic tables . . . Planters . . . Privacy screens . . . Strawberry barrels . . . Yard lighting

Cutting: A hacksaw or tubing cutter can be used to cut the tubing. The cutter makes a more accurate cut, but the tubing will need reaming afterward. The saw cut needs less reaming but must be filed smooth.

Joining: Besides using 90° elbow and T-butt connectors, ¾-in. tubes can be joined together by fitting a piece of ⅞-in. tube over them and securing it in place with Pop rivets.

Bending: You can make 5-in.-radius bends in the tubing with a simple jig. When making bends be sure to carefully line up the dimension marks on your tube with the index mark on the jig to insure properly fitting parts. Also clamp the tubing between the jig blocks to prevent it from sliding during bending. Pull slowly so the tubing won't buckle. To help apply pressure when you make the bends, brace yourself against the table.

FOOTSTOOL

The jig for bending the tubing is a 10-in.-dia. wood disc of ¾-in. stock (with index marks drawn through the center) and two pairs of support blocks. Each pair consists of a ¾ x 1¾ x 13-in. block and a ¾ x 1¾ x 17-in. block, with a ¾-in. space between them for the tubing. A successful project depends on your bending the tubing accurately. For best visibility, it helps to make the bend dimension marks on masking tape pressed on the tubing. If you lay the jig parallel to the table edge, you can easily check right-angle bends with a large square.

Step 1: On a 6-ft. length of tubing, mark off 24 in. from each end. Place one tube end in the support blocks, carefully match the tube mark nearest that end with an index mark on the disc, clamp and make a 90° bend. Pull slowly and apply pressure. Repeat on the other end to form a U.

Step 2: Make a mark at 13 in. from each tube end. Place the tube ends into the jig so that the upright part is vertical as shown while you make the third and fourth bends. Make a 90° sideways bend at both ends. Afterward mark off 10½ in. from the ends, which will be cut off.

Step 3: Tubing can be cut accurately with a tubing cutter. The cutter curls the ends inward, so they must be reamed before the joints can be fitted. You might prefer using a hacksaw, then smoothing the ends after cutting.

Step 4: Repeat preceding steps to make a second unit. Then join sections with two 5-in. x ⅞-in.-dia. pieces of aluminum tubing telescoped over the ¾-in. tubing ends. Drill two holes through one side of the tubing; secure with Pop rivets.

The covering is made from a 17½ x 37½-in. piece of canvas. Join the short ends with a ¾-in. seam. Sew a 1-in. hem with a ¾-in. turn-under on the sides.

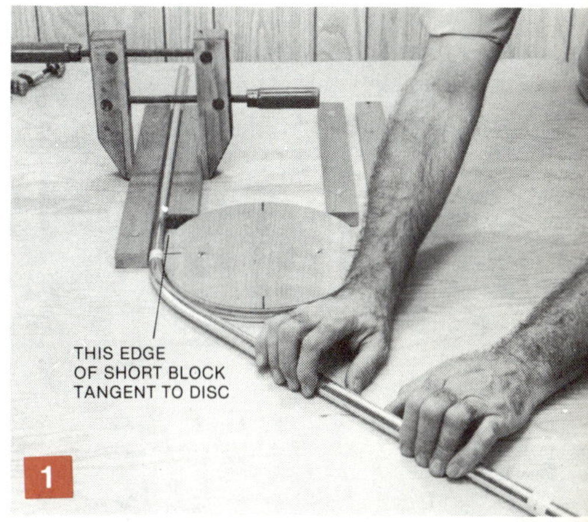

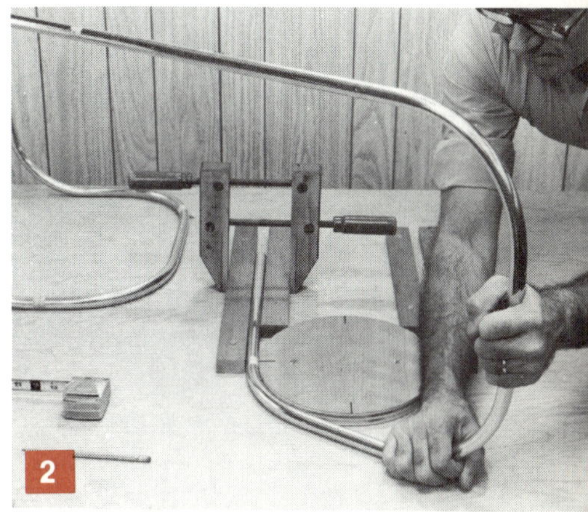

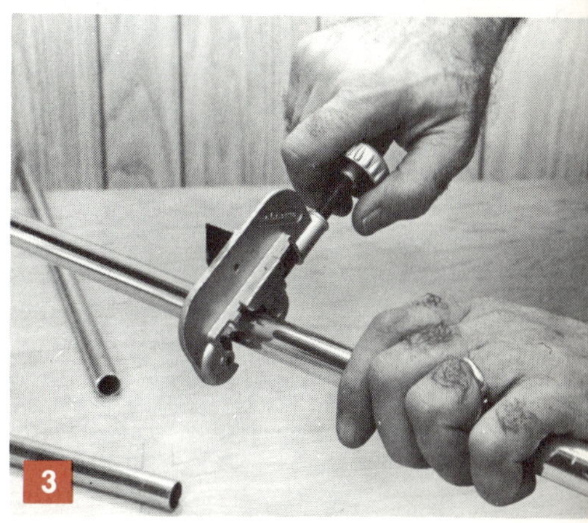

MATERIALS

6′ x ¾″-dia. tubes (2)
5″ x ⅞″-dia. tubes (2)
Pop rivets (4)
17½ x 37½″ canvas (1)

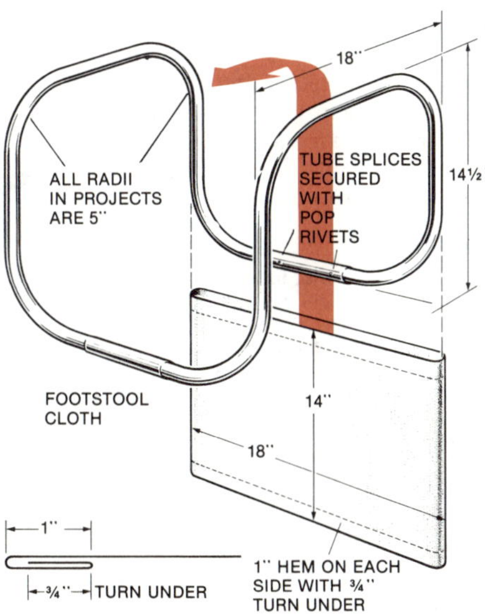

4

SMALL CHAIR

Step 1: To make the small chair, it's best to begin by making the chair back. Start with a 6-ft. length of ¾-in. tube and carefully mark off 23¾ in. from each end. Place a tube end in the bending block, match the tube mark nearest that end with the index mark on the jig and bend the tube 90°. Repeat with the other tube end to form a U.

Then give the back a slight backward bend for comfort. You can do this by marking off 17½ in. at both ends. Place the tube ends in the jig on edge and bend each side about 2½ in. off the axis.

To make the chair sides, begin with a 6-ft. length of ¾-in. tubing. Mark one end at 15⅜ in. and the other at 34¼ in. Placing each end in the blocks, match the

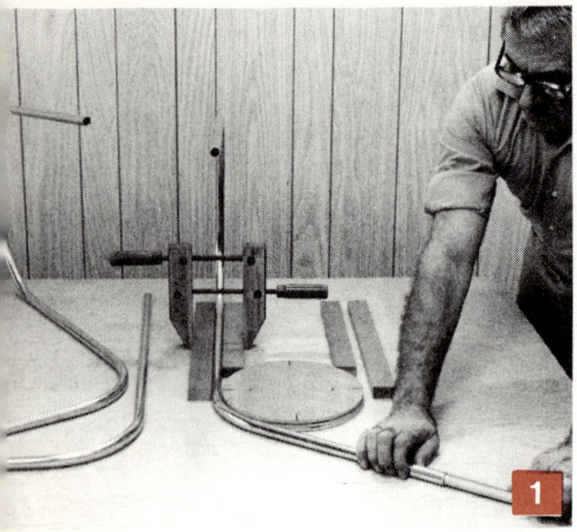

1

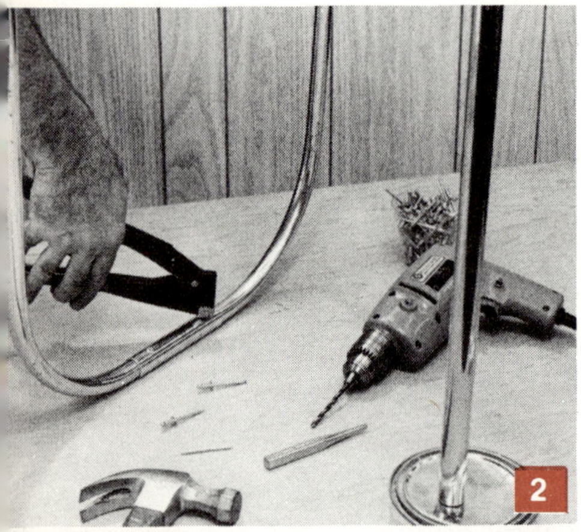

2

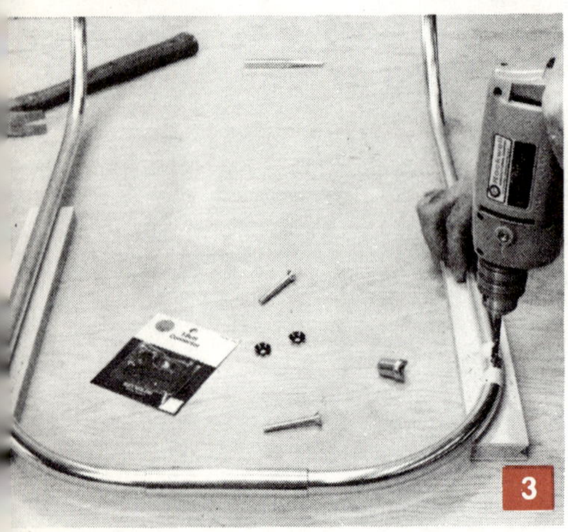

3

index marks with the tube marks nearest the end in the blocks and make 90° bends at both marks.

Now make a mark at 19¼ in. from the longer end and place the "U" part of the tube in the jig on edge. Grip the tube end to make a sideways bend which will be the third bend. To provide leverage to bend the short tube end, inset a ⅝-in. dowel into the tube as shown. This short length is the base of the chair.

Repeat the process for the second side, but make the third (base) bend in the opposite direction so the two sides (left and right) will join.

Step 2: Make a mark at 7⅜ in. from the base end of each side and cut off that excess. Join the two sections with a ⅞ x 5-in. tube splice secured with two Pop rivets.

Step 3: T-butt connectors (8) are used to assemble the parts. Allow an extra ⅛ in. for them when you're cutting the two cross tubes on the chair front and marking the base for the holes. For example, spacing between the chair sides is 17½ in., but the cross tubes are cut 17¼ in. to allow for the two connectors. The top cross brace is 13¼-in. high and the bottom cross brace is 2-in. high. The T-butt connectors consist of a locknut, connector and ¼-20 oval-head bolt.

To install the cross tubes, use a punch to get an accurate start, then drill a ¼-in. hole in the outside tube as shown. Use the oval-head bolt that comes with the connector to dimple (recess) the hole for a neat appearance. Lay the tub on a 2 x 4-in. board that has a ⅜-in. hole drilled in it to accommodate the bolt. Insert the bolt and strike its head with a hammer to make a neat dimple.

Step 4: After the bolt is inserted through the hole, place the connector over it and attach the locknut. Insert the tube as shown and tighten the bolt. The locknut spreads out against the tube wall when the bolt is tigthened.

Step 5: After you attach the sides to the two front cross tubes, insert the back into the base and then into the horizontal ends. The T-butt connectors can be removed, then reinserted. Later, the back will be loosened to insert the seat cloth.

Step 6: Cut the back cloth to the dimensions given. Finish the curved area with bias tape and fold the cloth in half. Make a ¾-in. side seam and a 1-in. bottom hem with a ¾-in. turn-under.

Step 7: Cut a 23½-in. canvas square for the seat. Make 1-in. front and back hems with ¾-in. turn-unders. Then sew 1½-in. side hems with ¾-in. turn-unders.

MATERIALS

6′ x ¾″-dia. tubes (3)
3′ x ¾″-dia. tube (1)
¾″ T-butt connectors (8)
5″ x ⅞″-dia. tube (1)
20½ x 31½″ canvas
23½ x 23½″ canvas

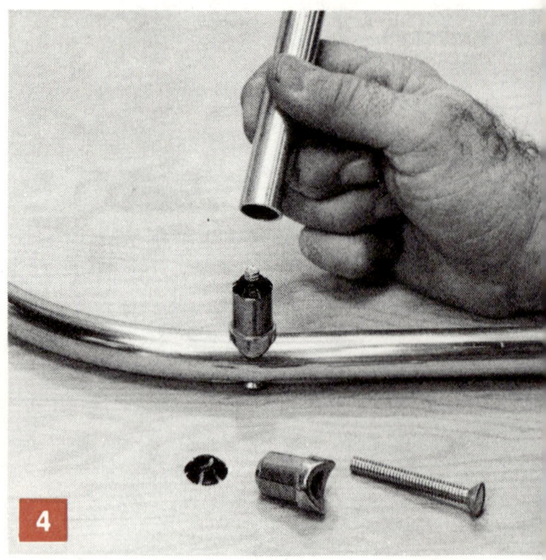

4

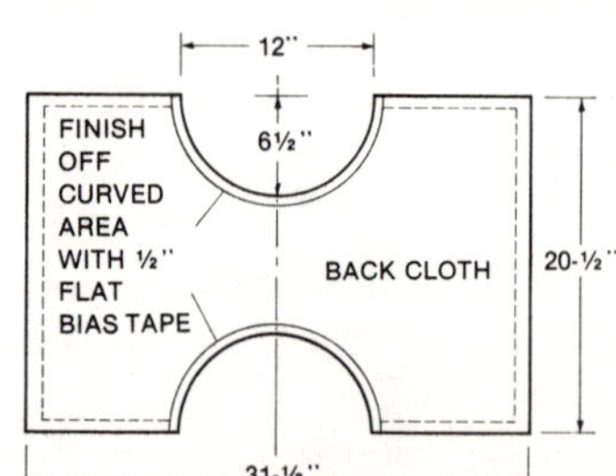

6

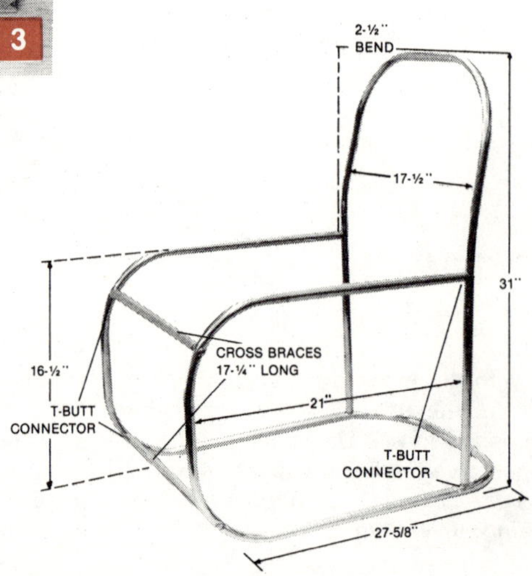

5

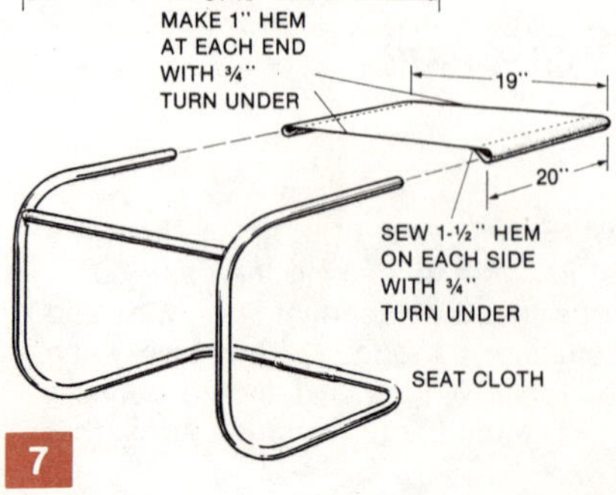

7

LARGE CHAIR

Step 1: To make the two sides, begin with an 8-ft. length of ¾-in. tube. Make marks at 8¾-in. and 39¼-in. from each end. Place the tube ends in the block and make the 8¾-in. bends at right angles on both ends. (Since only a small piece of tube will be held in the block, join a scrap piece of tube to the short end with a dowel and clamp firmly.) Next place the long middle part of the tube in the blocks and make the 39¼-in. bends to close the rectangle as shown. Join ends with a 5-in. x ⅞-in.-dia. tube splice and two Pop rivets, then make the second side.

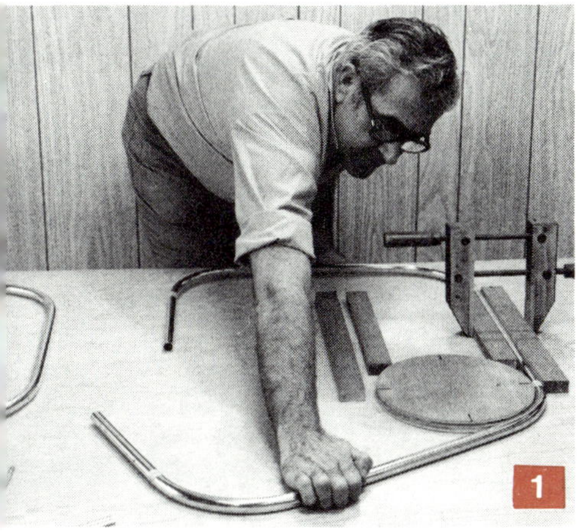

1

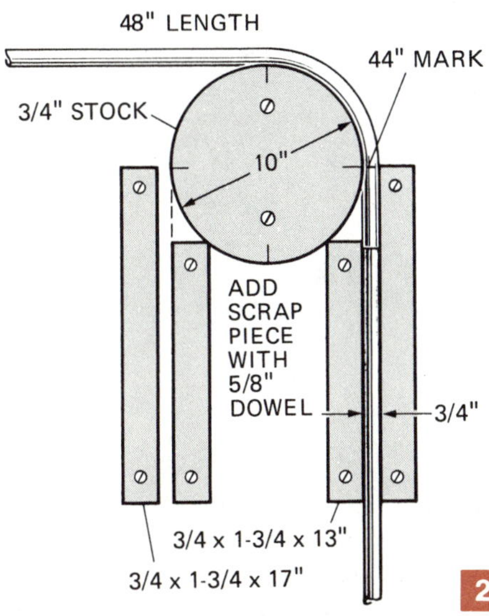

2

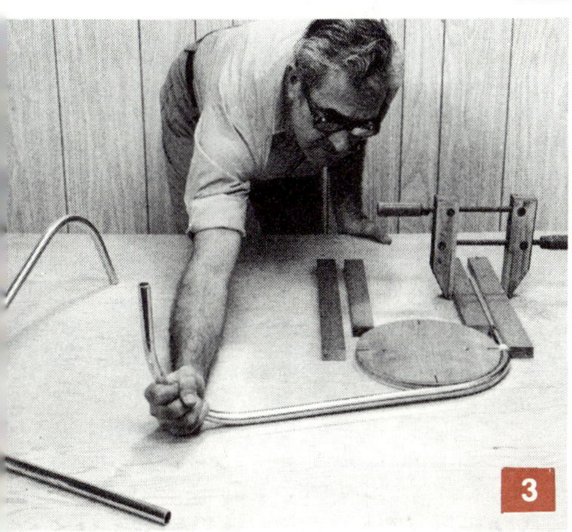

3

Step 2: To make the back, begin with a 48-in. length of tube (8 ft. halved) and mark one end at 44 in. Again add a temporary piece of scrap tubing with a ⅝-in. dowel as shown in the drawing so a sufficient amount of the tube can be held in the jig blocks. Bend two pieces in this way to 90° angles, then cut off ½ in. at their shorter, rounded ends.

Step 3: Still working with the two back pieces of tube, mark off 13 in. from their straight ends. Place the straight end of the tubing in the jig so the short bent end is held vertically in the air and makes a 104° angle. This will be the angle between the back and seat. You can mark the angle on the worktable as a guide. Bend one piece to the left, one to the right.

Step 4: You can make the upper back joint by inserting a piece of ⅝-in. hardwood dowel between the two tube ends. Two small nails will prevent the dowel from shifting and keep the joint secure. (A ⅞-in. tube splice as used before would make a bump in the canvas cover.)

Step 5: The front cross tube that is part of the seat is attached with a pair of 90° elbow fittings. Cut the cross tube to 17¼-in. length. (Elbow fittings have a 1⅛-in. makeup to complete the 19½-in. crossbar dimension.) Twist the fittings on either end of the tube clockwise to tightly secure them. Insert the free end of the elbows without the locknuts in the open end of the seat tube as shown.

Step 6: The elbow ends in the seat tubes are sécured with a self-tapping setscrew driven into the casting, as shown in the photo, when canvas is in place. Next cut three pieces of 19¼-in.

MATERIALS

- 8′ x ¾″-dia. tubes (4)
- 5″ x ⅞″-dia. tubes (2)
- T-butt connectors (6)
- 90° elbow connectors (2)
- 1⅝″ x ¼-20 oval-head bolts with nuts (2)
- 5″ x ⅝″-dia. dowel (1)
- Pop rivets (4)
- ⅝″ setscrews (2)
- 23½ x 58¼″ canvas (1)

4

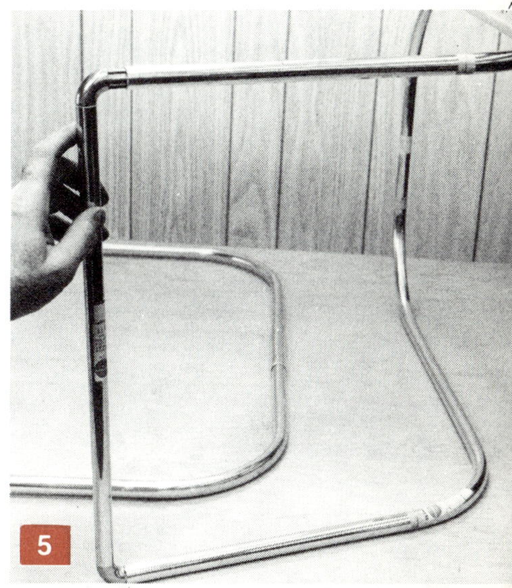

5

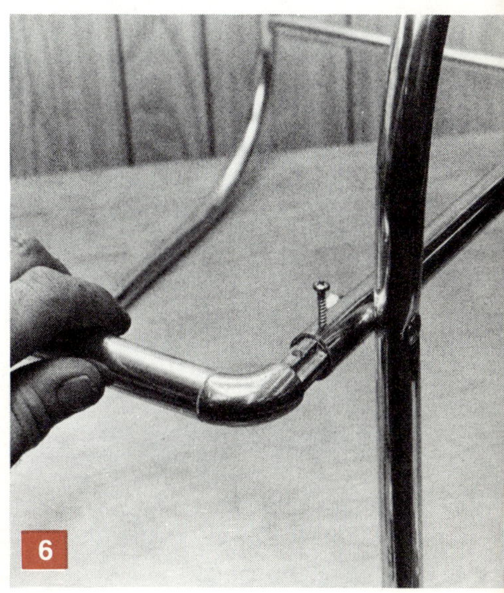

6

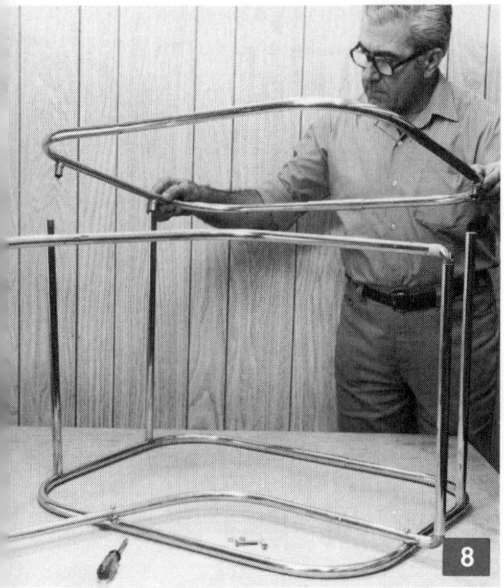

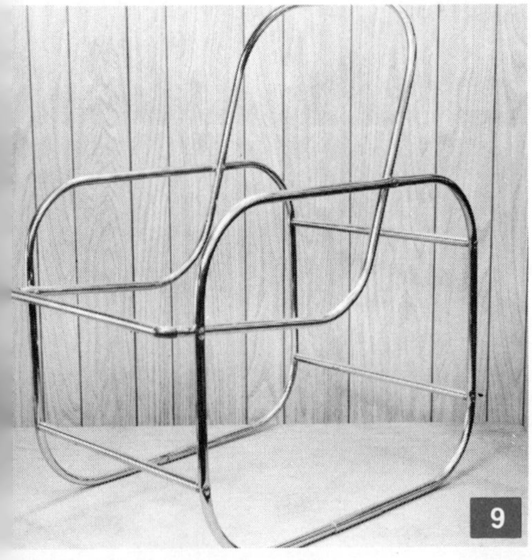

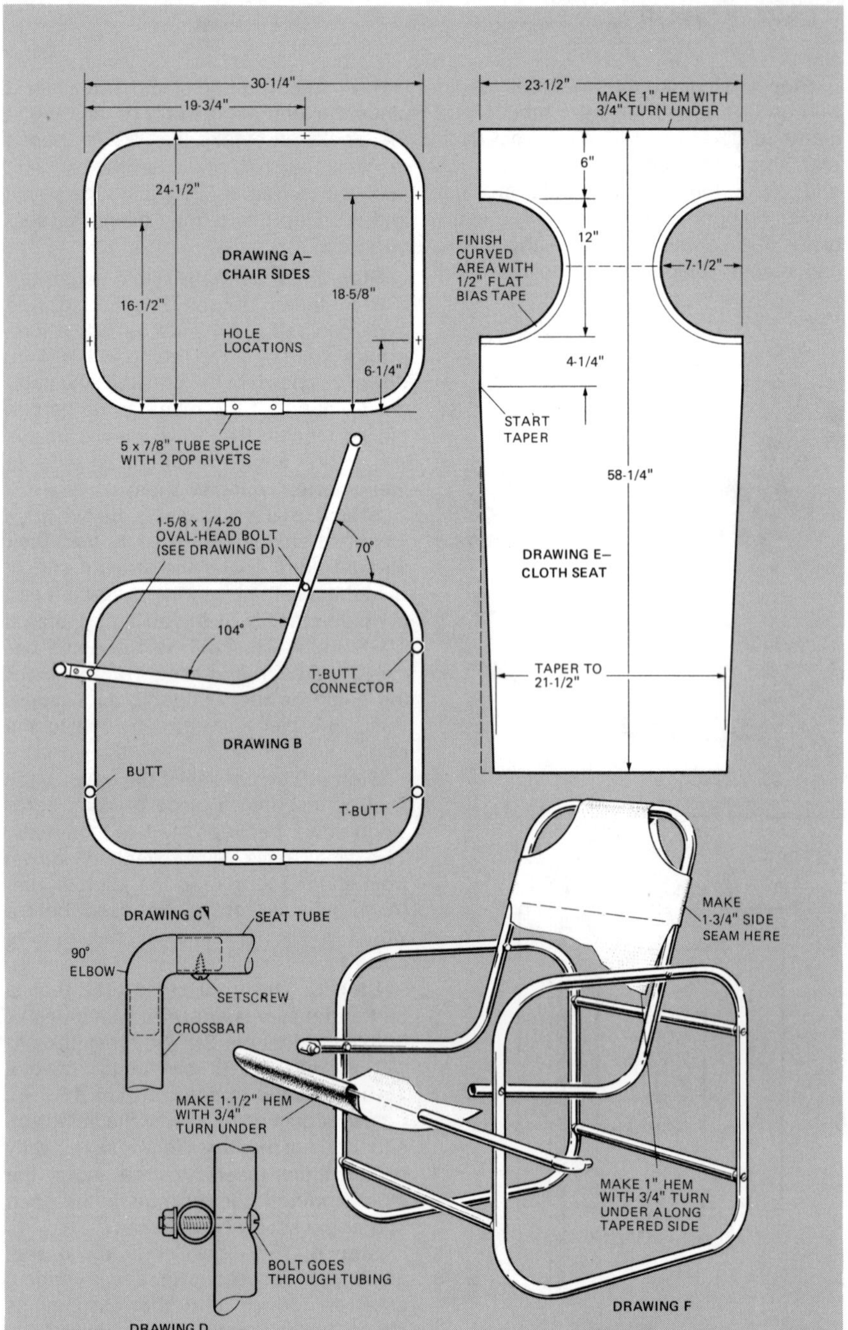

tube for the lower front crossbar and two back crossbars.

Step 7: Now you can drill the sides to receive the assembly bolts. Locate holes as shown in drawing A. Dimple the holes and insert the T-butt connectors and bolts as indicated in drawing B. Clamps and masking tape make an otherwise difficult job easy. Parts can be held together with tape to check alignment.

Step 8: Assembly should be done by first attaching the seat to one side, installing the three cross tubes with T-butt connectors, attaching the seat section with bolts as in drawing D, then adding the other side. All bolts should be tightened firmly after assembly.

Step 9: To make the cover, cut the canvas as shown and finish the curved area with bias tape, then taper the sides. Make a 1-in. top hem with a ¾-in. turn-under, then fold the top part over. Sew a 1¾-in. side seam as shown in drawing F. Make a 1-in. side hem with a ¾-in. turn-under along the tapered sides. Finally; sew a 1½-in. bottom hem with a ¾-in. turn-under. Then slip the canvas over the back; slide seat bar through bottom hem.

Rotary mower 'gases' lawn?

I've been told that rotary mowers with two-cycle engines—in which lubricant is mixed with fuel—damage lawns by exhausting gases and particles of unburned oil. I have noticed that many lawns have a yellowish-gray color a few days after mowing. Is this caused by the mower?—L.W., Ohio.

Could be, if the engine is in poor condition or the exhaust system is misdirected or damaged so that exhaust gases are directed downward onto the turf. I don't know that any tests have been run to determine if lawn damage results from engine exhaust. Offhand, I'd say this does not cause the condition you describe. Other possibilities are: mower set to cut too low, resulting in "scalping" the entire lawn or areas that may be slightly rolling or undulating; turf allowed to grow abnormally high between mowings; a dull blade which doesn't cut the grass cleanly.

Shingles 'washing' away

My home is only a year old and recently I noted that the gutters contain a quarter to a half inch of the fine particles with which the shingles are coated. The roofing is supposed to be good quality, but I'm wondering what's happening. Is my roof washing down the drainpipe?—G.S., Tenn.

I'd put this "problem" out of mind for the next 15 or 20 years. It's quite normal for asphalt roof shingles to shed the particles of slate with which they are coated. Some are loosened just in handling and applying. Others, not too solidly embedded, are loosened by rainfall, snow and sleet. Just clean them out of the gutters so that rainwater will flow freely.

Plaster patch shows

Before redecorating I patched an area about 1 ft. square on the ceiling. It shows under two coats of latex paint, although the second coat made it look much better than did the first. Did I omit something that should have been done?—D.E., Nebr.

I assume you used a prepared patching plaster but did you follow all the instructions? Check with a straightedge and you may find it's a little lumpy, which would cause high places to cast a shadow. Perhaps you can salvage the job by sanding flush, applying an undercoat of paint (same as used as top coat) and then spot-finishing the area. Better yet, apply another coat to the entire ceiling, as spot-finishing is not always satisfactory, although it can be done if you are careful to feather the edges.

Cracks in flooring

I live in an old house with wide floorboards, the cracks between the boards being about ⅛ in. wide. I've tried various fillers. No good; these break up. What can I use to fill the cracks permanently?—John Stanlow, Reading, Pa.

Slight movement of adjacent boards will tend to break up ordinary fillers or caulking. Assuming the boards are butted—not tongued and grooved—I know of a case where cracks were filled just below flush with the artificial rush used in caning chair seats. Then the cracks were filled flush with white lead paste colored to match the boards. Ample drying time before use must be allowed. Another method is ripping thin wedge-shaped strips from matching wood and tapping these into the cracks edgewise. Then the floor is sanded and refinished.

Latex over oil paint?

My old house needs repainting. Original paint seems to be in fairly good condition, needing only to be wire-brushed and sanded here and there. But I've got a question: Can I use a newer latex paint over the old paint?—J. Hendrickson, Sioux City, Iowa.

Latex paint can be used on a surface that has been painted previously with an oil-based paint if the surface is sound, clean and dry.

Basement water damage

Last summer, about 2 in. of water seeped into my basement and remained long enough to rust casters on my wife's washer, my workbench legs and two other castered pieces of furniture. I succeeded in brushing away most of the rust but the flooding can happen again. Is there any way to prevent damage to casters, other than blocking everything up?—F.D., Okla.

Seems to me it would be better to concentrate efforts to prevent more flooding. You do not say where the water is coming from—through walls or floor—but seepage through the walls can be prevented, except in extreme cases, by coating the walls with a masonry waterproofer. If water is seeping in at the point where the floor joins the walls, then a fillet of waterproof cement or caulking should seal it out. When applying the material, it is essential to follow instructions in all details; otherwise the application may not be successful.

Temporarily, however, you can purchase a number of fairly heavy plastic sacks and slip these over the casters when there is likely to be flooding.

THESE PROJECTS show Lincoln's talent as a do-it-yourselfer. He wove the seat for this rustic chair using hickory splint (right). The plans for the reproduction (left) include ash splint that resembles hickory.

A chair and a bootjack from Abe Lincoln

By DAVID WARREN

■ LINCOLN'S FATHER, Thomas, was a carpenter and the woodworking skills Lincoln learned as a young boy helped him later in life. In 1835, as a young man living in the frontier community of New Salem, IL., Lincoln moved from home to home and used those skills to help earn room and board. While boarding with Caleb Carman, Lincoln wove a new splint chair seat, as we show you how to do on page 652. Years later, as a practicing lawyer in Springfield, he made and used a simple bootjack (see page 655). We also show how to build the chair, following the plans on page 653.

SEE ALSO
Antique reproductions . . . Cupboards, china . . . Finishes, wood . . . Furniture, care of . . . Gossip benches . . . Hutch tables . . . Staining, wood . . . Varnish . . . Veneering . . . Wood finishes

selecting the chair's height

By today's standards, the original chair, photographed and measured at the Pennsylvania Historical Society, is low. The average person was shorter 150 years ago. We retained the original dimensions in our reproduction (it's a comfortable height for putting on shoes, boots and rubbers) but you may wish to lengthen the legs a couple of inches. Any addition in height should be made just above the tapered chair feet.

The original chair was constructed of maple and hickory. We used white maple from Craftsman Wood Service, 2727 South Mary St., Chicago, IL. 60608.

turning the legs

Begin construction by turning the legs to size. Since the back legs are over 36 in. long, a lathe bed longer than the standard 36 in. between centers is necessary to turn them. If such a lathe is

LINCOLN MADE this simple bootjack for his own use when he was a lawyer in Springfield.

REPRODUCING THE LINCOLN CHAIR

THE BACK chair legs are 39 in. long, too long to turn on a 36-in. lathe bed. See text for alternate method.

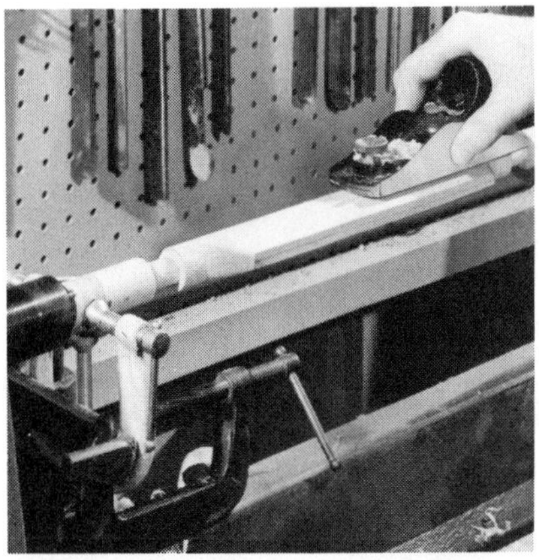

SEAT RAILS, designed to distribute strain on splints without padding, are turned off-center, then planed.

THIS SHOP-MADE V-block jig helps you bore leg holes at the proper angles for the seat rail and stretcher tenons.

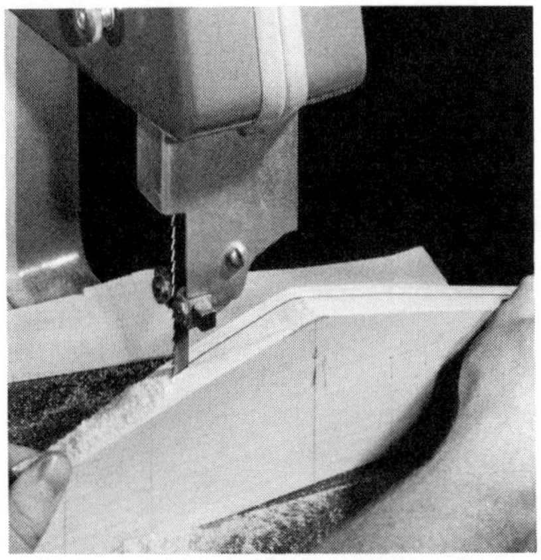

BANDSAW PROVIDES easiest method for cutting back splats. Use a fine-toothed blade to minimize sanding.

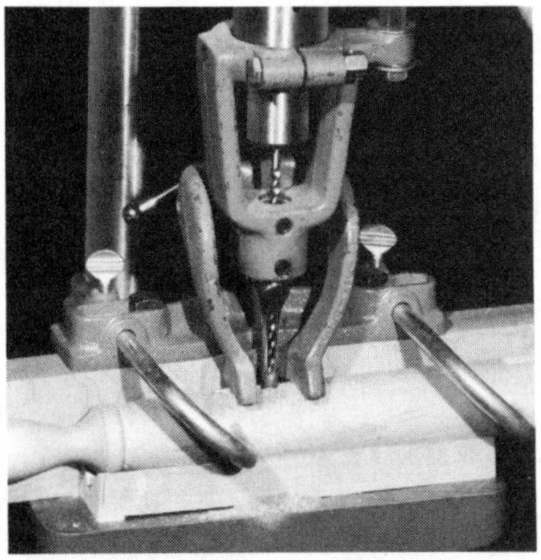

MORTISES FOR BACK splats can be made with a drill press attachment (shown) or with hand drill and chisel.

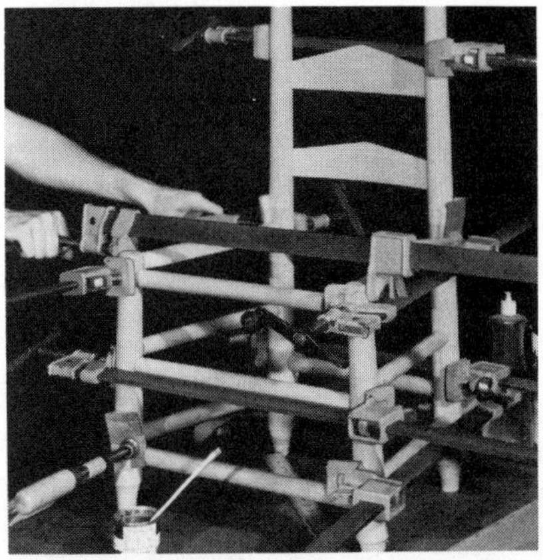

TO AVOID possible stain problems caused by glue squeezeout, wipe with a hot, wet rag after clamping.

WEAVING THE SEAT

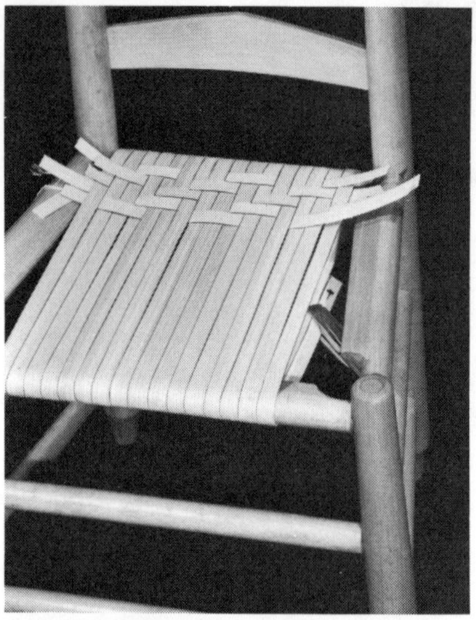

SCRAP STRIPS of splint show how three-over, three-under pattern looks.

TO PLAN WEAVE, make a cardboard squaring tool to fit your chair seat. Use it to lay out rectangular work area the full width of back rail. Apply warp to rectangular area first as shown in following photo sequence. For other patterns, see booklets from H. H. Perkins, 10 South Bradley Rd., Woodbridge, CT 06525.

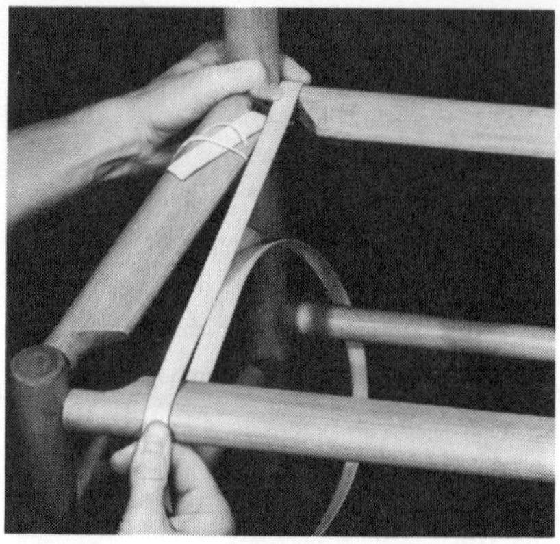

TO MAKE WARPERS pliable, soak for half hour in flat gallon dishpan filled with warm water and three or four tablespoons of glycerin. To begin stringing, fix end temporarily to left side rail with cord. Determine smooth side from rough underside by bending sharply and feeling for splinters.

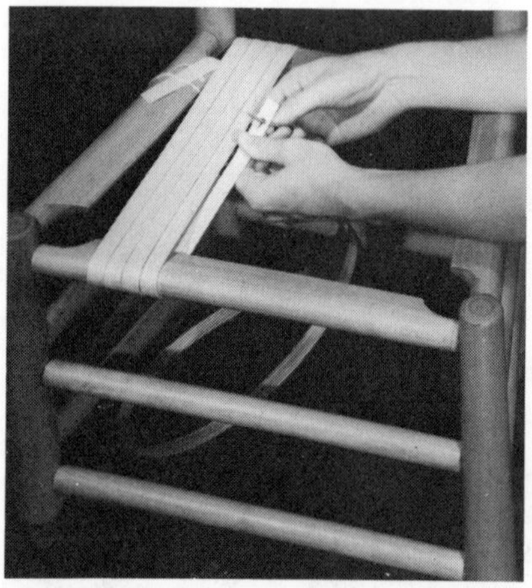

CONTINUE TO wrap warpers perpendicular to front and back rails. Keep strands equally taut. Join new strips with tied or threaded splices.

TO MAKE threaded splices, use paper punch to start hole and make arrowhead notches. Then finish hole and arrow with a small, sharp knife.

SPLICE ON a strand long enough to make transition from warp to weave. Rest of triangular spaces to right and left of rectangular warp are filled later.

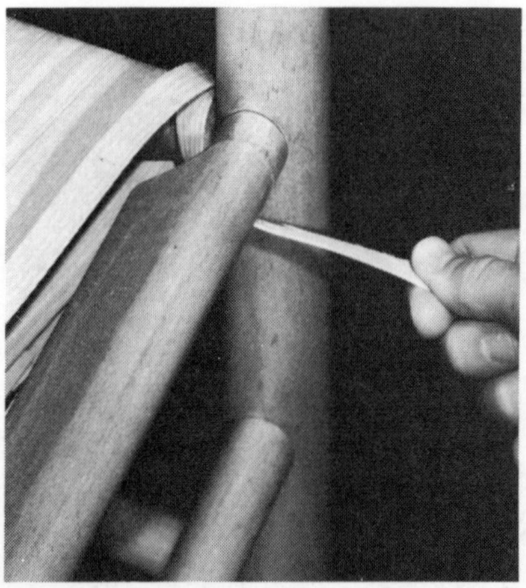

TO WEAVE across warp, wind last warper over back rail and around side rail.

THEN BEGIN threading the weavers, right to left. Keep smooth sides up.

WEAVE THE underside as you did the top—three under and three over.

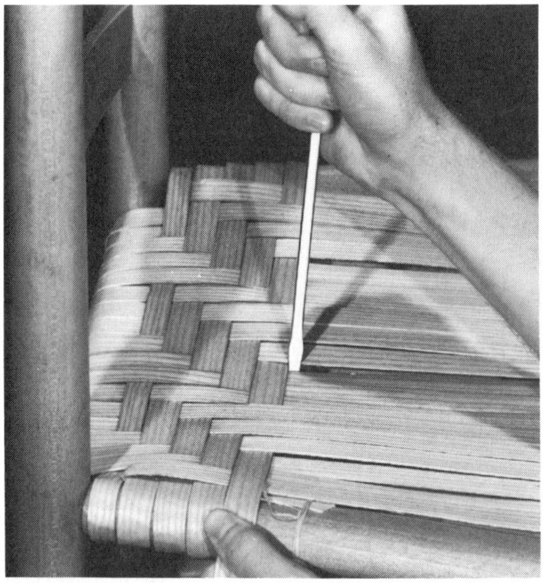

USE A SCREWDRIVER to tightly force the weavers together. Some shrinkage will occur later.

not available, make two turnings per leg and join them at the top finial.

After turning the four legs, turn the lower stretchers and seat rails. Since the seat rails are off-center turnings, they must be run at a slow lathe speed. The rails were designed to provide seating comfort and a wider area for the splint to rest on so it won't crack under strain around narrow edges. Padding the rails is not necessary. Shape the seat rails with a block plane while the work is held between centers.

boring the mortises

Next, bore round mortises in the legs for the stretchers and seat rails. An adjustable V-block jig helps you bore these angled holes accurately (see photo, page 651). Size the diameter of each

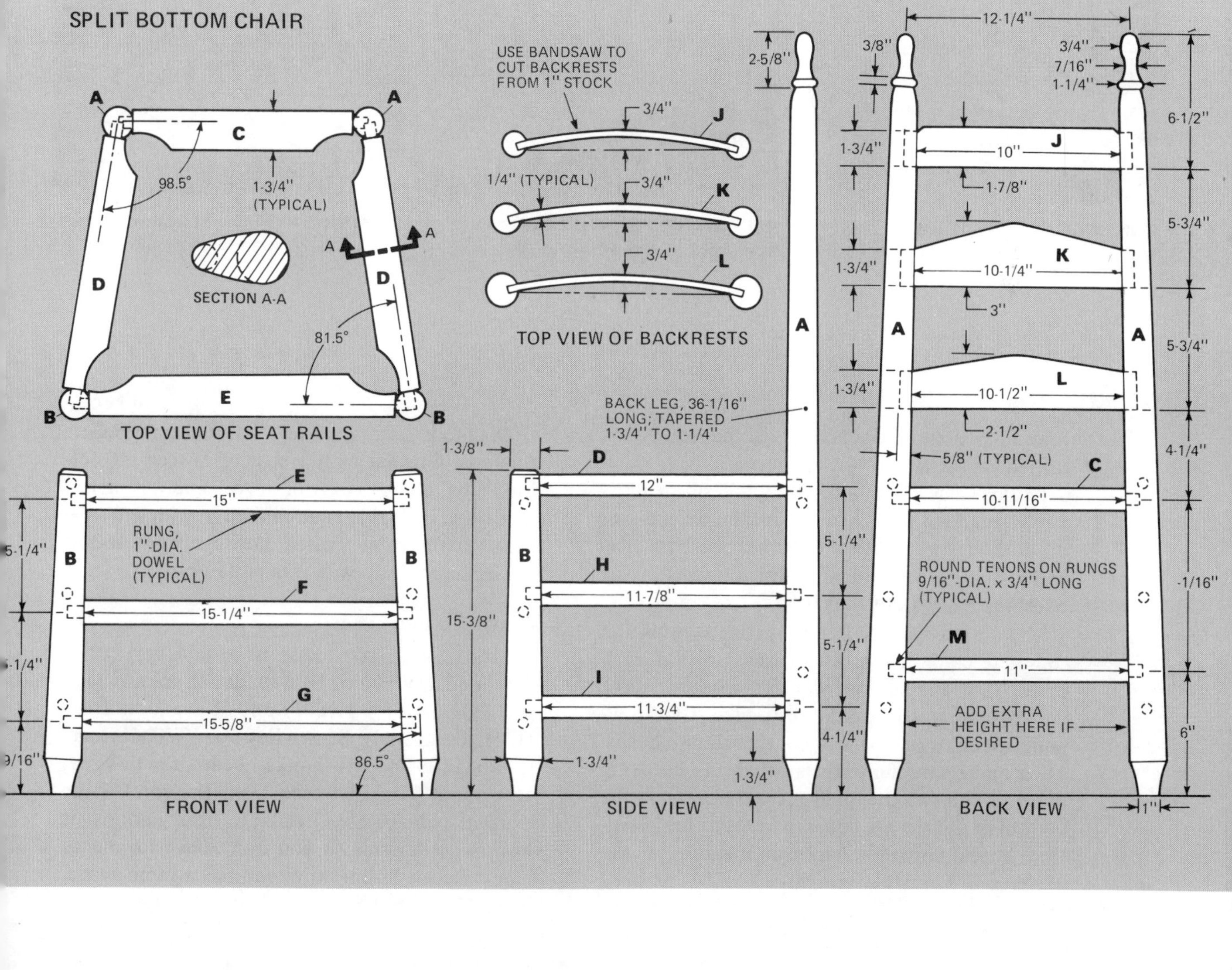

WHEN WEAVERS reach point where gap between warper and rail is ⅝ in., add additional warpers.

ADD A WARPER to bottom side, also.

WHEN NECESSARY to conserve splint, make splices on top and hide under warpers.

CONTINUE TO add shorter and shorter warpers as you carry weavers forward.

KEEP WARPERS moist as you weave front rows. A screwdriver helps.

CONTINUE threading of last weaver to underside; tuck end under, and trim.

round mortise to the actual size of the tenons you turned on the lathe.

At this stage, make a dry assembly of the parts you've made so far. Then cut out the back pieces on a bandsaw or with a chairmaker's bow saw. Sand all sides smooth. Cut slot mortises in the back chair legs to fit the tenons.

Make a second dry assembly, this time of the complete chair. Then disassemble, inspect each piece, and sand smooth where necessary. Make final assembly with plastic resin glue. Clamp all joints being sure to cushion the clamp heads. Then make sure the chair is square by checking to see if the two diagonal measurements at the bottom of the feet are equal to one another. Similarly, check the diagonal measurements at the top of the seat. Let dry overnight.

Do a final sanding as necessary. Our reproduction was finished with a coat of linseed oil, followed by several coats of 50/50 solution of linseed oil and clear shellac rubbed in with 4/0 steel wool. In a few days, when thoroughly dry, a coat of carnauba paste wax was buffed on.

weaving a splint seat

Lincoln may have made his own hickory splint for the seat. We used ⅝-in.-wide ash splint which is a lookalike for hickory and is available from H. H. Perkins, 10 S. Bradley Rd., Woodbridge, CT. 06525. The two hanks needed for this seat cost about $14. Flat reed from the core of the tropical palm is also available from Perkins. It has longer strands so you don't have to join as many pieces. Splint, however, has a more rustic,

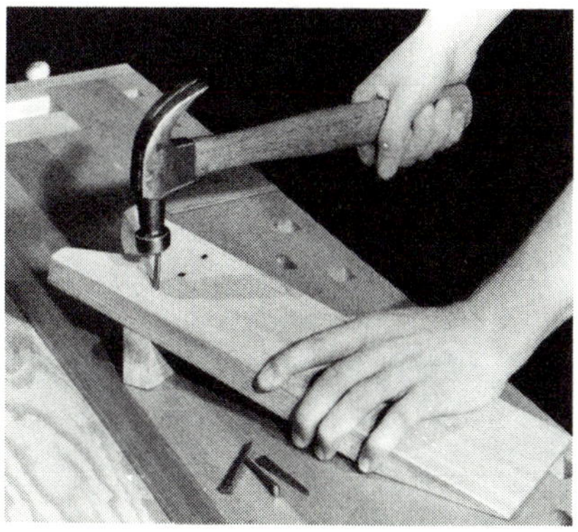

THREE CUT nails add authentic look. Pilot holes provide less holding power, but minimize danger of splitting.

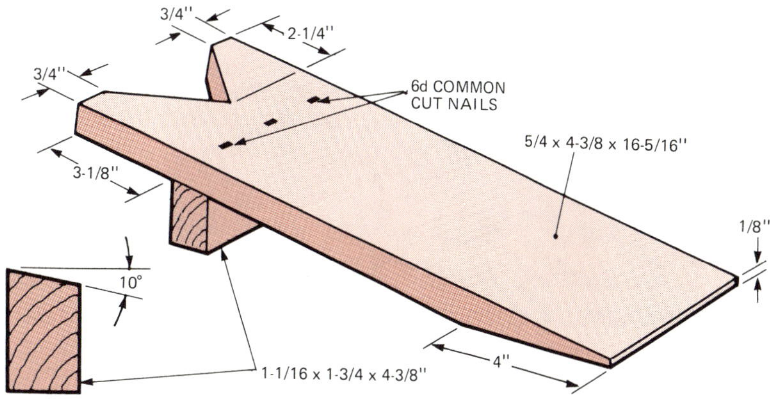

LINCOLN'S BOOTJACK

When Lincoln left Springfield, Ill., for Washington he gave his bootjack to a neighbor. Now that relic is at the Lincoln Library and Museum of Lincoln College, where PM photographed and measured Lincoln's handiwork for reproduction.

Boots are once again fashionable with men and women and, just as in Lincoln's day, they can be hard to pull off. This bootjack will help you remove them. To build it, cut the 5/4-in. board to shape shown. Then lay out and cut the V-notch. If the cut is not perfect, don't worry—Mr. Lincoln's cut was slightly off center, too. Saw the bevel on bottom end next. Sand exposed surfaces and cut out the leg. Assemble the two pieces with 1½-in. finishing nails and glue.

Lincoln used a softwood, probably Illinois white pine, and varnished it. If desired, old-fashioned cut nails are available from Tremont Nail Co., Box 111, Wareham, MA 02571.

pleasing texture. You will also need a small bottle of glycerin from your druggist and a half pint of linseed oil.

A splint or flat reed seat is easier to weave than a cane seat. You can use our sequence of photographic instructions to weave a splint seat either for this reproduction or for any similar post and rung chair that needs reseating. When reseating an old chair, first note the size of the existing splint and weaving pattern, then remove all old material and any padding. Clean and repair rails as required.

warping and weaving

Splint is woven in two directions. First, the splint is wrapped around the back and front rails until the entire center area is filled. This step is called warping. The open triangular area which remains on either side is filled in later during the weaving. Then the splint is woven at right angles to the warpers. The sequence of weaving is shown in the photos.

MATERIALS LIST—LINCOLN CHAIR

Key	Pcs.	Size and description
A	2	2 × 2 × 36 1/16" white maple
B	2	2 × 2 × 15⅜" white maple
C	1	1 × 1¾ × 12 3/16" white maple
D	2	1 × 1¾ × 13½" white maple
E	1	1 × 1¾ × 16½" white maple
F	1	1" dia. × 16¾" white maple
G	1	1" dia. × 17⅛" white maple
H	2	1" dia. × 13⅜" white maple
I	2	1" dia. × 13¼" white maple
J	1	1 × 1⅞ × 11¼" white maple
K	1	1 × 3 × 11½" white maple
L	1	1 × 2½ × 11¾" white maple
M	1	1" dia. × 12½" white maple

Misc.: Plastic resin glue; linseed oil; shellac.; carnauba paste wax; 2 hanks, ⅝" ash splints (see text for source); glycerin.

THE SAFEST WAY TO CUT DOWELS into pins on your table saw at production-line speed is to run a blade through them in a notched paddle. It keeps fingers away and automatically sets the length.

TACK SCREEN WIRE to a wood block and you have a marking gauge that will let you rule a fairly accurate line along the edge of a board. A pencil is placed in the proper hole in the wire mesh.

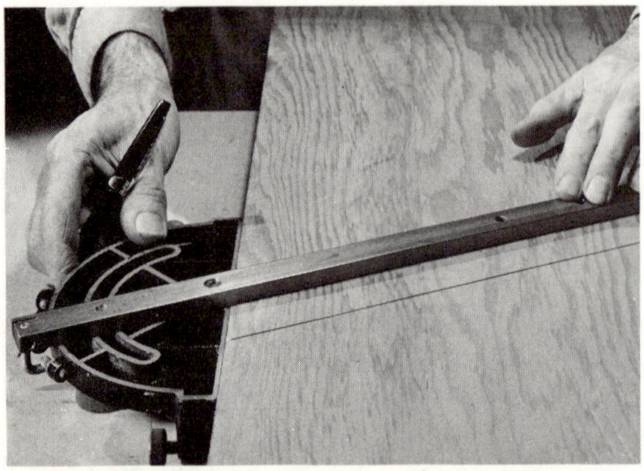

FOR A KING-SIZE T-BEVEL, remember the miter gauge on your table saw. The desired angle is set by the protractor on the front and the angle is marked by inverting the gauge.

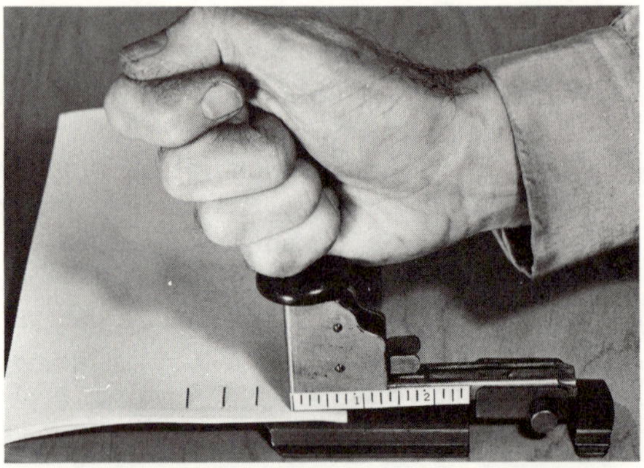

INCH MARKS ON A STAPLER will let you spot staples accurately when it's important that they be a certain distance from the edge. Stick gummed tape to a stapler and ink the marks.

SAVE THE RING CLAMP from a discarded looseleaf binder and attach it to your shop wall. It's a neat holder for a goodly supply of sandpaper. Punch holes along the edge to fit the rings.

INSIDE CALIPERS, handy for spacing shelves, can be improvised from two thin sticks and two wood clothespins. The pins are placed over the sticks and small bolts are inserted through holes in the legs.

THE TESTER measures line voltage and checks outlet wiring (see table below). Designed for three-wire grounded outlets, it can also check three-wire adapters used in two-wire outlets; here, yellow light shows that the "ground" screw isn't really grounded

CONDITION	METER READING	LAMPS
PROPERLY WIRED OUTLET	NORMAL LINE VOLTAGE (U.S. AVG. 117 VAC)	I_1 ○ ○ I_3, I_2 ●
OPEN GROUND	NORMAL LINE VOLTAGE	I_1 ● ○ I_3, I_2 ●
OPEN HOT WIRE	ZERO	I_1 ● ● I_3, I_2 ●
OPEN NEUTRAL WIRE	ZERO	I_1 ○ ● I_3, I_2 ●
HOT-NEUTRAL REVERSED	NORMAL LINE VOLTAGE	I_1 ● ○ I_3, I_2 ○
HOT-GROUND REVERSED	ZERO	I_1 ○ ● I_3, I_2 ○

LEGEND: ○ LAMP ON ● LAMP OFF

PARTS LIST

I1, I2, I3,—Set of three neon indicator lamps with built-in dropping resistors (Set: Radio Shack No. 272-338).

M1—0-150-v.a.c. voltmeter (Calectro D1-926 or equivalent).

Misc.—Phenolic case with 5⅝ x 2⅞ x 2-in. panel (Calectro J4-717); three-wire line cord with U-ground plug; solder.

Build an electric outlet checker

Are your grounded outlets really grounded? You can use this easy-to-build electric outlet checker to find out and check your line voltage at the same time

By RUDOLF F. GRAF and GEORGE J. WHALEN

■ ARE YOUR GROUNDED OUTLETS really grounded? Will the center screw of your ungrounded outlet be a safe connection for the pigtail ground wire of a three-wire adapter plug? Is the outlet's polarity correct? And what's your line voltage? Plug in this easy-to-build checker and you'll have all the answers.

Like commercial testers, it has three lights to indicate polarity. But because it also has an extension plug, you can read it easily even when your outlet is difficult to see or reach. And it checks voltage, too.

Parts are all readily available, and construction is simple. Take care when making the holes in the case. For the meter hole, drill a ring of small holes first, then carefully chip out the material between them. Holes for indicator lamps are first drilled small, then carefully reamed to size to avoid cracking the panel.

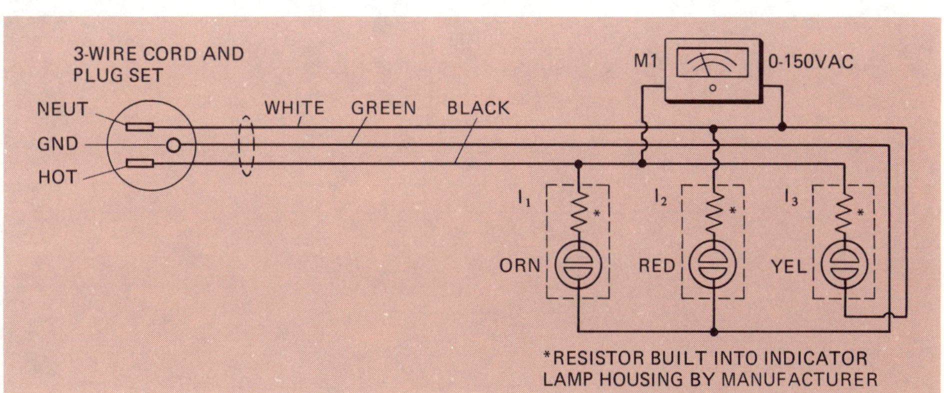

A chess set fit for a king

Whether you feel like a king, a queen or a pawn, this handsome chess set will make you feel like a champ if you make it yourself. As a matter of fact it copped a first prize at a Michigan Industrial Education Fair amongst tough competition

By BILL FIFER and WALTER LANGE

THOUGH ITS EXACT origin is unknown, a generally accepted theory is that chess was imported to Europe from the Orient more than 1500 years ago. The game as we know it today, except for minor changes, is at least 600 years old. The rules, pieces, and board have not changed through all those years.

While the shapes and sizes of the chessmen may vary, the checkered playing board is standardized around the world and consists of 64 squares—32 light colored and 32 dark. Here we present an elegant modern version of the old board and pieces. In our version, the board is of ½-in. plywood and the squares are made by tilting the table saw blade to 45° and running shallow V-grooves at right angles.

SEE ALSO
Air games . . . Backgammon tables . . . Bridge sets . . . Bridge tables . . . Cribbage boards . . . Game tables . . . Metal-lathe techniques . . . Modelmaking

The contemporary chessmen are machined on a metal lathe. One set is of brass while the other is of aluminum so the opposing men can be readily identified. Other combinations of metal could be used or, both sets could be aluminum with one set being anodized. To protect them when not in use, they are snugly stored in rattleproof drawers lined with styrofoam. Pieces can be placed here when captured, or stored here when the game is not in use.

Making the chessmen: Start by cutting the stock to length—allowing two chessmen to each length—except for the kings and queens. Cut a chessman out on one end of the stock, then reverse the stock end for end and turn the second chessman. Dimensions for all the chessmen are given with a high degree of accuracy in the diagram on page 658; use standard metal-lathe prac-

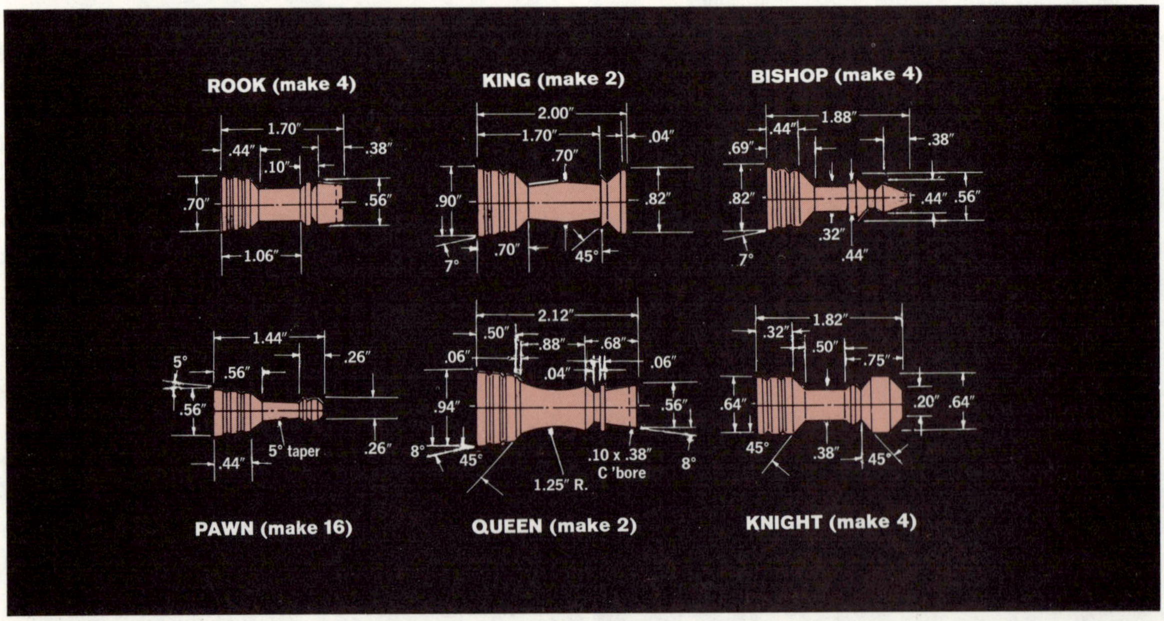

tice to cut them. The stylized king's crown is made using a jeweler's file. Carefully file the notches about $^1/_{16}$ in. wide and $^1/_{16}$ in. deep. The other pieces can all be made using just the metal lathe. Note that the knight is not the traditional horse.

Finishing the chessmen: After each piece has been turned, leave it mounted and polish it dry with 240-grit emery cloth, then with oil. Next use 320 grit, also dry and then with oil. Use lacquer thinner and tissue paper to clean the piece while it is still on the lathe. Once each of the pieces has been cleaned make certain that they are not touched with the fingers.

Heat the piece with a torch until just warm—don't overheat. Then apply three coats of spray-can lacquer to provide good, thorough protection for each piece. Finally, cut the piece off with a parting tool, making sure the bottom is flat. If there are any burrs, knock them off with a single-cut file or the piece may not sit flat.

Notice that the aluminum pieces were flocked (on the bottoms) with a royal blue flock and that the brass pieces received a light green flock. (Flocking is the process of applying powdered felt to paint while it is still wet. Here, of course, it is applied to lacquer.) The felt on the bases is optional but it does save the playing board from scratches which means it will look its best much longer.

LATHE-TURNED MEN in gleaming brass and aluminum, used and stored in a rich walnut case, make this handsome chess set a unique conversation piece that's worthy of your finest craftsmanship. Each set is stored in a drawer of its own and is cradled in a bed of styrofoam. The chess playing surface is scored and squares are stained contrasting light and dark colors. *NOTE:* The board, as shown here, is set up incorrectly. Each player should have a *light* square in his righthand corner. Decide whether you want the drawers to open *toward* the players, or to each *side*, before staining the squares.

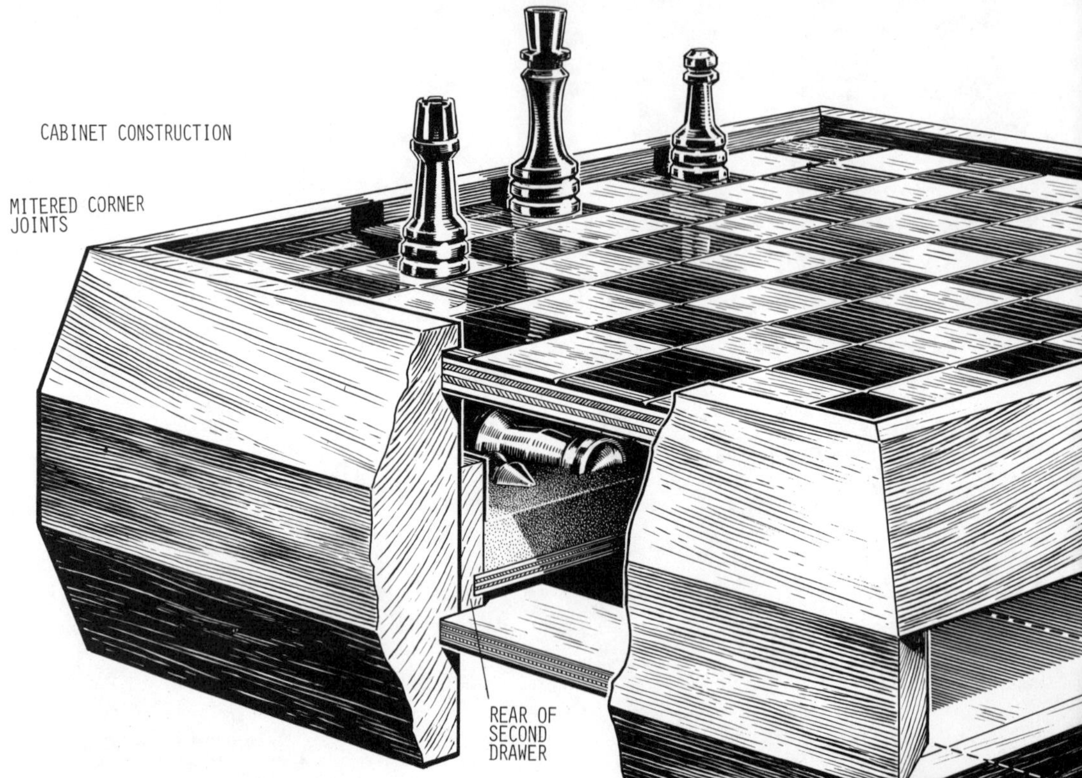

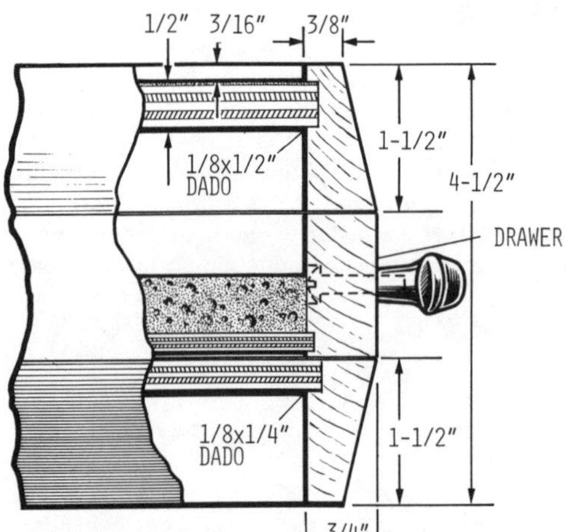

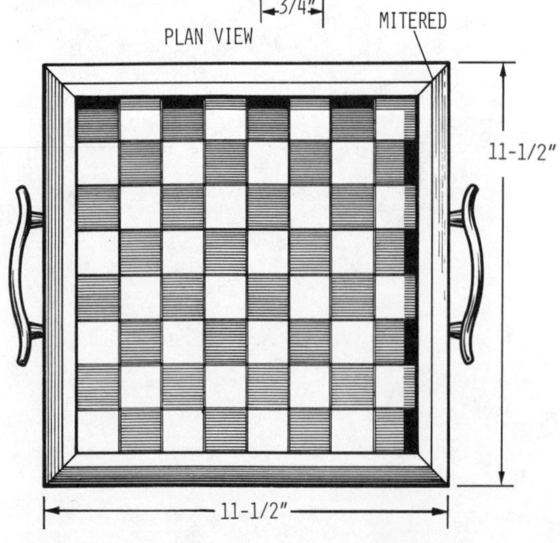

GLEAMING BRONZE HANDLES, accenting walnut used for cabinet and drawer fronts, were purchased at a local hardware store. The drawers do not require backs, but the styrofoam should be cut oversize to insure a press-fit. Drawer bottoms can be of plywood as shown or, if preferred, of ¼-in. tempered hardboard.

Making the cabinet: Start by cutting the playing board to size. Be sure you allow an extra ⅛ in. on all four sides for inserting the plywood into dadoes in the cabinet sides. After grooving the squares, sand the board thoroughly, and stain alternate squares, using an artist brush and walnut stain. (See special note in caption on page 659).

Next make the box. There are no tricky or unusual cabinetmaking techniques called for, but work carefully so that the finished product will have the look of elegance it deserves. The sides are cut to shape on the table saw. Notice that the corners are mitered as are the mating ends of the drawer fronts. To insure a minimum

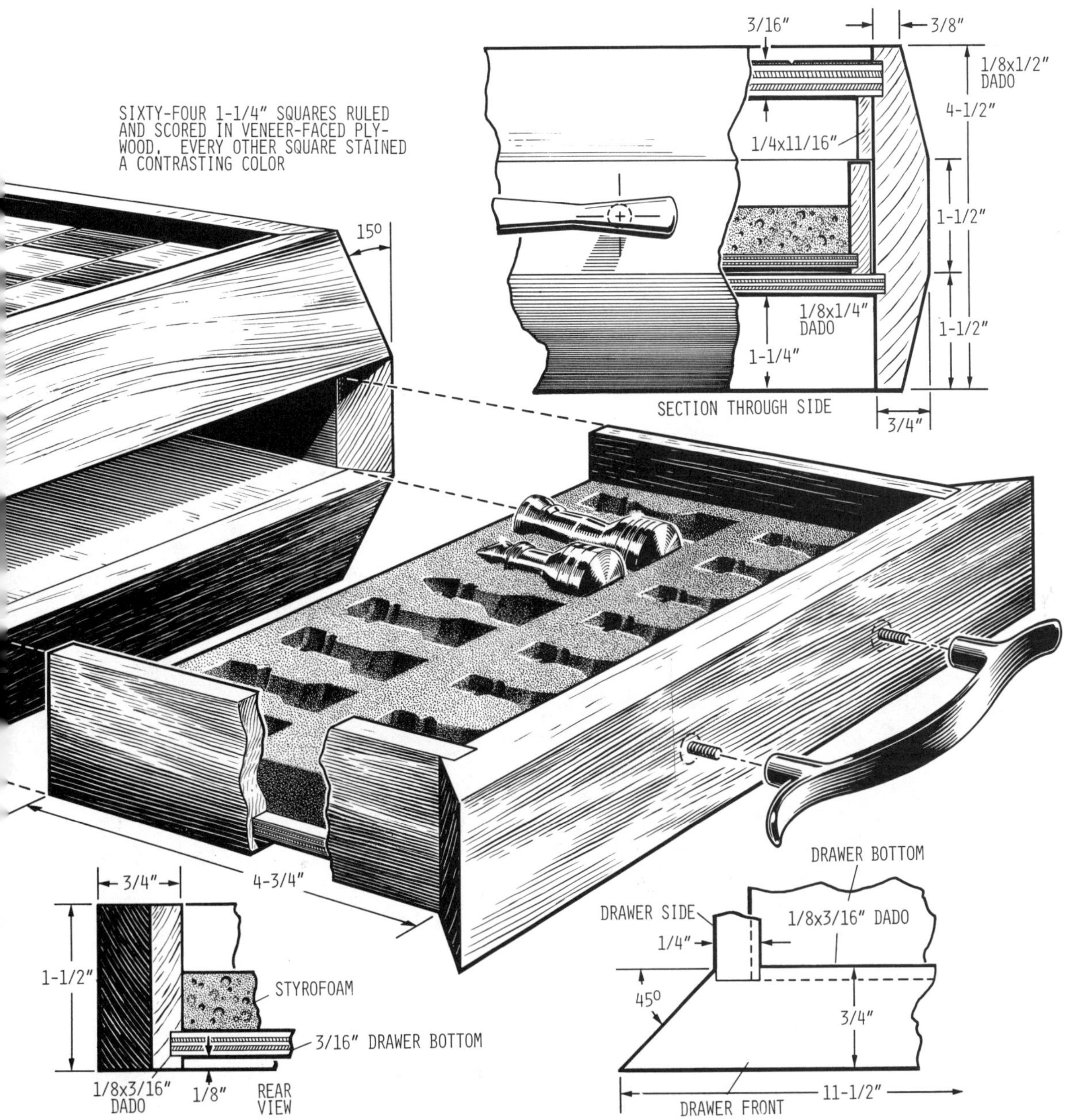

of saw marks on the bevels on the cabinet sides, use a hollow-ground cabinet blade to make the cuts.

With box and drawers assembled, cut both styrofoam drawer liners to size. Next, arrange the chessmen in two rows as they appear on the board. Then, gently press each piece down into the styrofoam so that it will clear the drawer opening. Remove the pieces, paint the styrofoam top and front and then flock with the color of your choice. Allow ample time for the setup to dry before going on to the next step. *Caution:* Since certain paints will melt styrofoam, check the label carefully when selecting the paint.

Being an open-grain wood, the walnut does require filling. To do it, make a paste, mixed to about the consistency of heavy cream, using walnut filler and walnut oil stain. Rubbing with the grain, work the filler into the open pores of the wood. To remove the excess, wipe off with strokes across the grain so that the filler remains packed in the pores. This is standard procedure any time you use paste wood filler on a fine woodworking project. Allow the cabinet to dry for at least 24 hours. To finish, apply two or three coats of lacquer. When this is dry, apply a paste wax and buff it to a soft luster.

With the board and men finished you are ready to take on your opponent in the best of style!

Period pieces from stock moldings

A battered trunk and about $10 worth of appropriate molding combine to give this project the look of Old-World craftsmanship

By ROBERT WORTHAM

BARGAIN-PRICE cedar chest before moldings were applied. It was bought at a thrift shop for $2.

THERE ARE probably several good reasons why Spanish or Mediterranean-style furniture enjoys the designer and decorator status it does today. The massive, sculpted look of the deeply carved, recessed panels blends well with practically all decors. And the rugged-looking finish can take the abuse that it's certain to receive in a home with youngsters. Minor nicks or dents in the finish are practically invisible and, in fact, can add charm to the piece. Your youngsters can sometimes be your own antique specialists.

Happily, it's not necessary to be a woodcarver or woodworking artisan to duplicate the look. Using stock moldings available at any lumberyard, you can achieve the effect with simple butted joints. Take a trip to your nearby lumberyard and take a look at some of the stock moldings. The different moldings you find may give you original ideas for your own purposes. Or, you can make original moldings using your shaper or router. Though this is more work, it may give you just the look you are trying to achieve.

The cedar chest shown on the opposite page was purchased in a junk shop for a couple of dollars. It was battered, its veneer was half peeled off and it was shabby looking. (I think the shopkeeper is still amazed that he sold it.) No doubt you can also find one in a second-hand store, junk shop or even in your attic.

Back in the shop, I reglued the veneer, removed the old ball-type feet and sanded the piece down to bare wood. Sometimes an old chest can have many coats of paint or varnish as well as dirt on it, so make sure you get down to the bare wood when sanding. Once I decided which moldings to use, I made a scale drawing

MOLDINGS AT CORNERS are miter-joined; horizontals and verticals inside have 45° bevel undercut.

VARIATION ON AN old chest. In the original state, it had beveled drawer fronts and plain, flat doors.

of the piece to determine the on-center locations for verticals and horizontals. With this calculated, all I had to do was cut the required number of pieces.

I used miter cuts at the outside corner joints. On the inside strips of molding, I simply made straight crosscuts with a 45° bevel and butted the pieces. But, if the molding you select has a shaped edge, perpedicular joints will have to be made with either 45° saw cuts or by coping. Apply the molding to the outside corners first, then add the interior pieces. Here, since the chest was to be painted and antiqued, I used white glue and brads to assemble. The latter eliminated the need for clamping and kept the job buzzing along.

A final touch, though a matter of personal choice, is to add the small, beveled blocks of the same molding to each recessed square. Depending on the piece, this will often add a little extra charm.

SMALL CABINET

A chest in the Spanish style

By ROBERT WORTHAM

In this chest the accent is Mediterranean from the sculptured cabinet to the mosaic top. It's easy to build and blends with any decor

THIS HANDSOME SPANISH chest is as easy to build as it is to look at. The dark stained wood and mosaic-tile top will add richness to any room.

To determine the dimensions of your chest, first select your tile. Then, alter top dimensions to fit the tile chosen to avoid extra cutting.

On the chest shown, I used an imported mosaic tile which came in 1-ft. squares on paper backing. It cost $1.25 per square. After laying squares on the plywood top, add ½ in. (in width and length) to the plywood to give you a ¼-in. grout line around the perimeter. Ceramic tiles were available where I shopped in 4¼, 6 and 12-in. sizes, with thickness ranging from ¼ to ¾ in.

SEE ALSO
Cabinet furniture . . . Desks . . . Dining tables . . . Finishes, wood . . . Furniture, care of . . . Hinges . . . Joinery . . . Moldings . . . Storage ideas

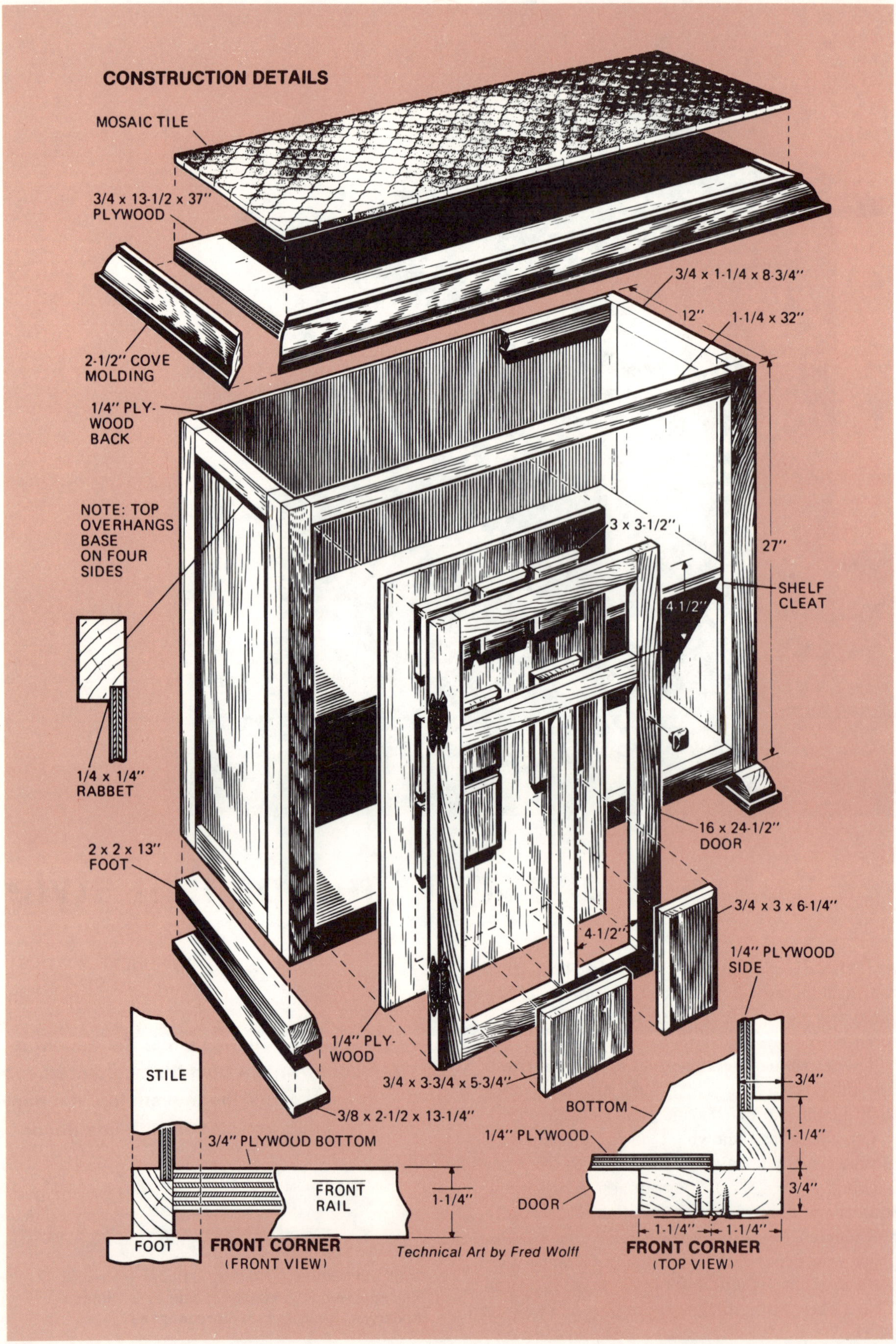

Technical Art by Fred Wolff

The 12 x 27-in. end panels were made with 1¼-in. framing (stiles and rails) ripped from ¾-in. stock and rabbeted. Then ¼-in. plywood was glued in the rabbets. Though the drawing shows the plywood let into edge-rabbets, it could be simply glued and tacked to the inside of the framing.

The doors were framed with ¾ x 1¼-in. stock and the ¼-in. plywood backup panel was glued and nailed to the frames with short brads.

Panel blocks were cut from ¾-in. stock and fastened to the plywood backing with small brads and white glue. For a sculptured look, bevel the blocks along the top edges with the table saw set at 45°. When you lay out the blocks, leave at least ⅝ in. around each block.

The feet were ripped 1½ in. wide from 2 x 4 stock and then beveled 45° at the front. These, in turn, were glued to the lower feet and the leg setup was then fastened to the cabinet with flathead screws.

Edge (cove) molding is fastened to the plywood top so that it sits above the plywood the thickness of the tile and mastic. With the molding placed before the tile, the former can then serve as a leveling guide when you lay the tile. Apply the mastic with a notched trowel and let it set about 15 minutes.

As you position each tile tap it lightly with a hammer and clean wood block to assure a tight bond.

Next day mix dry grout and water to the consistency of mayonnaise. Apply grout between tiles with a straightedge to rake it into the spaces. The grout should dry in about 30 minutes.

THE DOOR stiles and rails (top) are made of ¾-in. stock. Blocks are beveled 45° on the top edges and then glued to the ¼-in. plywood backing with ⅝-in. spacing on all four sides of each block.

THE PLYWOOD-TOP size is determined by the tile you use. In the case above, 1-ft. square mosaic tile was applied using mastic. Half tiles are used around the perimeter to complete the surface.

THE TILE GROUT is raked diagonally between tiles with straightedge (left). After a wait of about 30 minutes the excess grout should be washed off the surface of the tile with a sponge and water.

SEE ALSO

Beds . . . Desks . . . Drawers . . . Family rooms . . . Game tables . . . Modelmaking . . . Study centers . . . Toys . . . Wood finishes

This kid studies under his bed

Here's a novel solution to a space problem in a small bedroom. This combination bunk bed/desk gives room for sleep or study

■ NOT ONLY DOES this kid study under his bed, he sleeps over his desk. Far from being a mixed-up kid, he thinks he has the grooviest bunk bed/desk ever. This combination unit solves the space problem in a small room.

The two-in-one unit occupies a corner of the room from floor to ceiling to provide a regulation-size bunk bed and a kneehole desk with nearly a 4x7 ft. top. Ample in size for homework galore, the desk also presents a great hobby and play surface for model building, train and racing-car layouts—you name it. Three roomy drawers flank each side of the kneehole with a pencil drawer above.

Constructed of common white pine, the unit is pretty much a duplicate each side of a centerline. Like members are made the same except for being assembled left and right hand. This is particularly true when making the four hollow posts and the two separate drawer compartments.

Since the posts butt against the ceiling they have to be built in place. You can't expect to tip them up into place if put together on the floor. Each pair of end posts is joined with a panel of ¼-in. plywood, which can be plain or fancy with random grooves. If the bed is built in a corner, only the exposed end would require fancy plywood. If centered on a wall, both ends would be exposed. The distance between posts is set by the length of the steel bedrails. The original rails (and mattress) are from Sears and measure 75 in. long. They are for bunk beds without springs, and a pair costs about $6. After the rails are bolted to the posts of each end assembly, you

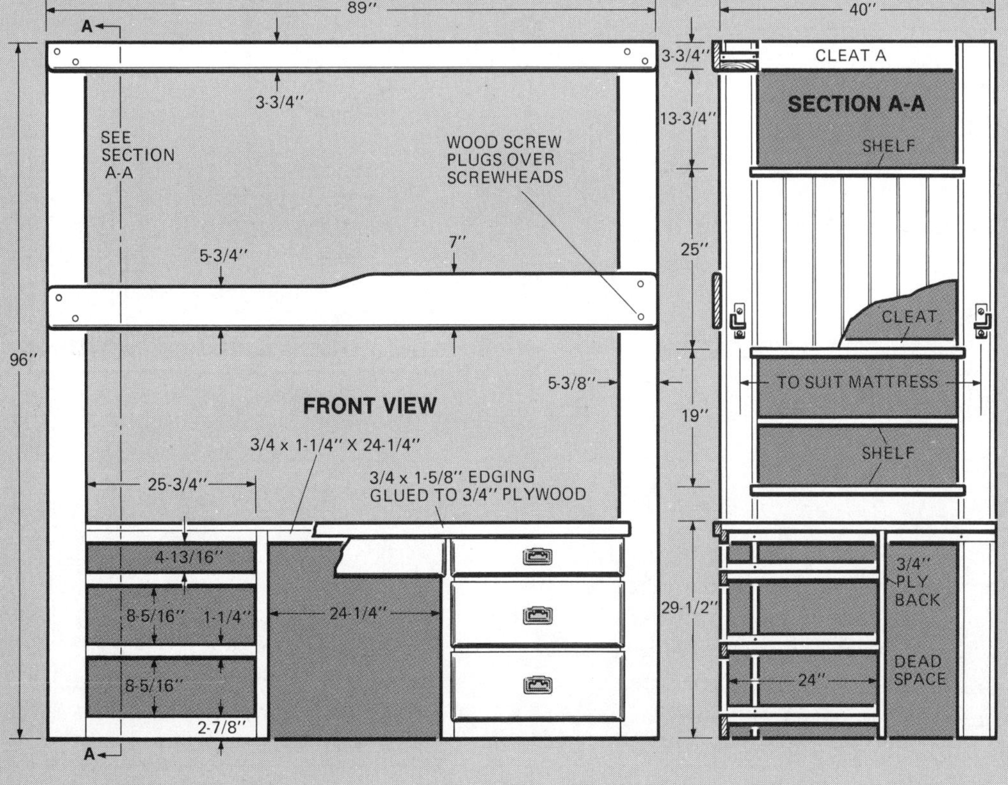

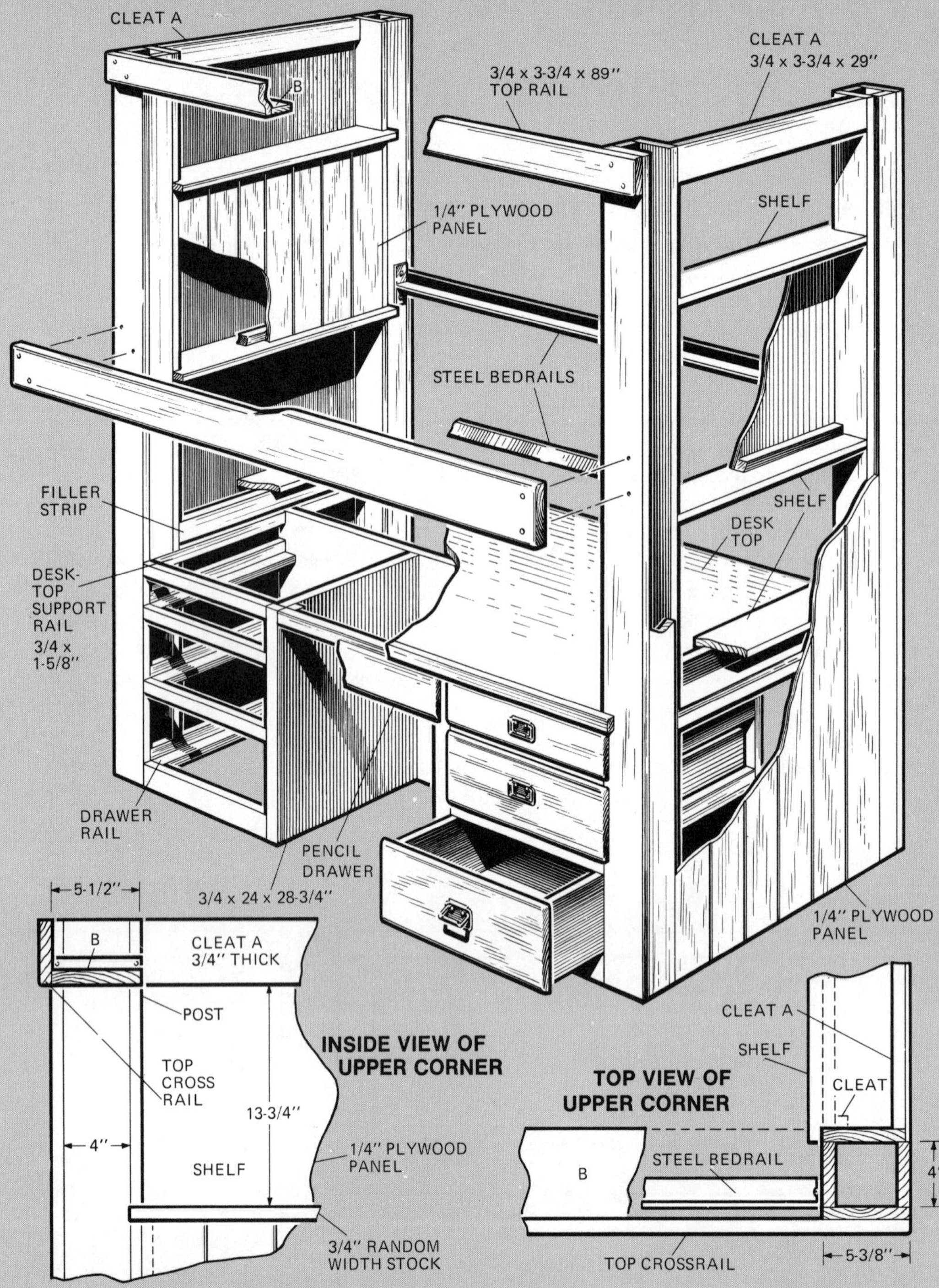

can proceed to add the connecting board across the top at the ceiling and the board that hides the bed rail. These are fastened with screws set in counterbored holes and capped with plugs.

The rails of the drawer compartments are attached to the front posts with dowels. Notice that a full-length plywood panel provides a back for each compartment and the kneehole. This panel also supports the outside drawer slides at the rear.

Make any minor adjustments to the dimensions to fit your particular situation. When construction is complete, the unit is ready for finishing to match the decor of the room.

Simple coatrack for a child

By MAX FARRELL

IF YOUR KIDS need a little help keeping their coats off the floor and their boots in one spot, this quick project is for you. Besides providing coat hooks at a height accessible to a child, it also incorporates a place to stow muddy boots by using a grocery carton as a disposable liner.

Cut members to length from 1 x 4 clear pine or fir. Eliminate sharp corners from head-level by rounding off upright members with a sabre saw (see drawing). Cut the stub tenons on the base's side pieces with a backsaw. Then use a coping saw to remove the bulk of the waste from the two sockets in the front piece to match the tenons, finishing with a sharp chisel. Assemble unit with glue and flat head screws, countersinking them to prevent snags and tears. Sand well, and finish with stain and polyurethane, or enamel paint. Add coat hooks and corner braces to hold box.

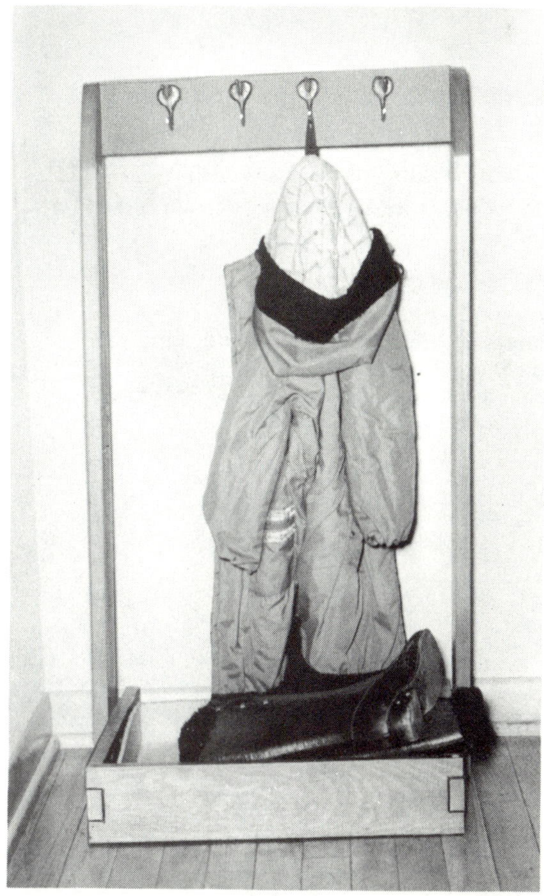

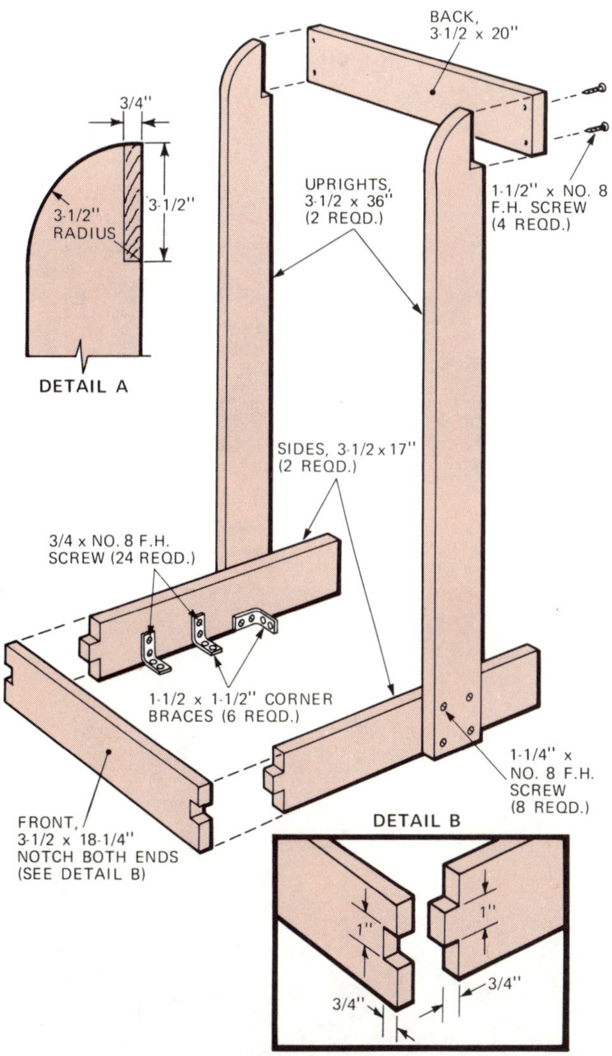

MATERIALS LIST—COAT RACK

Pcs.	Size and description
1	¾ x 3½ x 20" pine or fir
2	¾ x 3½ x 36" pine or fir
2	¾ x 3½ x 17" pine or fir
1	¾ x 3½ x 18¼" pine or fir
6	1½ x 1½" angle irons
24	No. 8 x ¾" fh wood screws
8	No. 8 x 1¼" fh wood screws
4	No. 8 x 1½" fh wood screws

Misc.: White or yellow glue, enamel paint or polyurethane and stain, corrugated cardboard box to fit coat rack base.

SEE ALSO

Desks . . . Family rooms . . . Finishes, wood . . . Hi-fi centers . . . Mobile furniture . . . Mudrooms . . . Painting, furniture . . . Storage ideas

Two quick projects for the kids' room

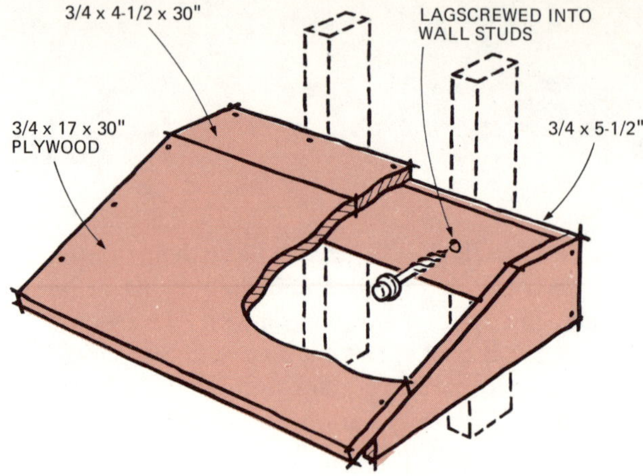

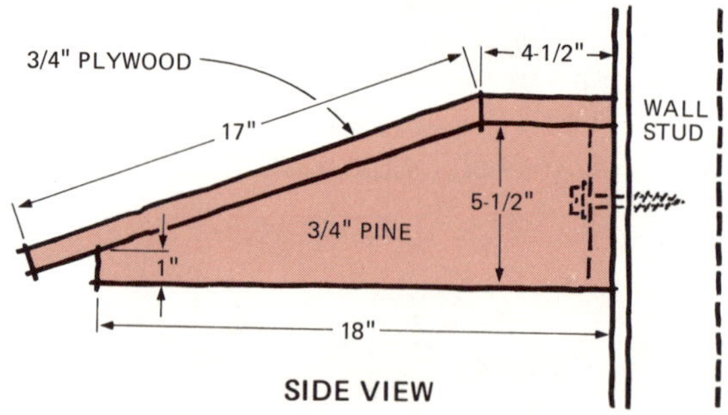

Furniture for children's rooms makes a good do-it-yourself project because it is basic and easy-to-assemble. Try your hand at the desk and bed table shown here

SEE ALSO
Bed tables . . . Bookstands . . . Desks . . . Game tables . . . Hi-fi centers . . . Painting, furniture . . . Pool tables . . . Sofa-beds . . . Storage ideas . . . Wood finishes

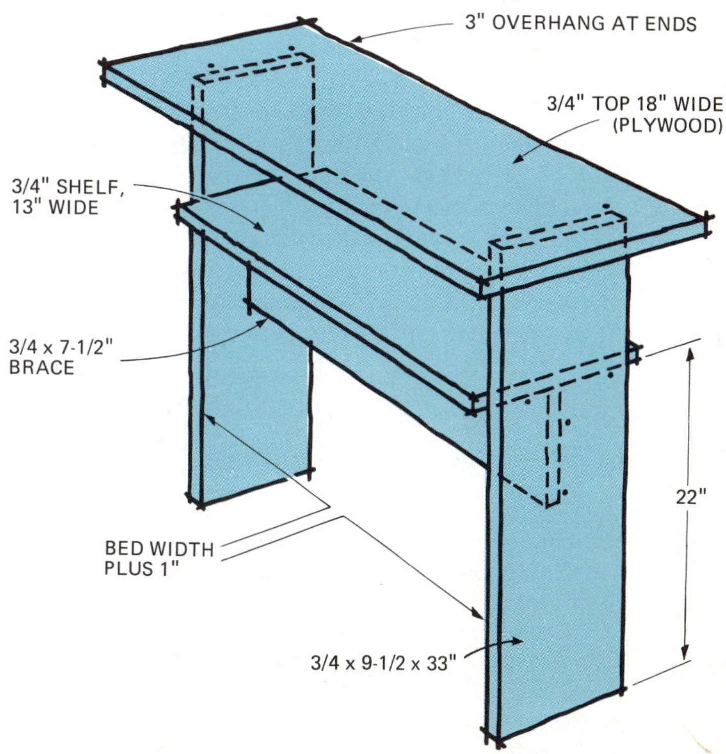

■ ONE THING ABOUT kids' furniture—it's usually simple to make, and that goes for this novel wall-hung desk and footboard bed table. Both require little more than a hammer and saw to build. You simply saw the pieces to size, apply glue, nail together, paint and you're through. The job is even simpler if you have your lumber dealer do the cutting for a small extra charge.

The wall-hung desk becomes plenty strong to work on when it's anchored to wall studs with a couple of husky lagscrews, and there's nothing underneath to bang knees on or interfere with cleaning. A good height from the floor is about 30 in. The desktop is slightly sloped for easier reading, writing and sketching. The footboard table is made to straddle twin beds placed end to end along a wall. To change the bedding, you just lift the table out of the way.

This bunk bed is only for one child, but it includes something instead—four built-in drawers under the mattress and more space at the head and foot

Bunk bed with a built-in chest

By LAURA LABARGE

■ NO NEED TO WORRY about getting this king-size bunk bed in and out of the room; it all comes apart with a twist of a screwdriver, thanks to special Selby Hardware connectors holding the 14 parts together.

The bed makes the most of space—four large drawers built in under the mattress swallow up lots of toys, extra blankets, sheets and pillow cases. Two "ladder" shelves at the foot of the bed provide still more storage space, and another shelf across the headboard will hold a lot of bedtime-story books. The bed accommodates a 36 x 75-in. foam-rubber mattress. The complete bed is built from ¾-in. fir plywood. Half-round molding covers the exposed edges of the sides. The bed cost John Doherty of Greenlawn, NY, about $75 to build.

The two-part connectors consist of a steel pin with a large head and a slotted 1-in. steel disc installed in the line with the pin. When the disc engages the pin and is turned with a screwdriver, it draws the joint tight. You'll need 28 connectors called Elite 25 with DU91 dowel. You can buy them from Albert Constantine, 2050 Eastchester Road, Bronx, NY 10461.

SEE ALSO
Bed tables . . . Beds . . . Desks . . . Drawers . . . Game tables . . . Occasional tables . . . Storage ideas . . . Study centers . . . Toys

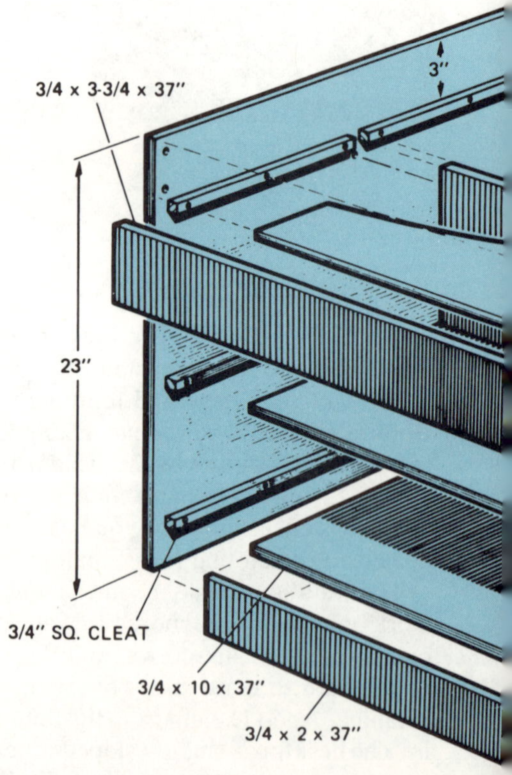

Technical Art by Peter Trojan

CLEATS SUPPORT plywood top where the mattress rests. They're glued and screwed 3 inches from the top.

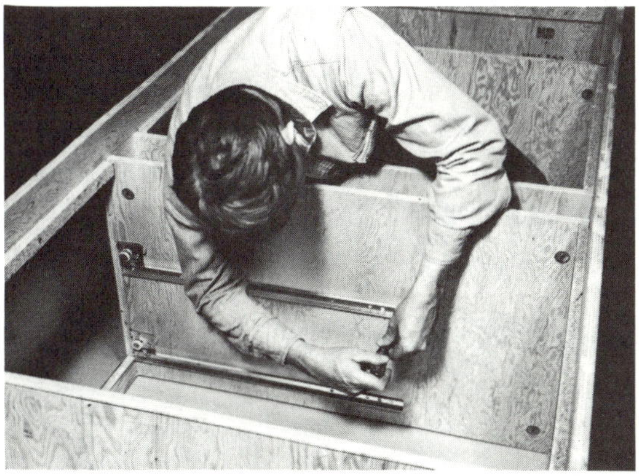

DRAWERS ROLL smoothly on standard metal guides which are screwed to the dividers and the drawer sides.

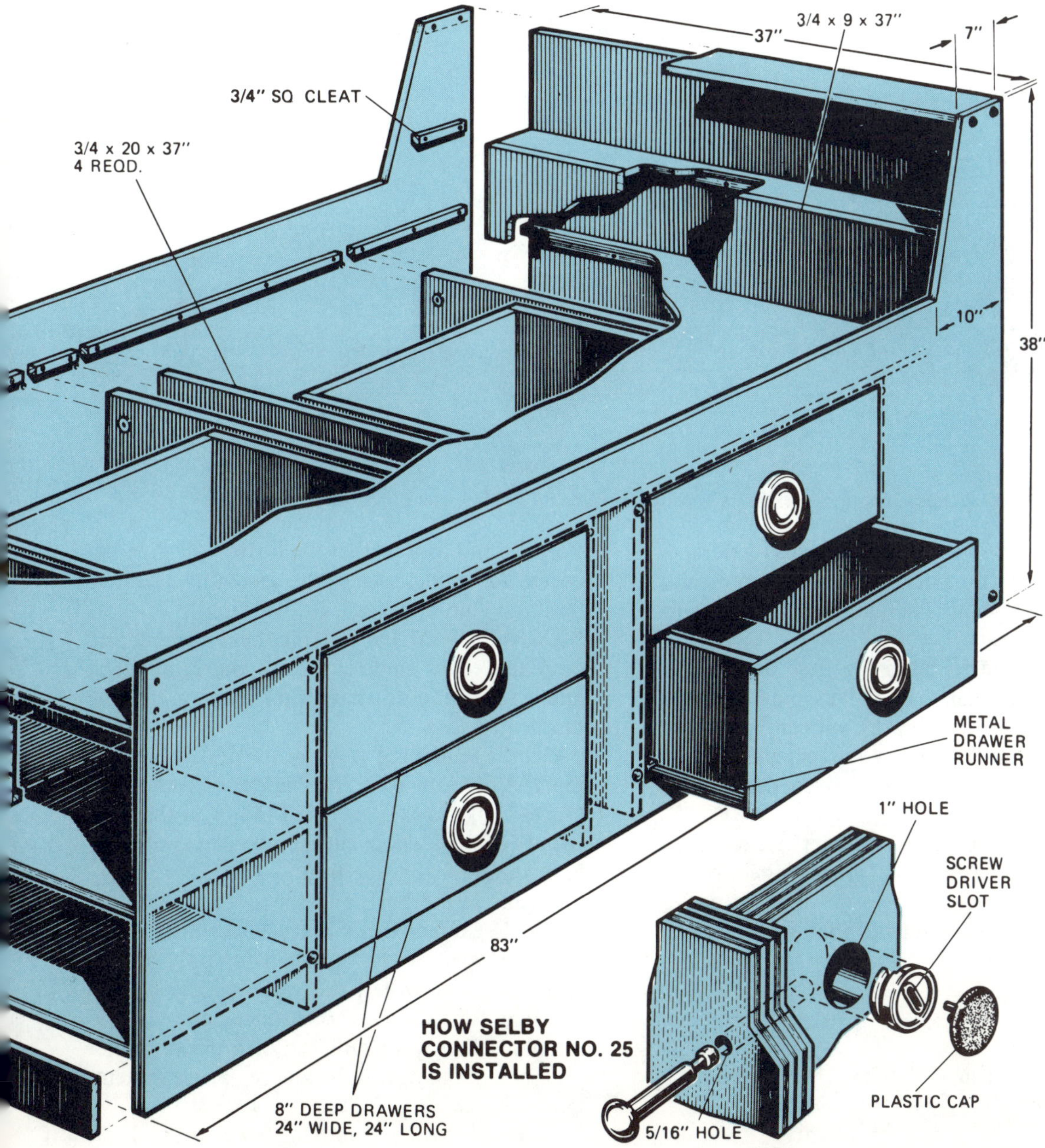

Build a rolltop desk for your youngster

By RALPH WILKES

THE ROLL-TOP pivots back, and the work surface slides forward for writing, coloring or other activities.

THE ROLL-TOP LOOK of this desk is a great attraction for youngsters. Contrary to the real thing, though, this desktop simply swings up as a unit.

Materials used to build the desk are readily available. I built this one of 1-in. pine (actually ¾-in. thick). It is easy to work with and produces a neat appearance. Pine is less expensive than birch-veneered plywood and looks nicer than fir plywood.

The 16⅝x24⁷⁄₁₆-in. work surface (E) is made up of four pieces of 1-in. stock. Glue tongues of the short pieces into the grooves on the ends of the center boards. This joinery helps to prevent warping and assures that the board will slide between the guides. Keep the assembly clamped until the glue dries (at least overnight).

Cut the sides (C) and clamp them together and sand the edges smooth. Finish the sanding by hand, using 150-grit garnet paper on a sanding block.

Cut the remaining parts for the desk frame: the top (A), bottom trim (D), guides (F) and (G), braces (H), front (I) and filler (M). Cut the back (B) of ¼-in. plywood; cut the two pieces of ¾-in. half-round for the side trim.

Assemble the back and the sides of the desk frame. Use a temporary brace across the front to hold the assembly rigid while you apply bottom and side trim. Install the work-surface guides, checking for fit with work surface before applying glue. Add front rail (I). Then install corner braces to hold the unit square. Remove temporary brace.

To build the false tambour front, cut ends (J)

SEE ALSO

Butcher block furniture . . . Desks . . . Drawers . . . Furniture, care of . . . Game tables . . . Mudrooms . . . Toys . . . Wood finishes

to shape and sand smooth. Fashioning the slat assembly is the time-consuming part of this project, unless you use the simplified procedure described later. I made the slats from two, 1-in.-thick, clear pine boards, each about 26 in. long.

Start by rounding all four edges of both pieces of pine stock. If you don't own a shaper, you can create the moldings using a router and rounding-over bit, or by hand with a block plane, rasp, surform tool and sandpaper.

Set the rip fence on your table saw to produce a ⅜-in. wide board and push the four edges through using a push stick. For minimum sanding, cut the moldings with a fine blade and use a slow feed.

To assemble slats to each other and to ends (J), temporarily tacknail a scrap piece of plywood to the back of the ends. Using a 1-in. brad as a drill bit, bore a hole near the center of each slat for nailing the adjacent slat. (*Editor's note:* Offset these nailholes slightly on adjacent slats so that brads won't interfere with each other.) Run a *thin* line of glue between slats, being careful to avoid getting glue on the surface. Use a damp cloth to immediately wipe up glue squeezeout.

MATERIALS LIST—'ROLL-TOP' DESK

Key	No.	Size and description (use)
A	1	¾ x 9¼ x 27″ pine (top)
B	1	¼ x 25¼ x 28″ plywood (back)
C	2	¾ x 16 x 30″ pine (side)
D	2	¾ x 3 x 16″ pine (bottom trim)
E	1	¾ x 16⅜ x 24-7/16″ pine (work surface)
F	2	¾ x ¾ x 15″ pine (bottom guide)
G	2	¾ x ¾ x 11″ pine (top guide)
H	2	¾ x 4½ x 4½″ pine (brace)
I	1	¾ x 3½ x 24½″ pine (front)
J	2	¾ x 8 x 9½″ pine (end support)
K	1	⅜ x 1½ x 24⅜″ pine (handle backing)
L	1	¼ x ⅜ x 3″ pine (handle)
M	2	¼ x ⅜ x ⅜″ pine (filler)

Misc.: ⅜″-dia: dowel, 1″ clear pine about 26″ long (or ¾″ half-round pine molding) to make slats, 6d finishing nails, No. 16 x ¾″ wire brads, 2 No. 10 x 1½″ rh screws, 6 No. 8 x 1¼″ rh screws, glue, sandpaper, stain, varnish.

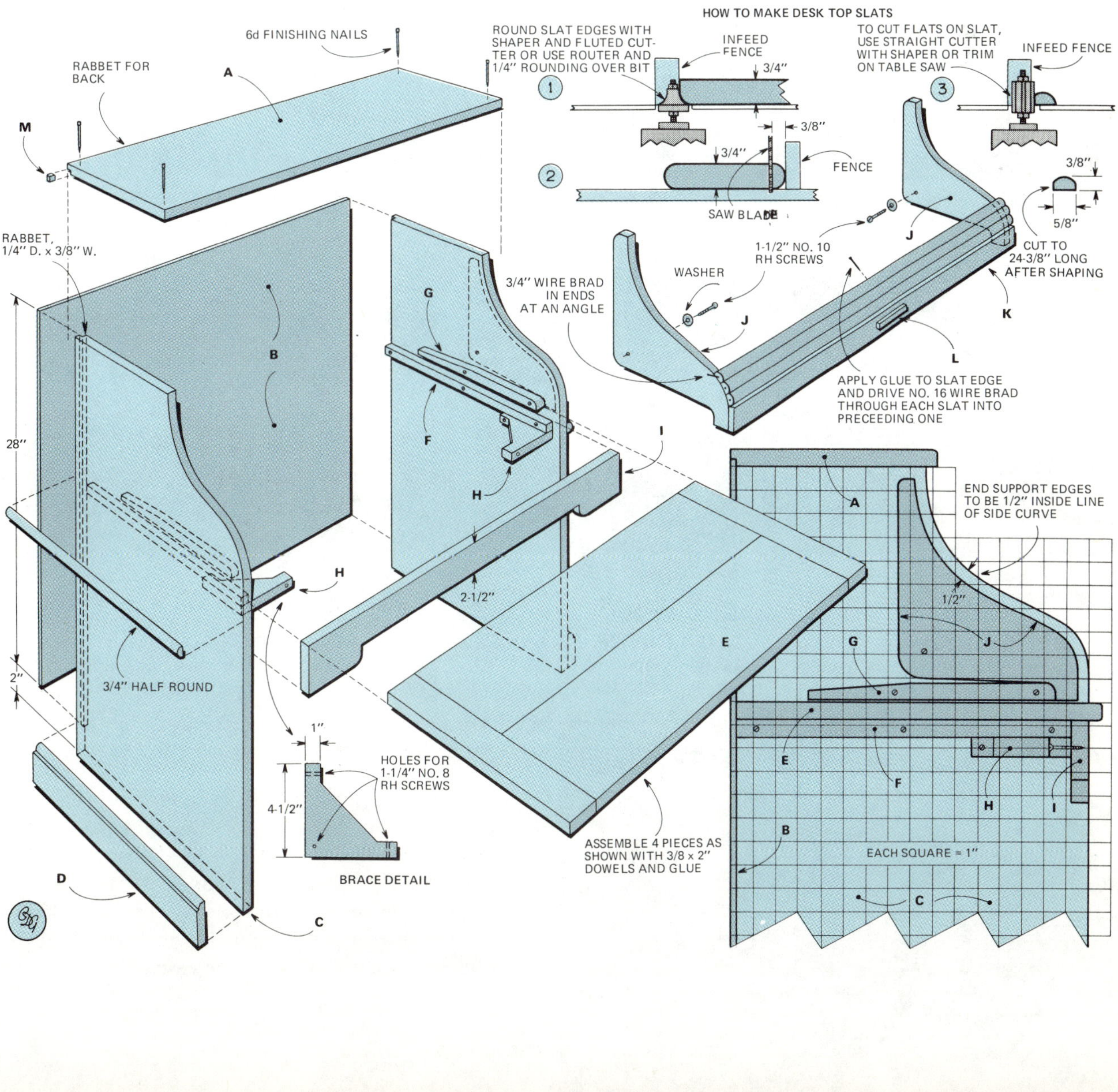

CLAMPING technique on wide pieces: C-clamps, boards prevent warping.

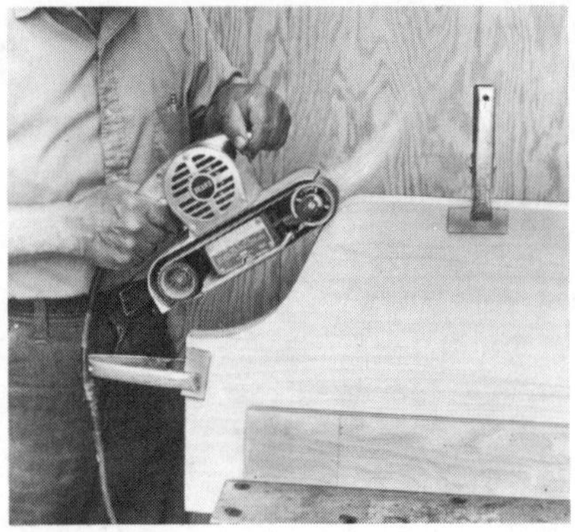

USE A 120-grit belt in sander to smooth contours of clamped sides.

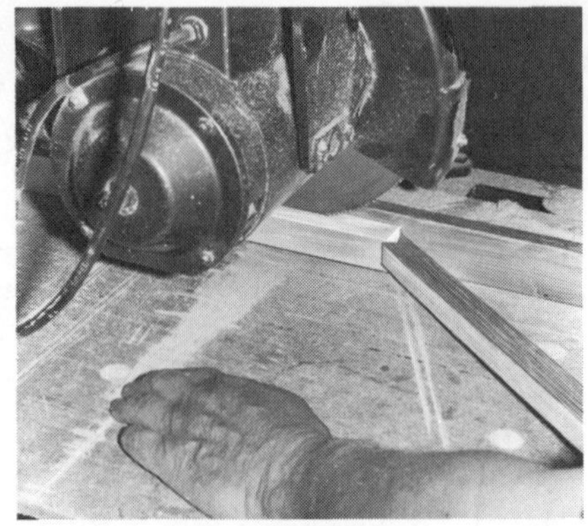

TONGUE-AND-GROOVE joints are used on work surface (E).

APPLY GLUE sparingly to mating surfaces, wait 30 seconds, then assemble.

CLAMP BOARDS, using bar or pipe clamps; leave to dry overnight.

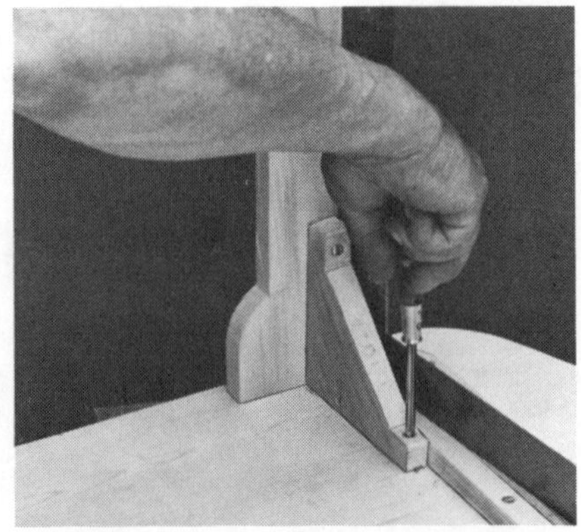

CORNER braces (H) are shop-made; install them using glue and screws.

CLEAR-PINE slat edges are rounded using shaper, router or block plane.

AFTER SHAPING slat edges, finish with 120-grit paper.

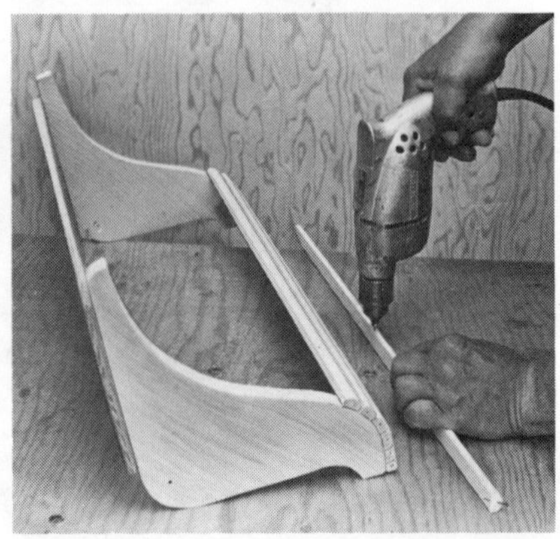

BORE SLIGHTLY offcenter hole in each slat using a 1-in. brad as bit. Run a thin glue line near back edge of slat.

BORE ANGLED pilot holes at ends, apply glue, set ¾-in. wire brads slightly. Temporary plywood back aids assembly.

Bore an angled hole at each end of each slat; use glue and ¾-in. brads to fasten slats to ends. Set the heads slightly. Use 1-in. nails at slat centers. An alternate, much simpler, procedure for making the roll-top front is to use ¾-in., half-round pine molding. But, the stain may "take" differently than on your pine case.

building the chair

To prevent cracking, make the seat double thick, with ¾-in. pine (on top) and plywood framed by pine (bottom). Glue and clamp layers securely together. Make the pedestal from 1-in. iron floor flanges installed on 1x7-in. black-iron or galvanized pipe. Or use a standard 1x6-in. pipe nipple instead; it saves the cutting and threading charge. But base pieces (I) must then be cut 4½ in. high instead of 3½ in. Finish all parts before attaching pedestal. Paint metal with black enamel. Use primer such as GalvaGrip on galvanized pipe and flanges.

Thoroughly sand all surfaces. Dust and wipe with a tack cloth. I used a mellow pine stain followed by two coats of varnish.

MATERIALS LIST—CHILD'S DESK CHAIR

Key	No.	Size and description (use)
A	1	¾ × 12 × 14" (overall) pine (seat top)
B	1	¾ × 9½ × 11" (overall) plywood (seat bottom)
C	2	¾ × 1½ × length trimmed to fit, pine (seat-bottom edge)
D	1	¾ × 1 × length trimmed to fit, pine (seat-bottom edge)
E	1	¾ × 1½ × 9" (overall) pine (seat-bottom edge)
F	1	¾ × 10 × 12" pine (seat back)
G	2	¾ × 5 × 9" (overall) pine (arm support)
H	2	¾ × 1½ × 10" pine (arm)
I	2	1½ × 3½ × 15" (overall) pine, fir or spruce (base)*
J	2	1" iron floor flanges
K	1	1 × 7" black-iron or galvanized pipe*
L	11	No. 10 × 1½" fh screws
M	3	Wood plugs
N	20	No. 10 × 1¼" fh screws
O	as reqd.	6d finishing nails

Misc: White glue. *If a standard 1 × 6" nipple is used, cut 1½ × 4½ × 15" base pieces (I) from 2 × 6.

PINT-SIZED executive chair (above) consists of three basic assemblies—seat, pedestal and feet.

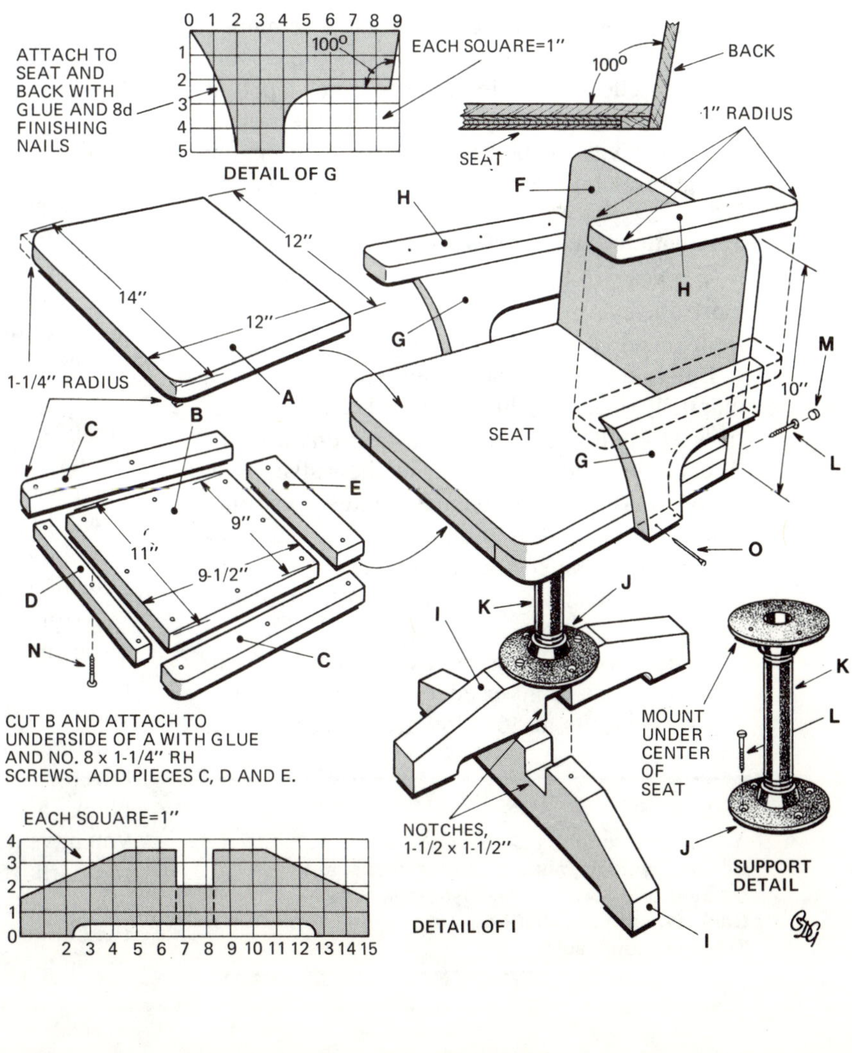

How to keep your choke working

By MORT SCHULTZ

The simple combination of fuel and spark isn't enough for the sophisticated car of today.

AN AUTOMATIC CHOKE can fool you. An inoperative choke, costing but pennies to fix, can produce symptoms that might lead you on a wild-goose chase. A hard-starting engine or one that stalls or uses excessive fuel may trick you into doing a major tune-up unnecessarily. Check the choke first.

Every carburetor has a choke valve designed to close over the throat when a cold engine is started. This reduces the air flow to the cylinders and enriches the fuel mixture.

If the choke valve didn't close, the mixture would be too lean and ignition couldn't occur. A "normal" fuel mixture is too lean for starting a cold engine because gasoline condenses on cold manifold and cylinder walls as it enters the system. The remaining vapor is not rich enough to burn. But once an engine starts, the fuel mixture would be too rich if the choke valve remained closed. Cylinders would flood and the engine stall. So chokes are designed to crack open at once and continue to open as an engine warms up. If the valve stuck partly open, the engine would probably run, but fuel would be wasted.

automatic vs manual chokes

Most choke plates open automatically. You close one by pressing the accelerator pedal to the floor once. It opens as the engine heats up.

But some foreign carmakers still believe in a manually operated choke valve. The driver controls it by pulling and pushing a knob on the dash. A cable connects the knob to the valve. Few problems result with manual chokes. Dirt may cause a choke valve to bind and physical damage, such as a kinked or bent choke valve, could occur, but manual chokes are mostly trouble-free.

Many drivers bothered by automatic-choke problems have converted to manual systems. Conversion kits at $6 to $9 are available from automotive parts and supply dealers. But conversion is a cop-out. Automatic chokes are reliable and usually need only occasional care, but you must know how to maintain them.

SEE ALSO

Alternators, auto . . . Carburetors, auto . . . Cooling systems, auto . . . Differentials, auto . . . Distributors, auto . . . Fuel systems, auto . . . Gaskets, auto . . . Misfiring, auto . . . Transmissions, auto

testing your choke

Testing choke operation if hard starting, stalling or excessive fuel consumption occurs is simple. With engine cold, preferably on a cold day, remove the carburetor air-cleaner assembly and look down the carburetor throat as someone presses and releases the accelerator pedal. The valve should close fully over the carburetor. If it doesn't, the trouble is:

- binding choke linkage,
- a binding choke valve,
- an improperly adjusted choke,
- a bad thermostatic coil spring.

Start the engine. The choke valve should crack slightly open immediately. If it doesn't, the extra air needed for cold-engine idling—still a rather rich mixture—won't be properly supplied. The choke valve is partially opened at this point by either a choke piston or a vacuum diaphragm unit responding to intake manifold vacuum. Either the piston or the diaphragm isn't working or the diaphragm is maladjusted.

Let the engine run. The choke valve should be wide open when engine temperature reaches its normal operating range. Full opening should take place in only 60 to 90 seconds in many 1973 and later models, since that was when manufacturers began adding electric-assist chokes. They're designed to ensure prompt, positive opening to cut back the rich-mixture period and reduce exhaust emissions. If the choke doesn't open wide, you probably have

- a binding choke valve;
- a damaged heat tube, or
- an electric assist that isn't working.

Before charging into a repair job, identify the basic choke system your carburetor uses. Likely it is a stove choke-control or manifold choke-control design. The stove control has the thermostatic coil spring in a housing on the carburetor body. If you see a round cover, usually black, attached by screws to a metal housing, you have a stove control. If no such device is on the carburetor, you have manifold control. To check, trace the long choke linkage attached to the choke valve. It will probably run into a housing on the exhaust manifold crossover. Or it may

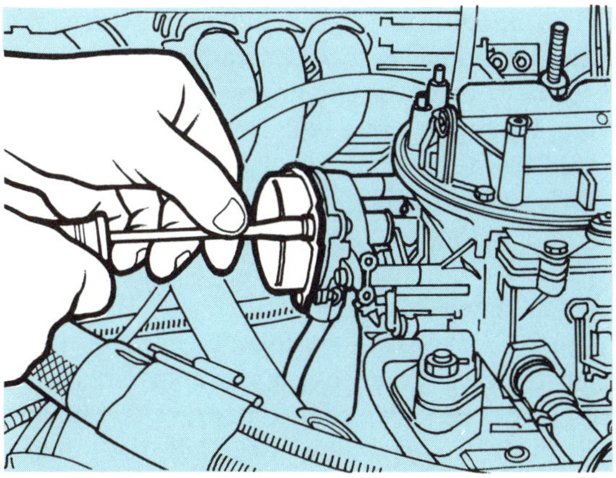

AUTOMATIC CHOKES are governed by thermostatic springs. Stove-controlled versions locate the spring in a housing on the carburetor body. They often get engine heat via a tube from the exhaust manifold.

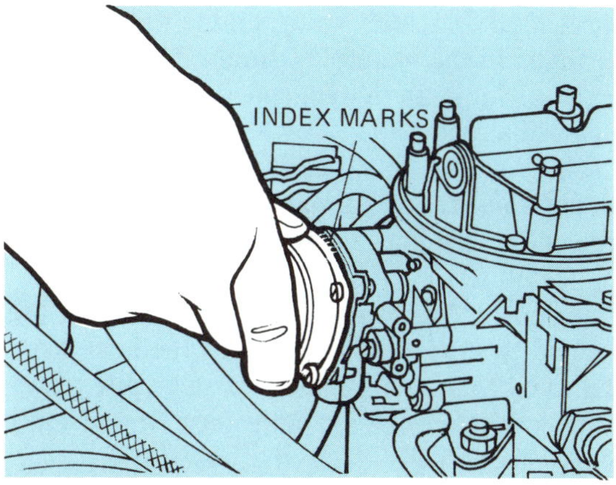

STOVE-CONTROLLED automatic choke has rich/lean marks on the cover. Turning the cover changes tension on the thermostatic spring, modifying how long it will keep the choke valve closed in the carburetor.

MANIFOLD-CONTROLLED choke has its thermostatic spring housed in a well on the manifold system—right at the heat source. A rod transmits the action of the spring to the choke valve.

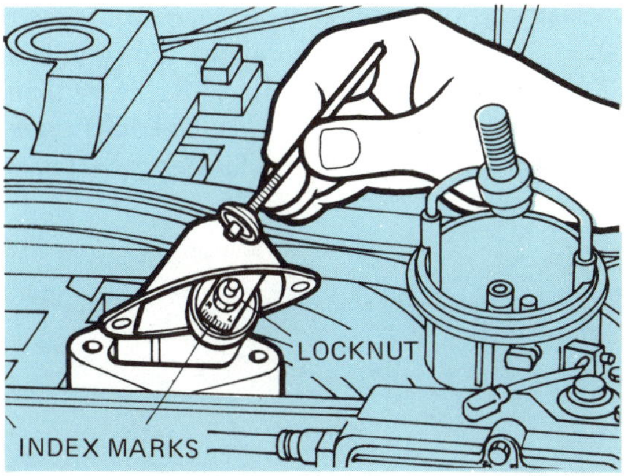

A MANIFOLD CHOKE must be lifted from its well for adjustment. Just loosen the locknut and turn the wheel one index mark toward the rich or lean side, according to the change you want in the fuel mixture.

go from the choke valve to a vacuum chamber high on the carburetor and from there to the manifold. The thermostatic spring is inside the crossover.

choke valve doesn't close

Buy a can of carburetor-cleaning solvent, lacquer thinner or denatured alcohol. Soak an old toothbrush in solvent and clean the choke linkage.

Inspect the linkage. Normally this is bent. If it looks unusually bent or obviously damaged, replace it.

Using the solvent-dipped toothbrush, clean the choke valve, especially its pivot points. This is easier to do with a spray can of choke-valve cleaner. You aim the solvent directly onto pivots. Examine the choke valve. It shouldn't be nicked or bent. A damaged valve should be replaced. *Caution:* Do *not* lubricate the linkage or choke valve. Oil attracts dirt and will cause the choke valve to bind.

To adjust stove-controlled chokes, loosen the screw or screws on the choke housing cover and turn cover to the index mark specified in service data. If the manifold heat tube is attached to the cover, it too must be loosened in order to turn the cover and adjust the choke.

A manifold choke control is adjusted by removing the thermostatic coil spring from the manifold crossover. Loosen the cover screws and lift the coil from the well in the manifold. Then loosen the locknut holding the spring and turn the wheel on which the spring rests until index mark is in position specified by the manufacturer.

If adjustment doesn't cure the problem, replace the thermostatic spring. It has probably lost tension.

It's important to know whether you have a vacuum chamber (also called a vacuum break) or choke piston to crack the valve slightly at engine start. Manifold units, in which the thermostatic spring is in the manifold, usually have vacuum breaks. Some stove-controlled units—but not all—use a piston.

The vacuum chamber is probably the most obvious indication of which system you have. The choke piston is accessible only through the stove-control housing.

If your choke has a vacuum unit, check the vacuum source by disconnecting the hose from the unit. Start the engine and put your finger firmly over the open end of the hose. If you don't feel a strong pull, check the hose for damage. Also ream out the vacuum port on the other end of the hose.

Test the vacuum unit with vacuum line disconnected at the unit. Depress and hold the stem of the diaphragm, and put your finger firmly over the vacuum opening. Now release the stem and watch it closely. It should not move more than $^{1}/_{16}$ inch in 10 seconds. If it does, the diaphragm inside the vacuum chamber is leaking, so replace the chamber.

The amount the vacuum unit opens the choke valve should be set to specification. If the break is too restricted, the engine may flood. If it is too wide, the fuel mixture will lean out too much for a cold engine, causing a stall. Check service data for the specification. When adjusting it, apply vacuum to the vacuum chamber by sucking on a vacuum hose connected to the vacuum port. Be sure the engine is cold.

Vacuum should allow the choke valve to set itself to spec. To check, insert a specified size gauge between edge of the choke valve and air-horn wall. If adjustment is needed, the linkage rod from the vacuum unit is normally rebent at the bend.

If your choke has a piston, disassemble the choke housing to reach the piston. Move piston to and fro. If it binds, take it out of the cylinder. Clean the piston and cylinder with a solvent.

Whenever you're working on a stove-controlled unit, don't fail to look inside the choke housing for carbon; it can impede spring operation as well as foul a choke piston's action.

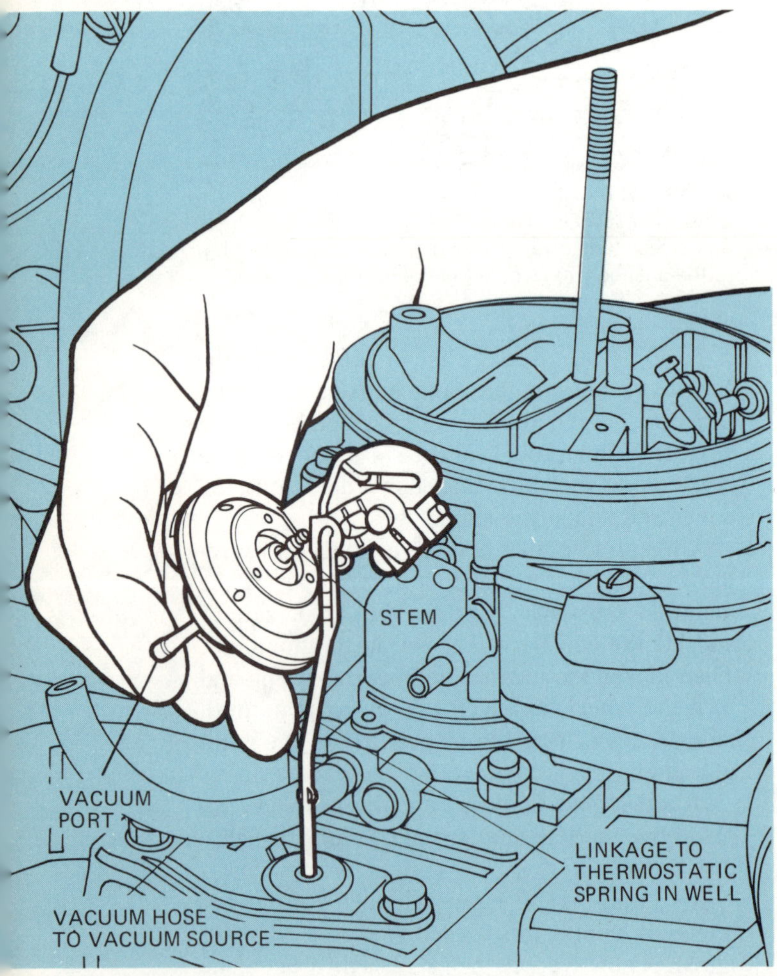

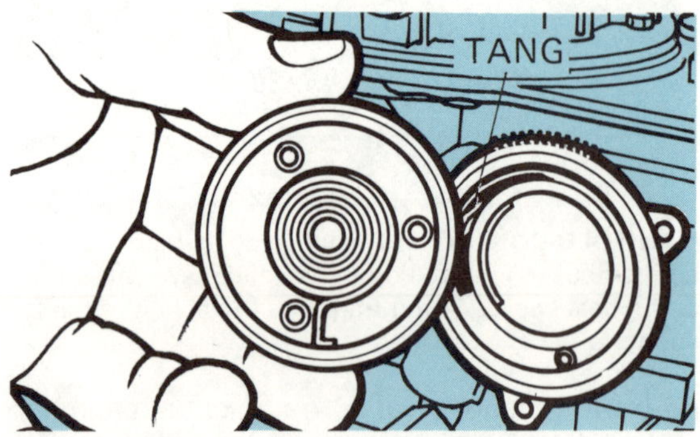

THE THERMOSTATIC SPRING is easy to replace in the cover of stove-controlled choke housing. But it's critical that you be sure to fit the new spring properly in the cover and that the control tang slides into the spring as it should. Otherwise rotating the cover will contribute little to adjusting the choke.

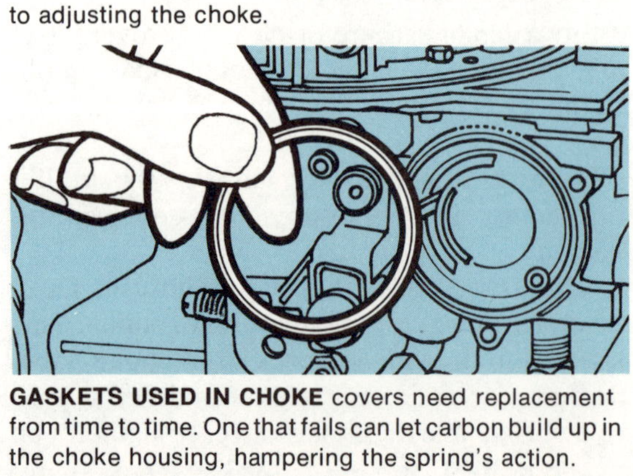

GASKETS USED IN CHOKE covers need replacement from time to time. One that fails can let carbon build up in the choke housing, hampering the spring's action. Vacuum chambers such as the one shown at left are used to modify the spring's action on some choke systems. You should check yours for vacuum leaks.

CHECK THE VACUUM BREAK by supplying vacuum as above. The choke should crack open slightly as if the engine had just started. Bend linkage (below, left) to adjust it. Where a piston (below, right) does the job, be sure it's clean and can move freely.

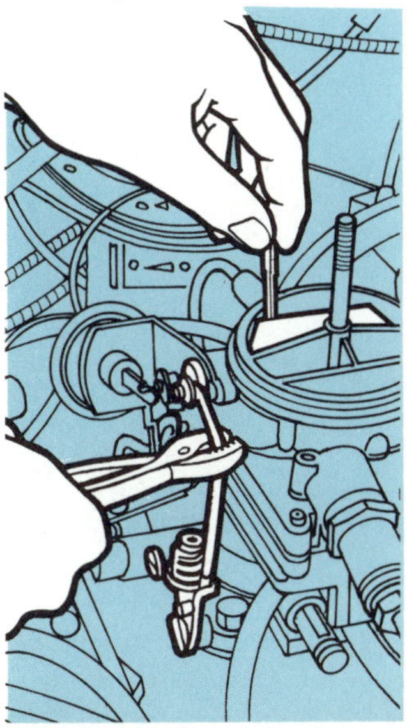

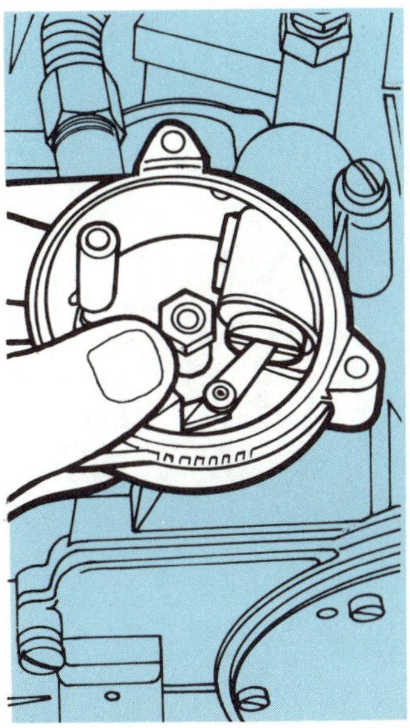

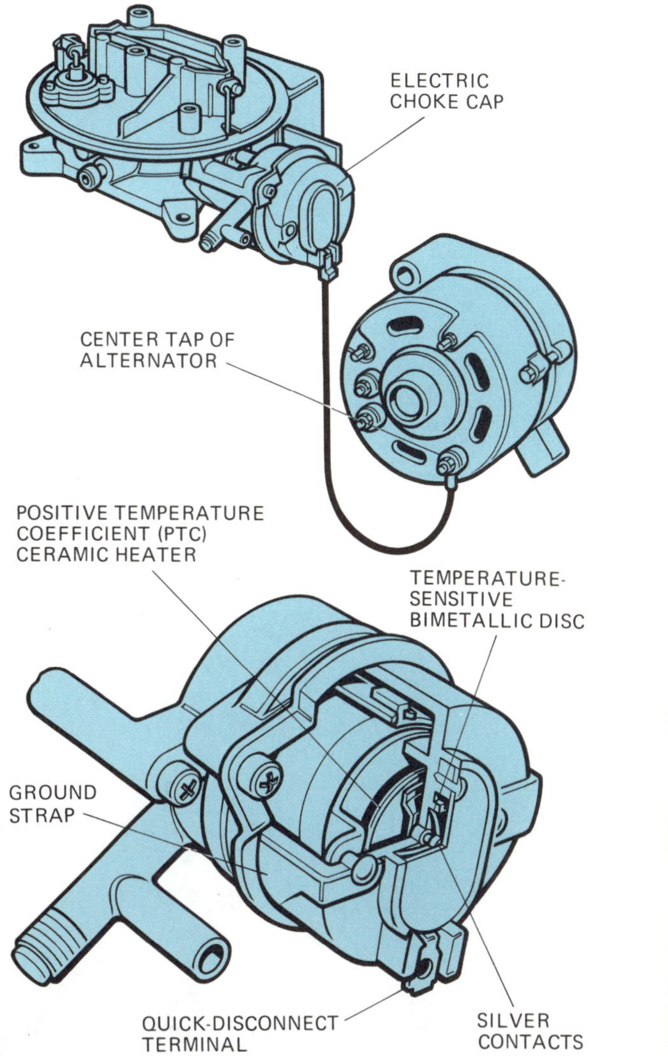

THE ELECTRIC CHOKE assist, in a version by Ford, uses current from the alternator. All components are inside the choke cap. If one should fail, the entire assembly must be replaced. It is grounded through a strap connected to the carburetor.

The carbon is due to air leaking into the housing through two spots. The gasket may be damaged, so replace it. The heat tube extending from exhaust source to choke housing may have cracked or developed holes. If so, replace it.

electric choke assists

Electric-assist units come in two types. One unit, used by Ford, has all parts (thermostatic spring, temperature-sensing switch and a ceramic positive-temperature-coefficient heater) in the choke cap. The alternator supplies current to the switch. (The similar device from Volkswagen draws current directly from the battery.) The Ford system is grounded through a strap connected to the carburetor.

At under-hood temperatures below 60° F., the switch is open. No current gets through to the heater, and the spring operates as if there were no electric assist. At 60° F. and above, the switch closes and current is applied to the heater. As it gets hot, the spring loses tension, and the choke plate opens faster.

To test Ford's electric choke assist, disconnect the electric lead at the choke-cap terminal and connect a 12-volt test light in series with ground. Start the engine. The light should glow at all times. If not, the alternator lead or ground is defective. Place light in series with the terminal on the choke and alternator lead. If it does not glow, replace the entire choke cap assembly.

The electric-assist choke used by Chrysler is designed somewhat differently, but it also can be checked with a test light.

Make greeting cards from your photos

By MARK FINEMAN

SEE ALSO

Bird photography . . . Christmas decorations . . . Close-up photos . . . Gifts, Christmas . . . Mountings, photo . . . Outdoor photography . . . Photography . . . Prints, photo . . . Slides, photo

WOULD YOU LIKE to send a truly unique card this year? Greeting cards which incorporate photographs are certainly that, and with a bit of care can be quite professional looking as well.

If making your own cards seems like too big a project to tackle, many commercial processors and photo and department stores offer services which combine your favorite prints or slides with a standardized holiday message. Most of the commercially composed cards are in color and vary in price from about 25 cents to 50 cents per card, depending upon their complexity. But cards you print yourself will undoubtedly cost less, and they can be made for all occasions.

Start with a good negative—one that requires no specialized printing techniques such as burning-in or dodging. Such tricks are too much trouble when you have to turn out cards by the dozen. The picture should have good contrast and be sharp, too.

Pick your envelopes as soon as you decide what type of card you want to make, since the envelope controls the size of the finished product. Most stationers stock envelopes in many different sizes and colors, but that won't help you if you've printed up a batch of cards for which no suitable envelopes are available. (Of course, you could always make your own envelopes, or design a self-mailing card with a flap that folds over to protect the picture and to carry the stamps and mailing address.)

One of the simplest cards consists of a photograph mounted on a piece of cardboard with space for a handwritten greeting or message.

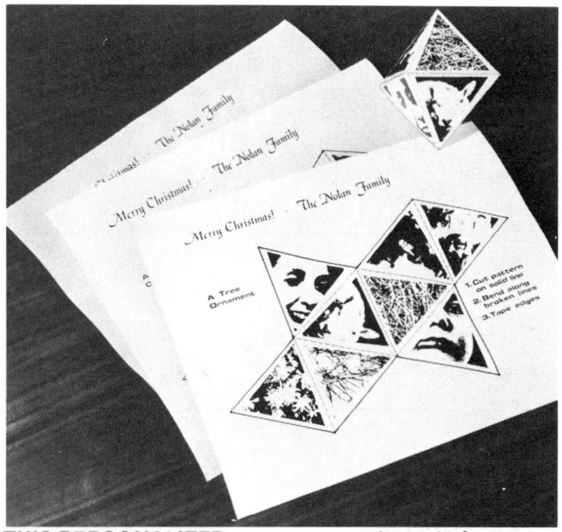

THIS PERSONALIZED tree ornament is made from one high-contrast negative combining greetings, directions on how to cut and fold, and eight triangular photos.

Mounting can be a problem, however. Dry mounting tissue is best, but it's also time-consuming and requires a dry-mounting press for best results. Kodak mounting cement or 3M spray-mounting adhesive will work reasonably well but may present difficulties if the prints are wrinkled. I've even used plain old rubber cement; with this the print may separate from the

BLACK-AND-WHITE cards are easy to make at home. For details on how these were made, see the text and photos.

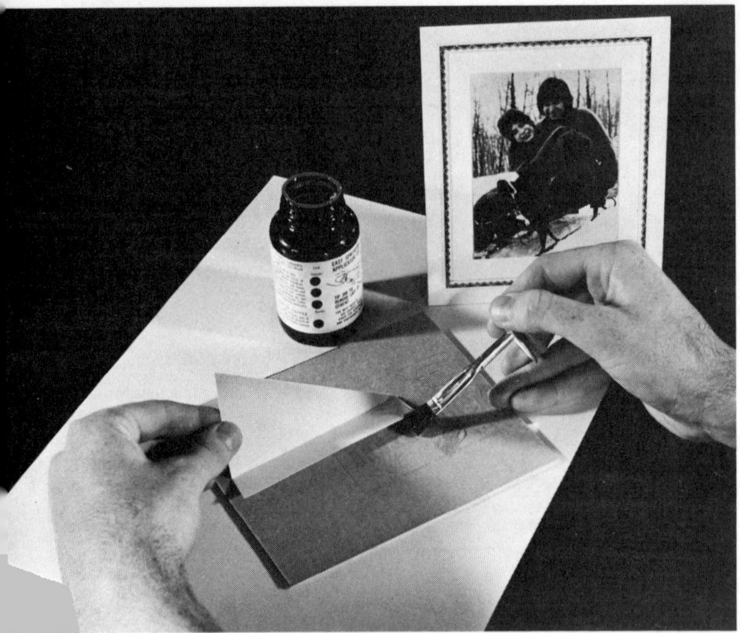

ADDING A SIMPLE EASEL BACK turns flat prints into stand-up keepsakes. The easel can be oriented for either horizontal or vertical photographs.

board over time and the solvents may effect the clarity of the print, but if you know that the card will only be viewed for a short period of time (no more than a month or two), rubber cement may be your best bet. It's easy, it's cheap, and excess amounts can be rubbed off with the tip of a finger.

Art supply stores carry an array of mounting boards, and I have found that an ordinary card can be transformed into a dazzler by picking the right color or texture for the surrounding mount board. Silver matte board, which lends a rich elegant tone to even otherwise commonplace black-and-white photographs, is especially effective.

Some card designs require tricky darkroom work; but if you're not adept at this, or lack time, you can take a lot of short-cuts with your camera. A time-honored way is to combine members of your family and their greeting in one shot by posing them with a letter sign bearing the proper message or with a symbolic prop, such as a Christmas tree.

I discovered still another in-the-camera card technique under the strain of making birth announcements for one of my daughters. I had taken a roll of 120 film of mother and daughter in the hospital, expecting to enlarge one frame for a birth announcement. The contact sheet of negatives was so interesting, though (at least to me and to our relatives) that I sent out contact sheets of the entire, 12-exposure roll, instead, less one frame for which I substituted the baby's name, birth weight and arrival time.

With some careful planning the contact-sheet method also can be used to make several cards at once. By repeating the same sequence of pictures three or four times, a single proof sheet of

COMBINING GREETINGS AND PHOTO on one negative for easy, one-step printing takes time in the beginning, saves it in the end. Here, greetings are lettered with Prestype onto high-contrast print; reshooting on high-contrast film results in a negative (right) from which you can make as many prints as you like.

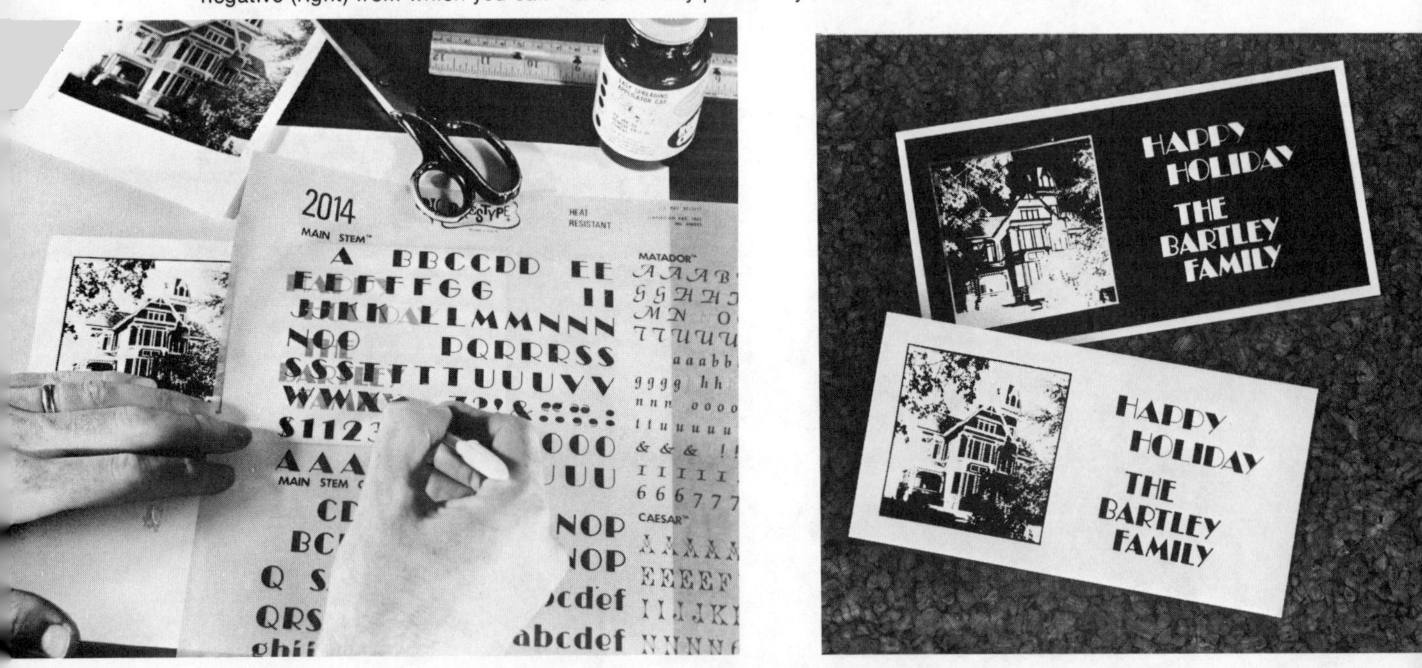

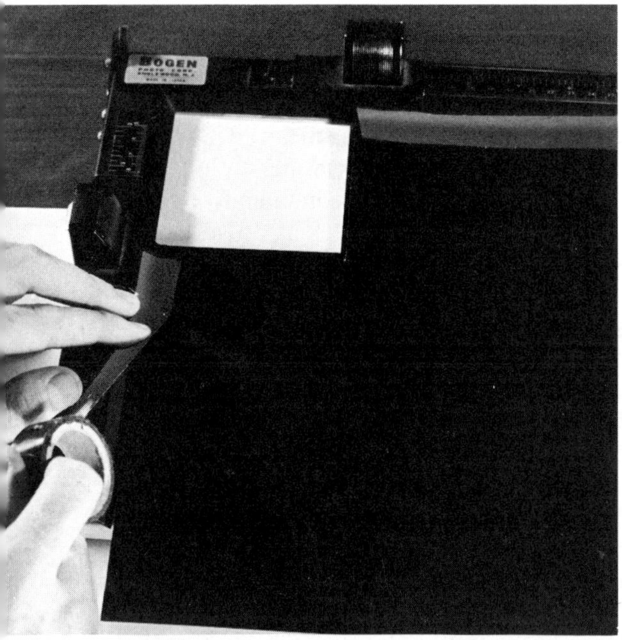

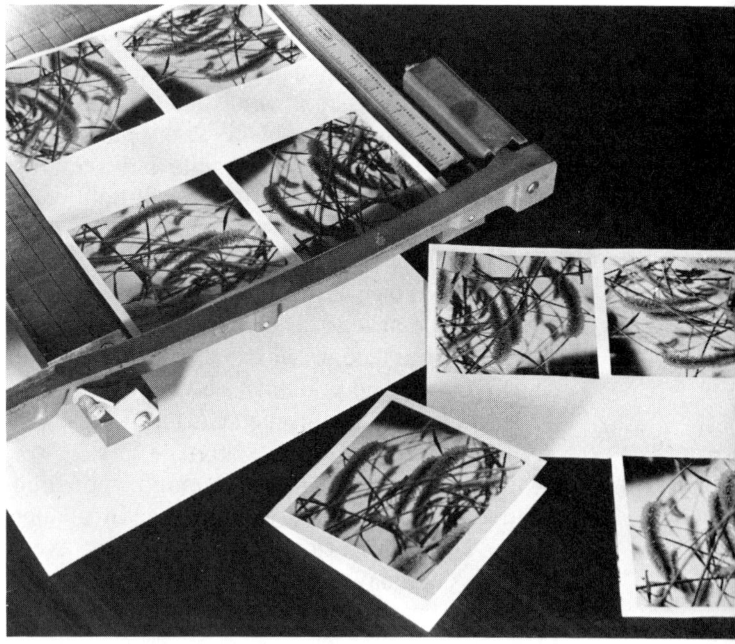

FOR EASY MULTIPLE PRINTING, mask off all but one corner of your photo easel with opaque cardboard (left) so that the cardboard swings up with the easel's masking frame. Insert paper for the first exposure, then turn it 90° for each of three additional exposures. Now you can process the four prints as one, cutting them apart (right) once they've dried.

120 film will yield several multiple-picture "cards" which can be mounted or sent as-is, a considerable saving in darkroom time. And since this type of card doesn't require an enlarger, it's ideal for those just getting started in darkroom work.

You can also put four *enlargements* on a single sheet of paper. It saves surprising amounts of time and aggravation: no more cutting paper in the dim illumination of a safelight, no more shuffling tiny chips of paper through the developer, stop-bath and fixer—instead, you just process one nice, big 8x10 for each four prints, then cut them apart in full room light when they're washed and dry.

Here's how: Make a simple mask by cutting a 3½-inch square from one corner of an 11-inch square of heavy cardboard. Adjust the easel's masking bands (if it has them) for a 3½-inch square print, then tape the mask to the easel's hinged upper masking frame with black tape. Insert the 8x10 paper, make the first exposure, then rotate the paper 90° for the second exposure. Continue, rotating after each exposure, until all four corners have been exposed. Then process the sheet and cut apart the individual prints to mount on your cards.

There are a lot of other darkroom tricks you can use for greeting cards, limited only by your skill and imagination. But high contrast techniques are probably the most important for home cardmaking.

That's because photographs are continuous-tone, with many gray values between black and white, while your written or printed greeting message should be high contrast—pure black and white with no intermediate gray tones, like printing.

Prestype lettering, available from art-supply

THIS TRIPLE PRINT was really made in the camera. The author shot the family together, then each daughter separately, repeated the sequence four times to fill the roll, then contact-printed all four sequences at once. Each strip of three is mounted on a card for mailing. A self-timer would get you into the picture, too. If you are planning on doing your own photographic cards, start early. Doing a quality job often takes longer than you'd expect it would.

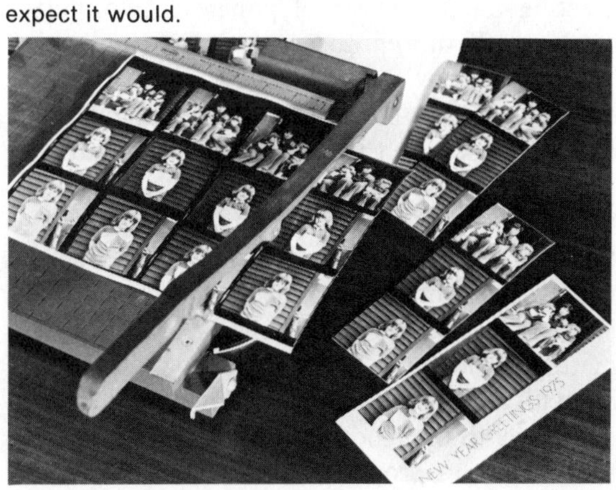

and some stationery stores, can be a big help here. If the picture you're using for your card has large, dark areas, you can print it through a clear acetate sheet the size of your final enlargement, with your message, in black Prestype, on the portion of the sheet overlaying the dark sections of your final print. The lettering will hold back the light, leaving unexposed "shadows" on the print which will stay white while the exposed areas around them develop and darken. The acetate must be at least as big as your final print, though, or its edge will leave a permanent shadow, too. And you must be very careful not to scratch the acetate or get it dusty, lest the scratches and dust "print," too.

If your negative is big enough, you can sandwich it with a Prestype message in smaller letters and enlarge the two together. However, the message may not be as clear a white, and sharpness may suffer.

combining photos and messages

You can also combine your photo and a Prestype message on a single, handmade card, then shoot a copy negative from which you can print photo and message in one step. The problem here is that the finished picture won't be as sharp as the original, and any white space around it will probably print as tones of gray, not pure white.

A better, but more complicated, way requires two negatives: The original, continuous-tone picture and a high-contrast negative for the written message, best made on Kodak Kodalith film. Since Kodalith, films like it and the special developers they require are commercial products not often sold in small quantities, you may find it cheaper to have Kodalith negatives made for you by a commercial photographer.

There are several ways to combine normal and Kodalith negatives to make your finished card. You can, for example, print your photo and greeting on one sheet of paper in two steps, masking off the photo area while printing the lettering, and vice versa. This is more time-consuming than most of the other techniques I've described, but the results are outstanding.

If your Kodalith negative is as big as your finished card, you could use it as a printing mask. First cut a "window" in the Kodalith, precisely where you want your picture to go. Then lay the Kodalith over the printing paper, and enlarge the picture through the window. Expose the lettering with a flashlight held directly above it and in contact with the Kodalith, to make sure the letters come out properly black; but be sure the flashlight doesn't leak enough white light (red light is all right, of course) to fog the picture area. To save time in making multiple copies, you might tape the Kodalith to the underside of your enlarging easel's swing-up mask so it will stay in place throughout your printing.

Still another way to combine Kodalith and continuous-tone negatives is to mount your negative itself in the Kodalith negative's window. If your picture negative is big enough to show up well in a contact print, you can use a Kodalith mask the size of your final card, as just described; but you contact-print, rather than enlarge, through the "window." If your main picture negative is small enough and your enlarger takes a big enough negative (a 4x5 or 2¼x3¼ enlarger and a 35-mm negative, for example), you could use a small Kodalith negative that will fit your largest negative carrier, with a tiny "window" cut for the picture negative, and enlarge both at once. If your enlarger has a glass sandwich carrier, you may be able to hold both negatives in place without tape.

The copy negative technique described earlier works with Kodalith, too. But here, the *lettering* comes out properly black and white, while the *photo* loses its intermediate gray tones. As you can see from some of the cards illustrated, the effect isn't always bad, and can be quite interesting.

several cards on one print

When you plan on making many prints from a normal or high-contrast copy negative, you can often save time by shooting several paste-ups at once onto a single copy negative. That way a single print will yield several cards in one operation—all you have to do is trim them apart afterward.

Some interesting cards combine photographic and nonphotographic ideas. The tree ornament (photo, page 713), a form of folded sculpture, is one example. I experimented with a number of layouts until a flat pattern was evolved which could be folded and taped into a solid. I filled each of the triangular areas that were to become the sides of the finished polygon with photos which I felt would work well in high contrast, and added both greetings and assembly instructions in Prestype on the portions of the card outside the pattern area. Then I shot the resulting paste-up on high-contrast film. The end product is a most unusual holiday greeting, one I know will stand out among the deluge of commercial cards.

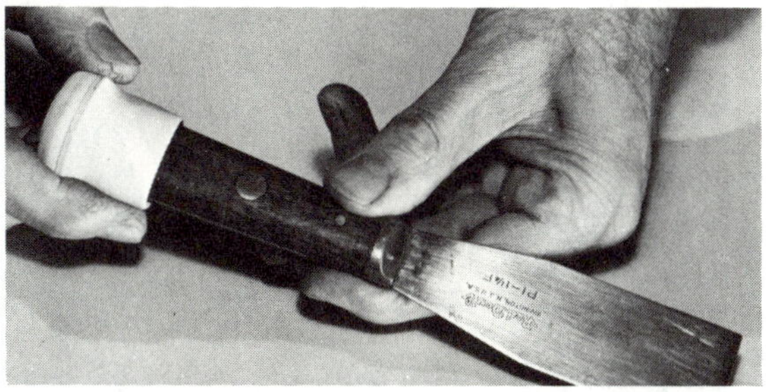

OFTEN, WHEN YOU remove a window pane or install a new one, it is necessary to give the glass a few light taps to loosen it or push it in place. If you slip a rubber crutch tip over the putty-knife handle, the latter can be used as a sort of "glazier's hammer" to do the tapping without any danger of breaking the glass.– *William Swallow.*

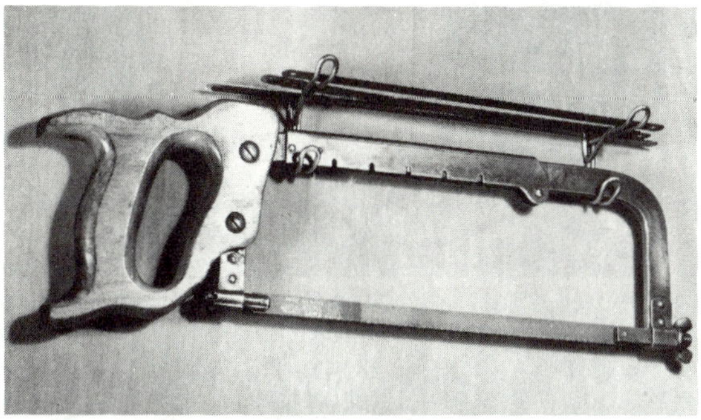

A COST-FREE and easy-to-assemble rack for your hacksaw can be fashioned from a couple of screw-type wire coathooks. Simply position the hooks to suit the saw's frame and screw them in the wall. The bottom hook of each hanger is used to hang the saw, while the upper hook is used to store extra hacksaw blades.–*William Swallow.*

IF YOU BEND a piece of hardware cloth in the shape of a U and fasten a wood block to each end, you'll have a drawer suitable for holding various shop parts such as those shown. This type drawer is particularly desirable where there is apt to be an accumulation of dirt, dust, or rust, because it falls through the wire, and the contents remain clean.–*B. W. Ervin.*

LACKING A TILESETTER'S nibbler when I recently tiled my bathroom, I found that a wire brush chucked in my bench grinder does a fine job of cutting tiles to fit around pipes and other odd shapes. The wheel bites the material more readily if you hold the back uppermost and, surprisingly, there is absolutely no flaking or chipping on the glazed side.–*D.L. Vaughn.*

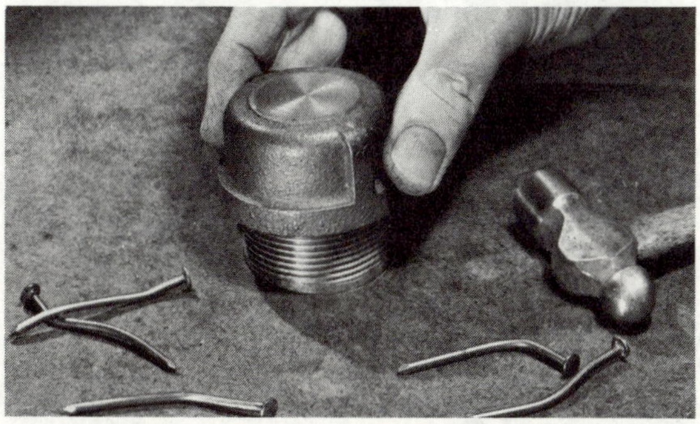

IF YOU FIT a short pipe nipple with a pipe cap and drop it in a dog hole in your workbench, it can be used as a mini-anvil. Because it is not feasible to straighten a nail or the like on the cap's round top, the center of the cap in the photo was "flattened" by machining on a lathe. If the cap has molded letters, these should be filed off.–*William Swallow.*

Christmas decorations that add holiday sparkle

By PENELOPE ANGELL

■ CHRISTMAS COMES only one day a year, but often the real joy and celebration is in the months of planning that precede it. PM craftsmen and designers have tried to come up with the most beautiful of decorations. We think the results on these pages will send you running to your workshop, too, to make sure your home will look its festive best at Christmas time.

1. This contemporary, plywood Santa welcomes holiday guests at your door.
2. Delectable-looking gingerbread ornaments are really hardboard with a lacy frosting of colored glue.
3. A flowerpot blooming with candles sheds light for the holidays. Clay pot is rimmed with colorful leaf imprints.
4. Cars of this train garland are painted hardboard, decorated with stick-on vinyl.

We've included material lists and complete how-to directions for making each item. For the most part, we've relied on novel design ideas that incorporate easily obtainable materials. The younger family members can make or have a hand in working on many of the decorations shown. If everyone pitches in, one afternoon plus several brief follow-up paint sessions is all it will take to produce a houseful of decorations.

5. Lively brass-studded hardboard horses paw air.
6. Christmas lights can shine through holes of these figures to lighten and brighten them.
7. Heirloom rockers give traditional touch.
8. Tinsel Christmas-tree wall hanging adds glitter.
9. Something special for rainbow lovers is this colorful wood mobile.
10. Reindeer table decorations can support place cards or hang on the tree.
11. Kids will get a boot out of candy cane holder.

GENERAL PAINTING DIRECTIONS

You can achieve a high-gloss look on painted wood projects with this technique:

Sand the project smooth by starting with 120-grit paper. Use 180-grit paper to finish. Dust the piece and wipe it with a tack cloth.

A fast, efficient way to seal small pieces is to use Krylon Clear Acrylic (No. 1301) spray. You might consider the alternative of using a mixture of equal parts 3-lb. cut white shellac and denatured alcohol. Rub lightly with 220-grit sandpaper, dust, and wipe with a tack cloth.

Apply a prime coat of Krylon All-Purpose White spray primer, Bin, or the primer made by the maker of the finish-coat enamel you plan to apply. Lightly sand with 220-grit paper, and dust and wipe with a tack cloth. Finally, spray on a coat of enamel; let it dry, sand lightly with 240-grit paper, dust, wipe with a tack cloth, and spray on a final enamel coat.

1 SANTA DOORPIECE

Layered pieces of plywood give this doorpiece a pleasing dimensional effect.

1. Make a grid on the plywood and draw pieces to size; see plan.

2. Cut out all parts with a scroll or sabre saw. Fill all edge voids with wood plastic filler. Sand with 120-grit abrasive, wipe with a tack cloth.

3. CANDLE POT CENTERPIECE

CANDLE POT centerpiece is a clay, flowerpot rimmed with foliage design.

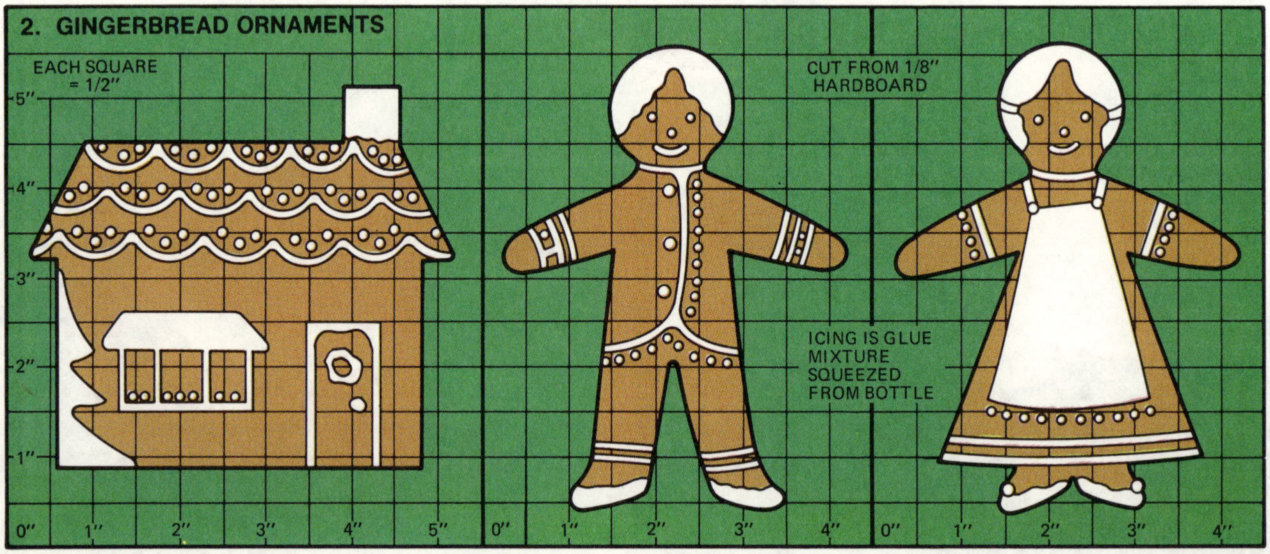

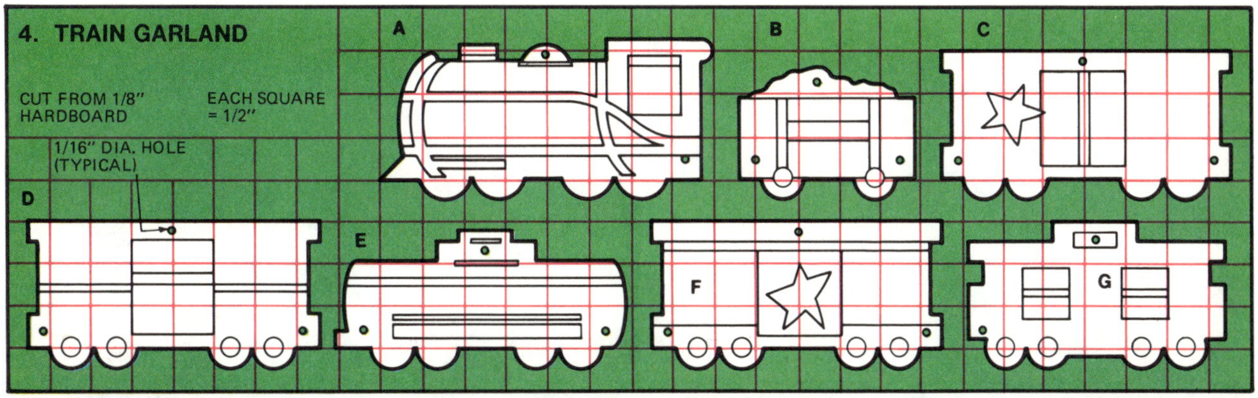

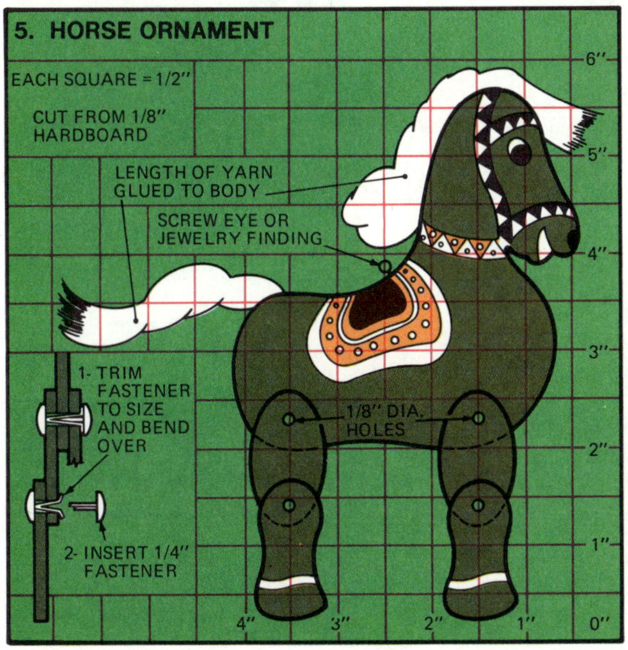

3. Seal, apply pigmented shellac undercoat as outlined in general painting directions.

7. HEIRLOOM ROCKER

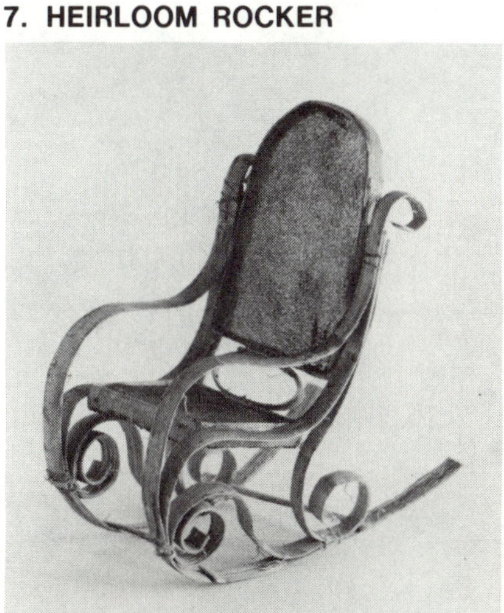

'BENTWOOD' rocker is formed with moistened strips of scrap cane binding.

4. Using the photo on page 690 as a guide, apply red and white paints. Also mix white and pink to make light pink and paint that area. Add white to dark blue and paint eyes. Let dry.

5. Next, paint pink cheeks, dark blue area of eyes and pink part of mouth. Let dry.

6. Glue parts, clamp and let dry overnight.

7. Install sawtooth wall hanger on back, making sure that it is centered. Hang by suspending from nail or picture hanger.

2 GINGERBREAD ORNAMENT

These gingerbread ornaments are simple projects that children will enjoy decorating.

1. Make full-size patterns for the gingerbread ornaments; see plan.

2. Transfer the patterns to the hardboard. Either draw around a cardboard pattern or use some carbon paper to trace a paper pattern.

3. Cut out the shapes using a sabre or jigsaw with a fine blade and a slow feed rate. When cutting toward narrow or pointed areas (i.e.; under arms), cut both lines toward the point and drop out waste.

4. To make the icing, remove about one tablespoon of glue from the bottle. Remove the nozzle cap and pour enough flour into the bottle to thicken the glue, keeping it so it can still be squeezed through the nozzle cap. Stir well with the skewer. Stir white acrylic paint into the mixture. (Use a squib about ¾-in. long if squeezed from a pigment tube.) If a color other than white is wanted, add drops of food color until desired tint is obtained. Mixture will dry slightly darker than it appears wet. Mix *very* well. Replace nozzle cap. Mix other colors as needed.

5. Practice a few lines and dots on scrap until you gain control; then decorate the ornaments. There will be air bubbles if the glue is recently mixed. These can be pricked with a pin. To avoid color bleed when two colors of icing touch, allow one to form a skin be-

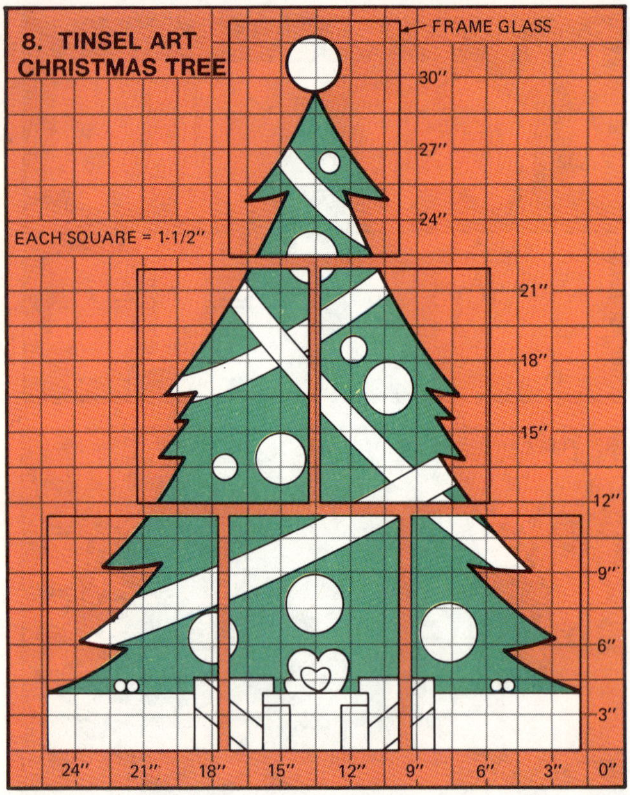

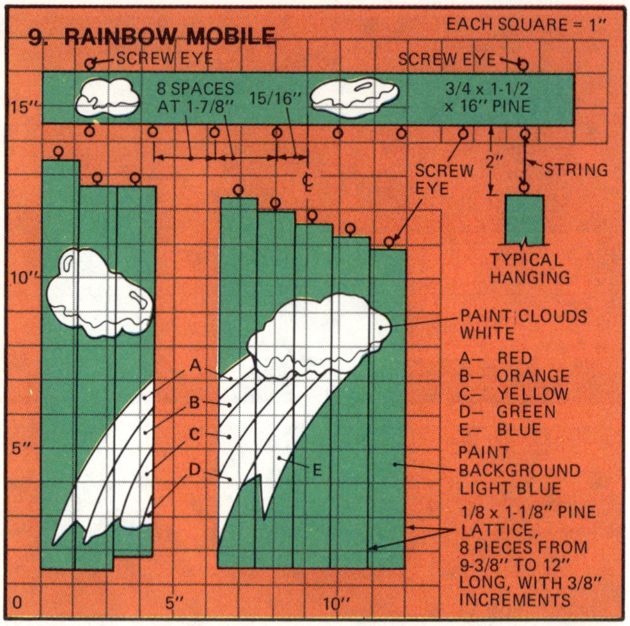

fore applying the second color. Let dry.

6. Spray completely with a clear coating such as Krylon No. 1301.

7. Decorate the back side of the hardboard.

8. Make a cord loop, trimming ends near the loop. Glue knot to top of ornament.

3 CANDLE POT CENTERPIECE

The flower-pot candle holder is a spectacular centerpiece when filled with Christmas balls and tapers or multi-colored candles of varying sizes. Sheets of color dye paper to make the designs are available in a kit called Nature Prints.

1. Color the flower pot with acrylic paint.

2. Cut a wood disc to make a false bottom.

3. Gather ferns, small leaves or other pleasingly shaped foliage. Flatten and dry it by sandwiching between pages of a newspaper and ironing with a hot iron.

4. Remove the top page of the newspaper and position a sheet of color dye paper (see materials list, page 696) face down over the leaf. Apply iron to transfer dye to the leaf.

5. To transfer the dye on the leaf to the rim fabric, place the leaf, colored side down, on the fabric. Cover with protective paper and apply heat. Continue flattening and dying foliage and then transferring color to the rim fabric as you desire.

6. Cement fabric to the pot.

7. Cover wood disc with aluminum foil and insert in pot.

8. Arrange Christmas balls and candles in holders in the pot.

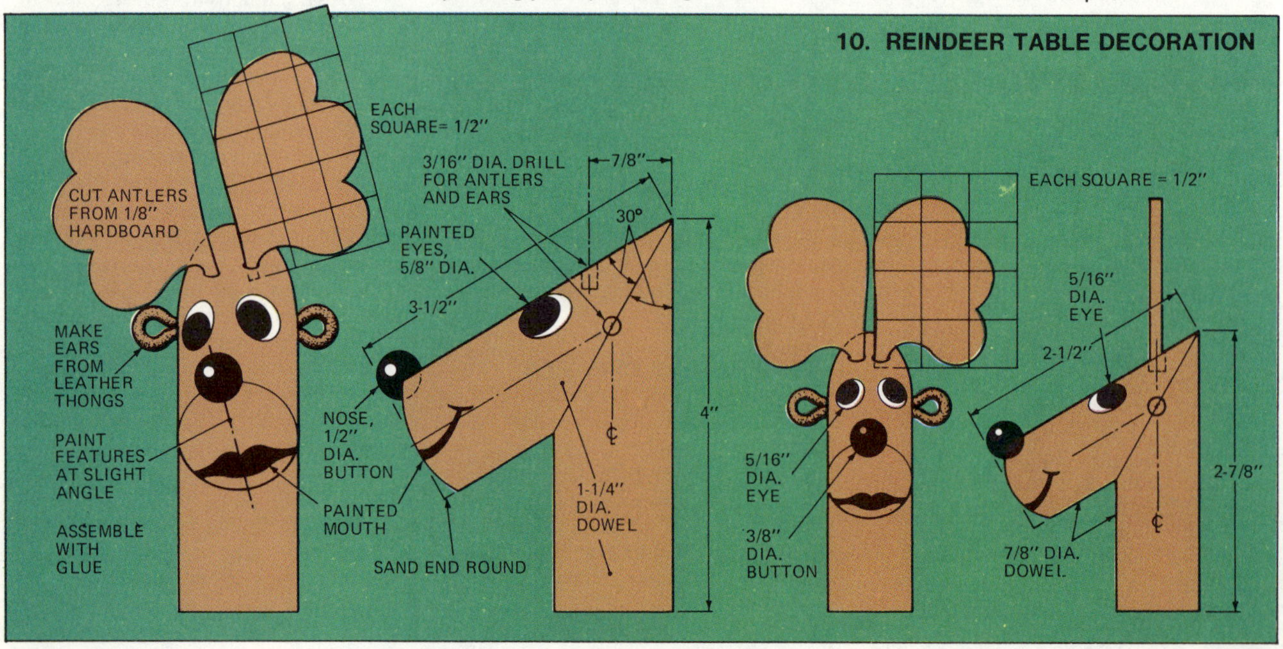

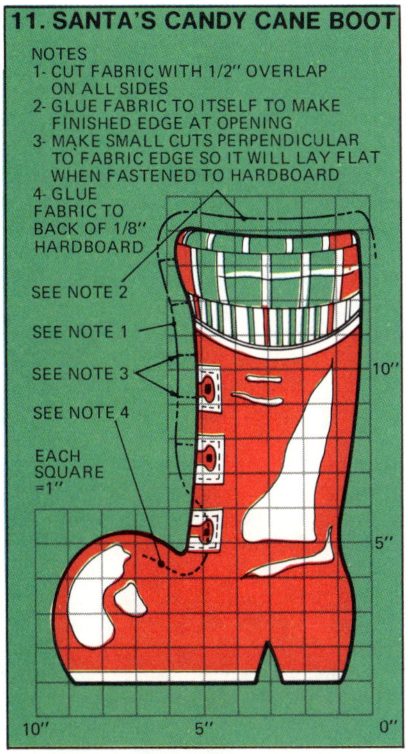

4 TRAIN GARLAND

You can make the train garland as short or as long as you wish. Each car attaches to the tree.

1. Make a grid and draw the full-size patterns (see page 693).

2. Transfer patterns to hardboard, either by tracing around a cardboard pattern or using carbon paper between the drawing and the hardboard.

3. Cut out cars using a sabre saw or jigsaw with a fine blade at low speed.

4. Using a 1/16-in.-dia. bit, bore holes in each car for connecting the cars together and for hanging them.

5. Spray on sealer, primer and enamel paint as directed in the general painting directions; sand, dust and wipe with a tack cloth between operations.

6. Cut out the self-adhesive plastic as shown or make your own designs. A paper punch makes small accent circles.

7. Join the cars with colored yarn.

8. Attach hanging wire or cord.

5 HORSE ORNAMENT

These show horses are brightly painted and assembled with movable joints.

1. Make grid and draw full-size pattern on it; see page 693.

2. Using graphite paper, transfer the pattern, outline only, to hardboard.

3. Mark and bore the holes for the paper fasteners.

4. Cut out the pieces using a sabre or jigsaw with a fine blade and slow feed rate.

5. Seal, prime and paint as discussed in general painting directions, sanding and dusting after each step but the final one.

6. Transfer the hoof, saddle and bridle designs onto the horse with graphite paper.

7. Paint the design backgrounds. Where two colors meet, let one color dry before painting the second color. Paint decorative dots on the bridle and saddle.

8. Assemble with paper fasteners as shown.

9. Glue on yarn mane and tail.

10. Bore hole for screw eye, making sure it is centered so the horse will remain balanced; attach screw eye and hang.

6 PUNCH-OUT ORNAMENT

You can make these ornaments as colorful as you want.

1. Make a grid and draw the full-size patterns on it; see page 693.

2. Using carbon paper, transfer the outline and hole positions onto the hardboard.

3. Use a ⅛-in.-dia. bit to bore the holes.

4. Cut out the pieces using a sabre or jigsaw with a fine blade and slow feed.

5. Spray sealer, primer and enamel on the shapes as mentioned in general painting directions, sanding, dusting and wiping with tack cloth between operations.

6. Decorate the ornaments with acrylic paints.

7. Hang with cord.

7 HEIRLOOM ROCKER

One little rocking chair requires less than 70 in. of scrap cane binding (the wider cane material used around the edge of a chair).

1. First soak the cane in warm water. Remove only the amount you can use at one time. See the materials list on page 696.

2. Cut the back piece (A). Color both sides with a marking pen. Since the cane is wet, the color will be subtle and will give an antique appearance. Shape the back; the bottom side should be 1⅜ in. wide. Overlap the cane ends near the bottom and glue. Then secure with thread.

3. Cut the seat (B). Color, and then bend in a square shape with each side measuring 1⅜-in. Overlap the ends ¼-in. Glue and bind with thread.

4. Cut, color and shape the arms (C), the rocker pieces (D) and the back supports (F). The arms and back supports both have curls. It is helpful to shape the curls around a nail, securing them for several minutes with bobby pins.

5. Upholster the back and seat with scrap nylon stocking. Begin work on the back by stretching a scrap of stocking over a mound of modeling clay that's been flattened in an area larger than the back. Secure the stocking on all sides of the work table. Apply glue with cotton swabs to the inside surface of the cane binding. Press the back into the stocking and clay and leave it until the glue dries. After an hour or so, remove the piece and trim off the excess stocking. Do the same with the rocker seat.

6. Glue and bind the arm, the rocker and the back support together, where they will attach to the back.

7. Glue and bind the arm and rocker at the bottom of the arm.

8. Glue and bind the bottom of the back support to the rocker.

9. Cut, color and shape the bottom side curls (E). Glue and bind them in place.

10. Glue the back to the side pieces, one at a time, by positioning a side piece on its side and balancing the back on it. (You can use the glue bottle and some cotton swabs taped to the bottle to prop the back until it dries.) **Note:** Inspect the assembly from all views to be sure the angles are correct.

11. Glue the seat to the assembly.

12. Cut, color and glue the bottom horizontal crosspieces (G).

13. Cut, color, glue and bind the oval (H). Then glue it in place.

8 TINSEL ART CHRISTMAS TREE

Tinsel art is an early-American craft. Our modern version uses crumpled tin foil to achieve a glittering effect.

1. Disassemble the picture frames; place the frame glass on drawing paper in a pyramid shape as shown on the art, page 694.

2. Trace the outline of each piece of glass and put glass aside.

3. Lightly draw a grid over the outlines of the glass on the paper. Then draw the full-size Christmas tree pattern on the grid.

4. Place the glass on the pattern and outline the pattern on the glass with black marker. Fill in the outlines with colored markers.

5. Paint a black background around the tree on the glass with black acrylic paint. Let it dry.

6. Cut pieces of aluminum foil ¼-in. larger than the cardboard backings of the frames. Crumple, and then smooth out the foil pieces. Tape them to the backings, shiny side outward.

7. Reassemble the glass (painted side inward) and backings in the frame and hang.

9 RAINBOW MOBILE

This colorful mobile can hang all year around. Plans are on page 694.

1. Cut wood pieces to size. Sand with 120-grit abrasive. Dust and wipe with tack cloth.

2. Prime-paint wood with pigmented shellac. Let dry, sand lightly with 180-grit paper, dust and wipe with a tack cloth.

3. Draw a grid to size and draw in rainbow pattern on tracing paper.

4. Clamp vertical parts together and transfer the rainbow pattern to the parts using graphite paper.

5. Outline the design using black acrylic paint and let dry overnight.

6. Paint sky background, rainbow and clouds on one side and edges, using the photo on page 691 as a guide. Let dry.

7. Repeat steps 4 through 6 on other side.

8. Install screw eyes as shown; cut cord and assemble mobile.

10 REINDEER TABLE DECORATION

The doe-eyed reindeer are so simple that you can make a herd at a time and use them as place-card props for Christmas dinner. Keep each in place with a pinch of Fun-Tak or modeling clay under the base.

1. Cut dowel parts; make the 90° base and muzzle cuts, and then make 30° cuts where the dowel pieces join. See art on page 694.

2. Soften the edge of the muzzle with 120-grit abrasive. Round the area where the nose will be.

3. Glue the dowel parts together, hold parts with masking tape, and let dry.

4. Draw a full-size grid on paper or cardboard and draw the antler pattern over it. Trace onto hardboard.

5. Cut out using a sabre saw or jigsaw.

6. Secure the dowel assembly in a vise and bore holes for antlers and ears. Make a small V-cut where nose will be positioned.

7. Sand the wood smooth with 180-grit paper, dust, and wipe with a tack cloth.

8. Apply spray sealer, primer and two coats of Spanish Brown as directed in the general painting directions. Sand, dust and wipe with a tack cloth between operations.

9. Repeat steps 7 and 8 for the antlers using Marigold Yellow spray enamel.

10. Cut leather for the ears and secure in place with glue.

11. Paint eyes and lips.

12. Glue antlers and nose in place.

11 SANTA'S CANDY CANE BOOT

This candy cane holder can hang on the wall or in front of the fireplace.

1. Draw a full-size grid and draw the boot on the grid using plan on page 695.

2. Transfer the boot outline onto hardboard. Either trace around a cardboard pattern or use carbon paper to trace a paper pattern.

3. Cut out the boot shape using sabre saw or jigsaw with a fine blade and a slow feed.

4. Trace the boot design onto white fabric. Then accent the lines with black marker.

5. Color the details with paint tubes, using the photo on page 691 as a guide.

6. Cut out the boot leaving a ½-in. border.

7. Make a perpendicular cut into the border every inch to form tabs around the boot fabric. **Note:** Do not cut tabs on the top edge of the fabric. Cut the tabs on the sides near the top of the boot somewhat shallower than the lower tabs to allow some slack when attaching the fabric to the hardboard.

8. Hem the top edge of the boot fabric with contact cement. Apply contact cement to the underside of the tabs and bend them around to fasten at the back of the hardboard. Allow slack when attaching the side tabs near the top. Let dry.

9. Place a hanger on the back. Then fill the boot with candy canes.

MATERIALS LISTS

SANTA DOORPIECE

One piece A-D exterior plywood, ½×26×48″

Misc.: wood plastic filler; pigmented shellac (Bin); denatured alcohol; Varathane colors in plastic or exterior enamel paints in the following colors: white, red, pink, dark blue; sawtooth wall hanger; resorcinol glue; sandpaper; medium and small paint brushes as needed.

GINGERBREAD

One piece hardboard, ⅛×4½×5″ per ornament.

Misc.: 2-oz. bottles of Sobo glue (one for each color of frosting); flour; liquid food color; white acrylic paint; skewer or stir stick; straight pin; a cord for hangers; a clear acrylic spray coating.

CANDLE POT CENTERPIECE

One 9″ top dia. clay flower pot; one piece heavy white fabric scrap, 2½ × 33″; one 8″-dia. wood disc (false bottom).

Misc.: Nature Print Kit; one tube acrylic paint in red or other bright color; foliage; contact cement; heavy-duty aluminum foil to cover wood disc; candle holders and candles as wanted.

Note: If you can't locate a Nature Print Kit at your local hobby store, you can order it for $6.98 postpaid from: Unicor Inc., Box 382, Champaign, Ill. 61820. Kit includes six colored dye sheets, 25 protective papers, one fabric test square and complete instructions for using the materials on fabric and paper.

TRAIN GARLAND

One piece hardboard, ⅛×4½×11″

Misc.: copper wire or other hanging cord; yarn; self-adhesive plastic such as Con-Tact; spray sealer; primer; enamel paints.

HORSE ORNAMENT

One piece hardboard, ⅛×5×6″

Misc.: rh brass paper fasteners with ¼ and ½″ shanks; spray sealer; primer and red spray enamel; assorted acrylic paints; yarn; tiny screw eye or jewelry finding; hanging cord; tracing paper; graphite paper; white glue.

PUNCH-OUT DESIGN

One piece plywood, 3/16×4¼×4½″

Misc.: spray sealer; primer and assorted enamel paints; assorted enamels in jars; small paint brush; hanging cord; carbon paper.

HEIRLOOM ROCKER

Key	No.	Size and description (use)
A	1	7″ cane binding (back)
B	1	5-¾″ cane binding (seat)
C	2	5-⅛″ cane binding (arm)
D	2	8″ cane binding (rocker)
E	2	4⅜″ cane binding (side curl)
F	2	4¾″ cane binding (back support)
G	2	1¾″ cane binding (crosspiece)
H	1	2¼″ cane binding (oval)

Misc.: white glue; thread; scrap nylon stocking; indelible marker; modeling clay; cotton swabs; nail; bobby pin.

TINSEL ART CHRISTMAS TREE

Misc.: six 8½×11″ picture frames; permanent felt-tip markers in black, light green, dark green, red, yellow, blue and orange; one tube of black acrylic paint; 1″-wide brush; large sheet of drawing paper; roll of aluminum foil.

RAINBOW MOBILE

No.	Size and description
1	¾ × 1½ × 16″ pine
1	⅛ × 1⅛ × 12″ pine
1	⅛ × 1⅛ × 11⅝″ pine
1	⅛ × 1⅛ × 11¼″ pine
1	⅛ × 1⅛ × 10⅞″ pine
1	⅛ × 1⅛ × 10½″ pine
1	⅛ × 1⅛ × 10⅛″ pine
1	⅛ × 1⅛ × 9¾″ pine
1	⅛ × 1⅛ × 9⅜″ pine

Misc.: 18 screw eyes such as Stanley No. V8450-216½; cord; graphite paper; sandpaper; pigmented shellac; the following acrylic paints: light blue, black, white, red, orange, yellow, green, royal blue; medium and small paint brush.

REINDEER

No.	Size and description (use)
1	⅛″ hardboard (antlers)
1	1¼″-dia. dowel (large reindeer)
1	⅞″-dia. dowel (small reindeer)

Misc.: white glue, leather shoe string; ⅜- and ½″-dia. plastic buttons; spray sealer; primer, Krylon Spanish Brown and Marigold Yellow enamels; red, blue, white acrylic paints; modeling clay.

CANDY CANE BOOT

One piece hardboard, ⅛×16×16″; one piece white fabric, 16×16″.

Misc.: contact cement; black felt-tip marker; Vogart Ball Point paint tubes: red, yellow, orange, green, blue; carbon paper; wall hanger.

What kind of faucet?

Recently I took apart a leaking faucet, thinking that it needed a new washer. A ball about ½ in. in diameter dropped out of it along with the washer, which was in pieces. Now I'm at a loss to know how to reassemble the parts. What goes where and what kind of faucet do I have?—A. Ashley, Salem, Ore.

According to your description you have a type of compression faucet. The ball, seated loosely at the bottom end of the stem, bears against the washer as shown in the illustration below.

The purpose of the ball is to effect a tight closure without turning the washer against a fixed seat. Replace the washer and parts as shown. While you have the faucet apart, it's a good idea to replace the packing to prevent possible leakage at the stem.

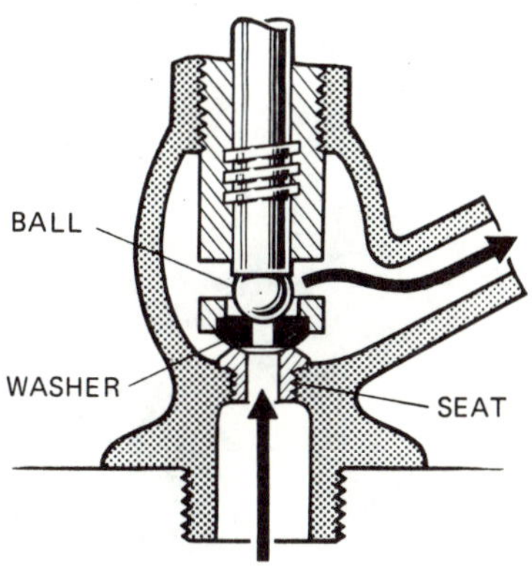

Those sweating sashes again!

Our home has steel casement sashes that sweat. Last winter, the water wet the frames, sills and the wall underneath, staining the plaster and loosening the wallpaper. The house is only one year old and we must find some way of preventing this damage. Can you tell us the cause and remedy?—C.E., Ala.

Ever notice the beads of moisture that quickly collect on a glass tumbler filled with cold water or a beverage on a warm summer day? Water collects (condenses) on the frames and panes of the sashes for precisely the same reason that it collects on the tumbler. The surface of the latter, cooled by its contents, is colder than the air with which it is in contact. Moisture in the air surrounding the glass is cooled to the dew point and condenses on the surface. The air in your rooms is warm and moisture-laden; the sash is relatively cold. Thus condensate forms on the frames and panes.

Most steel sashes can be provided with tight-fitting storm sashes and this usually solves the problem. The storms must fit tightly so there is no leakage of warm air into the space between the sashes. If your heating equipment is gas-fired, be sure it is properly vented to the outside.

Spotted faucet

I have hard water (no softener) and I've tried just about everything to clean the spotting off my new chrome-plated kitchen-sink faucet. Those horrid spots defy all my efforts and cleaners! Please, will you suggest something I can use without wearing myself out?—Mrs. Charles Wilson, Ottawa, Ill.

Must be you haven't tried cider vinegar. It takes some rub-a-dub with a soft cloth, as do most cleaners, but usually clears off the spots with minimum effort. Rinse off the vinegar residue after each cleaning with a soft cloth and wipe dry.

This is not a preventive; the spotting will come back. But if you wipe the plated parts dry after each use it will lengthen the time between periodic cleanings with the vinegar. Use it full strength, by the way.

"Burned" concrete

Last summer I poured a 15-ft.-long concrete walk, using a recommended mix. Now the walk is disintegrating and the surface is powdery. No salt has been used on it to thaw ice. What did I do wrong?—R.Y., Mass.

Assuming you poured the walk over a tamped gravel bed and troweled the surface in approved fashion, perhaps you did the job on a hot, dry and windy summer day, and the new concrete "burned out"—that is, it cured too quickly.

What to do? Break up the old walk and pour a new one, keeping it damp for *at least* 72 hours. Cover the walk with burlap, straw or anything else that will hold moisture after it has been wet down.

Derusting old tools

I've acquired some old tools, planes, chisels and the like, and the metal parts are rusty. What's the easiest, best way to take off the rust?—E.L., Fla.

There really isn't any "easy" way and the "best" way depends largely on the extent and depth of the corrosion. Surfaces deeply pitted are almost hopeless—unless you literally grind away the metal to obliterate the pits. Surface rust can be removed with a fine abrasive or an abrasive pad such as Scotchbrite. Chemical removers also are quite effective.

Old-fashioned decorations for Christmas cheer

BRIGHTLY PAINTED holiday candle holders are made of wood rings, crescents and spandrels available at hobby stores.

STRIKING WINDOW hanging looks like stained glass, but is made of easy-to-craft colored acetate and painted wood rings.

GLOWING FREE-FORM stars made of laminated pine add warm Christmas spirit to a buffet or other party table.

THE DELICATE LOOK of cut glass is easily duplicated in clear plastic as in the Santa and deer Christmas-tree ornaments.

THE ANGEL is etched with a plastic scriber that looks like a pen. Frost area is painted with solvent or sanded.

6

ORNAMENTS that glitter as they turn are made in short order with balsa wood and colored defraction trim.

SIMPLE SQUARE knots make the texture of this tree wall hanging. You might add a big red bow to the bottom of the tree.

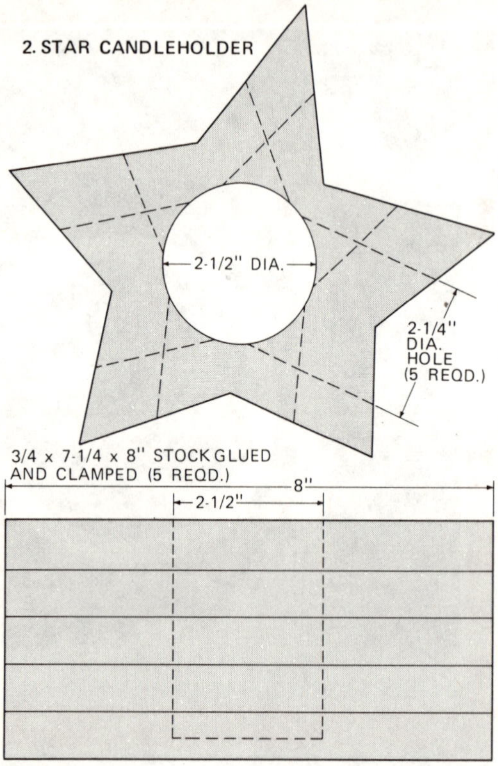

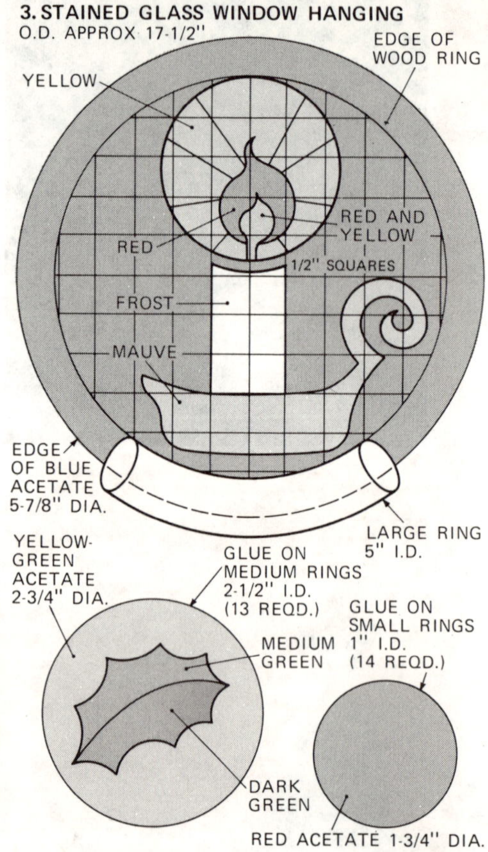

1. Wood-ring candlesticks

Holders shown are made of wood sections available at craft shops.

Crescent holder

Materials: 1″ i.d. wood ring, 16 crescents less than half circle with 2 to 2½″ o.d., metal candle spike, spray sealer, acrylic paint, white glue.

Seal and paint wood. Assemble holder upside down in small bowl, starting with ring. Glue ends of four crescents to ring. Make four layers of four crescents each. When dry, remove from bowl; glue spike to ring.

Loop-the-loop holder

Materials: 2 2¼″ i.d. rings, 1½″ i.d. ring, 3 1″ i.d. rings, spray sealer, acrylic paint and white glue.

Seal and paint rings. Glue two small ones together and two large ones together. Lay the medium ring on a table and glue larger ones upright on it. Glue a small ring upright inside large ones and place double small rings horizontally on large ones.

Wood-ring spandrel holder

Materials: 1¾″ i.d. ring, 3 1¼″ i.d. rings, 3 medium-size triangular spandrels, spray sealer, acrylic paint, white glue.

Seal and paint wood. Glue spandrels in triangular shape, corners touching. Glue large ring on top, followed by remaining rings.

Rattan holder

Materials: 2¼″ i.d. wood ring, 2 1¼″ i.d. rings, 3 crescents less than a half circle from 2¾ to 3¾″ o.d., spray varnish, white glue.

Varnish wood. Glue ends of three crescents to large ring to form a triangle. Glue two small rings together; then glue them to crescent tops. Wood sections are from Woodring Craft, 35 West 44th St., New York, NY 10036.

2. Star candleholders

Materials for one star: 5 pieces ¾ x 7¼ x 8″ clear pine, carpenter's glue, 180-grit abrasive paper, oil stain, varnish, scented candle in cup.

Apply glue to mating surfaces of five pieces of pine and clamp. Immediately, wipe off all glue squeeze-out with damp cloth. Let clamped star dry overnight. Using pattern above as guide, draw free-form star on block's top surface. Cut out star with bandsaw. On star top, mark somewhat larger dimensions than candle cup and bore its hole. Using 2¼″ multispur bit or holesaw, bore holes through each valley junction of star. *Caution:* Be sure star is aligned perfectly and clamped securely to drillpress table.

To finish, sand lightly with 180-grit paper, dust and apply choice of stain following maker's instructions. Let stain dry overnight, then apply thinned coat of semigloss varnish diluted 50 percent with turpentine. Let dry 24 hours, then apply varnish from the can. As the candle burns, light will shine through the holes.

3. Stained-glass window hanging

Materials: 14 1″ i.d. wood rings, 13 2½″ i.d. rings, 5″ i.d. ring, bottle liquid lead, Scotch Super Strength or model glue; Krylon spray sealer, Krylon Glossy White spray paint, one sheet each of these acetates: yellow-green, medium and dark green, red, frost, yellow, mauve, blue.

Draw design full scale according to plan. Seal and paint wood rings. Draw and cut out the blue, yellow-green and red disc shapes and other colored acetate shapes to be inlaid. From large and medium discs, cut out areas where inlays will be placed. Glue disc shapes of acetate to underside of the appropriate rings.

Center the large ring on an 18½-in. square piece of frosted acetate backing for reinforcement. Space small rings around the large one, glue to the backing and then glue rings together at their

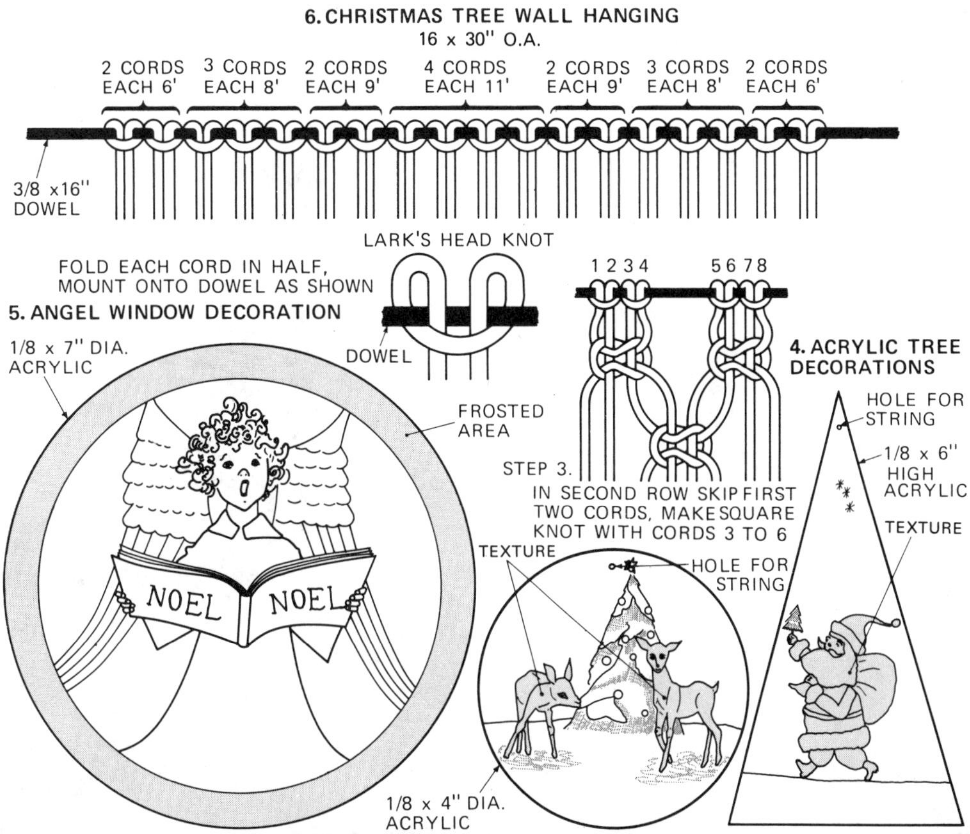

contact points. Position medium rings and glue them to backing and small rings. Arrange remaining colored acetate shapes on discs and tack-glue. Squeeze liquid lead in a line around color borders. Attach cord and hang. Rings are from Woodring Craft.

4 and 5. Acrylic decorations

Materials: ⅛″ acrylic plastic such as Plexiglas or Acrylite, indelible ink marker, red and white polishing rouge.

Beginning and finishing procedures are similar for all decorations. Cut the plastic to the shapes shown with jigsaw or sabre saw. Draw design on acrylic. Etch design in plastic as described below. For the finish, polish plastic to remove ink with either red and white rouge or toothpaste on a soft cloth. Wash with mild liquid soap.

Angel

Frost border by rubbing with medium-grit sandpaper after taping off clear area. Etch outline with an X-Acto carbide-tipped scriber. Finish as above.

Deer-tree decoration

This requires a Dremel, Foredom or other hand-grinder-type power tool. Etch tree with scriber or power tool with cutter accessory—deeply for foregrounds; lightly for backgrounds. Etch deer with round steel burs in power tool. Begin with large burs and work to small burs. Finish as above.

Santa-tree decoration

Etch the entire design with large and small burs in a power tool and finish.

6. Macrame wall-hanging Christmas-tree

Materials: 60-yd., 5-ply, 28-lb. ball of green jute twine, 2″ metal ring, 20 red 20-mm large-holed wood beads, 2 28-mm large-holed natural wood beads, ⅜″ dia. x 16″ wood dowel, 2 yds. red cord or yarn, 18 x 24″ Styrofoam knotting board, T-pins, white glue.

Cut the cords to size and tie them to wood dowel as shown. Begin tying by making a square knot with the first four cords. Repeat with the next four cords. Complete first row of nine knots.

In second row skip the first two cords at left and join cords three and four with cords five and six to tie a square knot as shown above. Continue along this row (eight knots), leaving two free cords at each end.

Continue this alternating knot pattern in row three by taking cords one and two (not used in previous row) and knotting them again with cords three and four. Complete row (nine knots).

In row four begin to decrease the knots by tying one less square knot every *fourth* row. Slip red beads on the spare two cords on both ends. In the fourth row slip beads between knots two and three, four and five, six and seven. To complete design, continue to decrease or drop two cords on both ends each fourth row. Add red bead in triangular design to accent tree shape.

At the top of the tree, secure the eight cords around a metal ring with red cord and trim. Turn the tree over and pull the beaded side cords through adjacent knots, glue and trim. Attach eight 12-in. cords in the center of the wood dowel, secure them with red cord and trim, glue large beads on the dowel ends.

7. Glittering tree decorations

Materials: ⅛″ balsa wood, acrylic spray paint, metalized film with adhesive backing (sometimes called defraction trim; available at hobby and automotive accessory shops).

Using a utility knife, cut trees, circles or other shapes out of balsa wood and spray-paint. When dry, apply shiny trim cut in small circles, squares or narrow strips. Pass a needle through the balsa to thread it for hanging.

1

2

Decorations for table and tree

5

6

■ FILL YOUR HOME with the spirit of Christmas. Deck the house with our festive Christmas decorations—we've included a complete materials list and step-by-step directions for making all the decorations shown here.

Our design collection ranges from traditional, brightly colored and highly polished wood projects to contemporary designs made of clear plastic. You can try your hand at molding and carving

7

3

4

plastic, shaping and soldering tin and applying colored wood veneers to make these holiday designs.

Many of the ornaments are made of common household items, hardware and scrap wood. Refer to the Shopping Guide in this article for items you have a problem getting locally.

Handcrafting decorations is a great way to involve the family in the holiday season.

8

1. Bird candleholders with finely-chiseled look are cut out of glued-up wood blocks. 2. The light of a dozen candles shines from this tree of life made of dowels, balsawood and hardware. 3. Centerpiece consists of pine trees turned on a lathe. Link them with dowels—or use them separately. 4. Brightly painted rocking chair ornaments are thoughtful gifts for little guests. 5. Make candy stripes on this candleholder by painting dowels white and winding red tape around them 6. Candlelight plays on prismatic film of this wall sconce to get a stained-glass glow. 7. Gutter strainers fit around sections of dowel to make stylized balloons. 8. True heirloom ornaments, these are colored veneer overlays on plywood backing.

9. Hang these colorful, old-time toys—ball and cup, tops, zizzer—on the tree. Give them to young guests as gifts. 10. Although these ornaments have the look of antique glass, they're of casting resin poured into plastic tubing. 11. Make these cookie cutter shapes in an afternoon. 12. Sparkling minitree is made of sheet acrylic and circles of prismatic film. 13. Santa moves in all directions at Christmas. Santa window hanging is carved on a plexiglass disc. 14. Make this pine bough window hanging by pouring casting resin into a pie tin in layers sandwiching embedded objects.

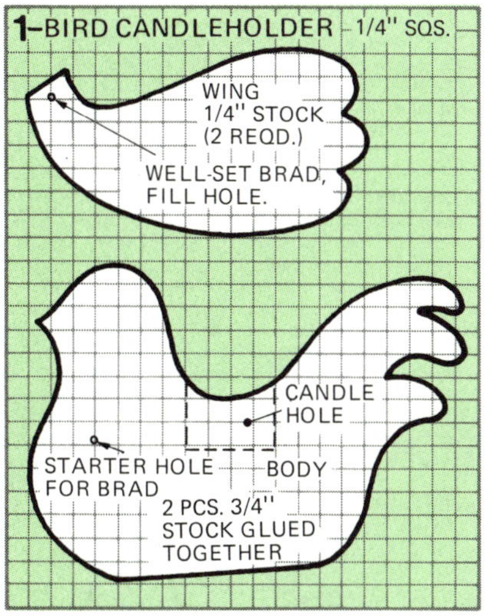

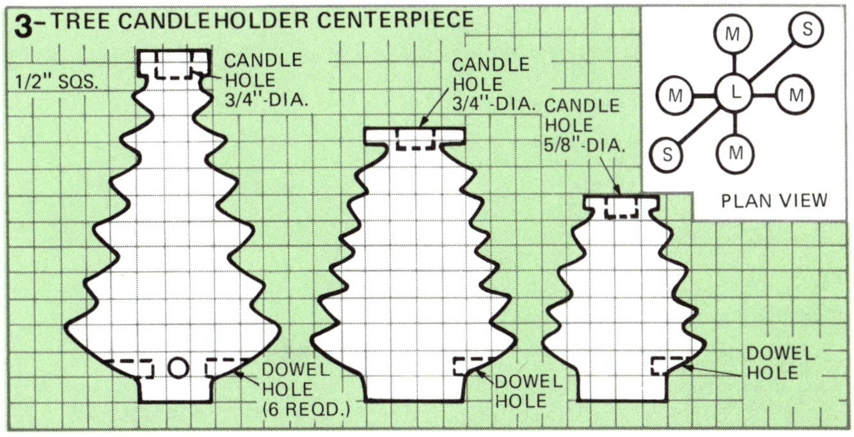

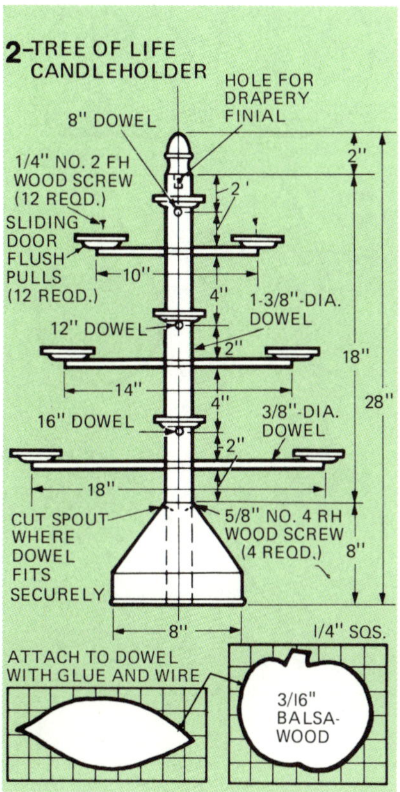

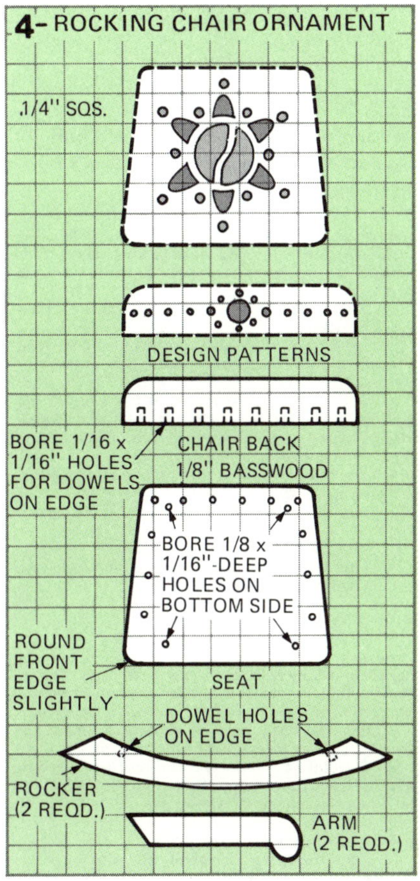

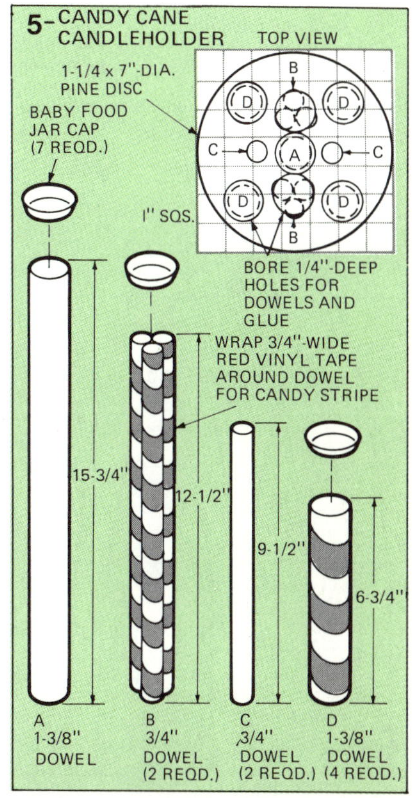

General painting directions

Sand smooth, starting with 120-grit paper and working up to 180-grit.

Thoroughly dust, wipe with a tack rag and apply two light coats of Krylon Clear (No. 1301) spray. Or seal with one coat of 3-lb.-cut white shellac thinned 50 percent with denatured alcohol. Rub lightly with 220-grit paper between coats. Dust, wipe with tack rag.

Apply a prime coat of Krylon All-Purpose White (No. 1315) spray primer, or prime with a pigmented shellac such as BIN. (Note: If you use the latter, the sealing step mentioned above can be eliminated.) Lightly sand with 220-grit paper, dust, wipe with tack rag. Then spray on a coat of enamel, dry thoroughly, sand lightly, and spray on a final coat.

1. Bird candleholders

Materials for each bird ¼x2x3¾-in. piece of lattice for each wing; 2 pieces ¾x4x5-in. stock glued together for body; ⅞-in. brads, white glue, plastic wood filler, sealer, primer, Krylon antique white spray enamel (No. 1503).

1. Cut ¾-in. stock to length; glue up pieces for body. Apply glue sparingly to mating surfaces; expose to air for 30 seconds, press parts together. Clamp immediately, dry overnight.

2. Trace body from pattern above, cut out, sand all edges.

3. Trace and cut out wings. Locate entry point for brads. Nip off head of a brad one size smaller than the ⅞-in. brads used and use it to bore pilot holes for the attaching brads in the wings and body. Sand parts smooth, dust, wipe with tack cloth.

4. Bore candle hole.

5. Sand parts smooth, dust and wipe with tack cloth.

6. Seal, prime and spray paint according to general painting directions.

7. When paint is dry, affix wings to body with glue and brads. Support wings if necessary until glue dries (overnight).

8. Fill brad holes with plastic wood filler, let dry and sand smooth. Touch up with paint.

2. Tree of life candleholder

Materials: heavy duty funnel; 1⅜-in. dia. dowel; ⅜-in. dia. dowel; 3/16-in. balsawood; light-gauge wire; drapery finial top; 4, ⅝-in. No. 4 rh wood screws; 12, ¼-in. No. 2 fh wood screws; 12 sliding-door flush pulls; white glue; sealant; primer; white, red and green spray enamel.

1. Cut funnel as required. Bore four holes through funnel equally spaced near the top opening. Cut 1⅜-in.-dia. dowel to size and position in funnel. Mark entry position for four screws to secure funnel to dowel. Bore holes in funnel and dowel and attach screws.

2. Mark and bore holes in large dowel for smaller dowel branches. Cut dowel branches and bore small holes in them at random to later attach wired leaves and apples. Leave room at ends for door pulls to hold candles.

3. Bore holes for screws to attach door pull candleholders; slide branches in place and glue. Attach door pulls.

4. Bore hole and attach finial.

5. Seal, prime and paint tree white as explained in general painting directions.

6. Cut apples and leaves out of balsawood. Make a small hole for attachment wire with an awl and glue wire. Seal, prime and spray paint. Glue leaves and apples in place.

3. Tree candleholder centerpiece

Materials ⅜-in.-dia. dowel (2 pieces 4¾-in. and 4 pieces 3 in.); 1 block of wood 4¾ in. sq.x10 in.; 4 blocks 4 in. sq.x10 in.; 2 blocks 3½ in.x6 in.; sealer; primer; green spray-enamel paint.

1. Glue up wood to create blocks (see materials list) for turning.
2. Turn blocks in lathe as indicated to make two small trees (S), four medium trees (M) and one large tree (L).
3. Bore candleholding hole while tree is in lathe. Or clamp tree to drill-press table to bore hole at center.
4. Bore holes for dowels on tree bases as marked. Use scrap wood beneath each tree plus hand screw clamps to assure tree being level (90° to drill bit).
5. Seal, sand and then finish by applying several coats of green spray enamel. Sand lightly between coats and wipe with tack cloth before applying next coat.

4. Rocking chair ornaments

Materials: ⅛-in. basswood; 5, 1/16x2⅛-in. dowels for back; 2, 1/16x2¼-in. dowels for back; 4, 1/16x⅝-in.

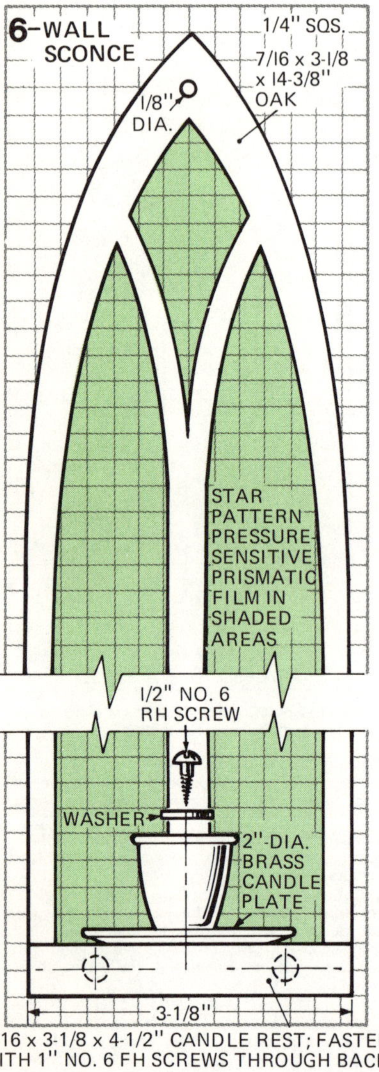

Balloon ornament is gutter strainer shaped and taped around a 1-in.x1-⅜-in. dowel.

dowels for arms; 4, ⅜x1⅛-in. dowels for legs; 2, 1/16x⅞-in. dowels for leg crosspieces; white glue; sealant; primer; spray enamel and bottled enamel paints.

1. Cut all dowels and basswood pieces. Sand edges smooth.
2. Use an awl or nail to bore holes for attaching dowels on chair back, arms, seat (top and under sides) and rockers.
3. Glue the two long dowels at the ends of the chair back with the five shorter dowels in between. Let the glue set several minutes and glue these dowels to the seat.
4. Glue the arm dowels into the arm and glue this assembly to the back and seat.
5. Glue the rocker assembly together. Let it set somewhat, then glue the cross dowels in place.
6. Glue the rocker and seat assemblies together.
7. After glue dries, seal, prime and paint following general painting directions.

5. Candy cane candleholder

Materials: 1⅛x7-in.-dia. pine base; 1⅜-in.-dia. dowels; ¾-in.-dia. dowels; 7 small baby food jar lids; Permabond-Super Glue; Sherwin Williams Marvethane satin polyurethane varnish; primer; green and white spray enamel paints; ½-in.-wide red vinyl tape.

1. Cut pine base. Mark off dowel placement and bore holes ¼-in. deep. Sand base smooth.
2. Cut dowels to size. Varnish and paint dowels white or leave natural as indicated on plan. Wind red vinyl tape around white dowels for candy stripe effect.
3. Glue dowels into base.
4. Spray paint jar lids green, glue lids in place, add candle cups and candles.

6. Wall sconce

Materials: 7/16-in. oak or other hardwood; prismatic film; ⅞-in. brass candle cup and 2-in.-dia. brass candle plate; ½-in. No 6 rh screw and washer; 2, 1-in. No. 6 fh screws; dark wood stain; polyurethane clear finish; white glue.

1. Cut wood pieces, stain and apply finish.
2. Mark prismatic film patterns on backing, checking that star patterns coincide on longer film cutouts. Use utility knife to cut.
3. Trace window outlines lightly on wood for proper placement. Peel off backing and press film; it will adhere instantly.
4. Attach the base to the back with glue and screws. Secure candle cup and plate. Bore hole to hang sconce.

7. Balloon ornaments

Materials: gutter strainer; 1x1⅜-in. dia. dowel; 1-in.-wide colored vinyl tape; white glue, acrylic paints in several colors; Christmas tree hook; adhesive mailing label to make top flag.

1. Cut dowel to length.
2. Shape gutter strainer around dowel.
3. Secure with white glue and colored tape.
4. Hand-paint decorations on strainer band and vinyl tape.
5. Attach Christmas tree hook. Glue on mailing label and cut to flag shape.

8. Veneer ornaments

Materials: Colored veneers (Write to Albert Constantine and Son Inc., 2050 Eastchester Rd., Bronx, NY 10461)—white, blue, red, green, yellow, purple, gray, orange, pink (or color white with pink felt-tip pen); ¼-in. plywood; white glue; off-white or other complementary color paint for plywood back and edges; clear spray lacquer.

1. Make drawings (see plan).
2. Cut three pieces of ¼x3½x6-in. plywood for

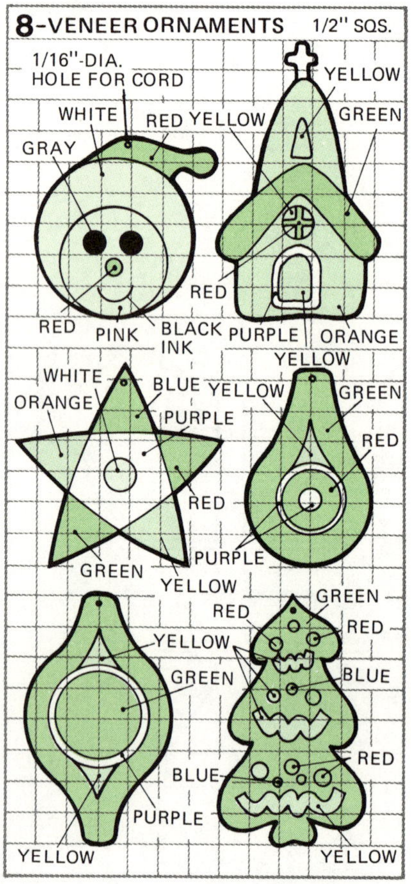

Christmas tree, large bulb and church. Cut three pieces of ¼x4x4-in. plywood for Santa, small bulb and star.

3. Cut and apply background veneers to the plywood: green (tree), blue (large bulb), orange (church), red (Santa), green (small bulb) and leave the star blank. To apply veneer lightly and evenly coat the plywood with white glue. Press down the veneers and weight or clamp. Don't clamp directly on the veneer—protect it with scrap wood.

Also cut five points and center for star. Glue center in place and weight or clamp until dry. Glue points one at a time, pressing until dry.

4. While panels are drying, cut out veneer overlays for all decorations. Cut with several passes with the point of a sharp utility knife. Cut small discs with paper punch for Santa's eyes and tree decorations.
5. When dry, cut out star along outside lines with a coping saw. Glue on center disc. Remove other panels from press and sand veneers smooth with medium, then fine-grit sandpaper. Use carbon paper and pencil to trace outline of church, tree, Santa and two bulbs on appropriate panels. Cut along outline of each design with coping or jigsaw. Apply veneer overlays to each decoration with very thin coat of

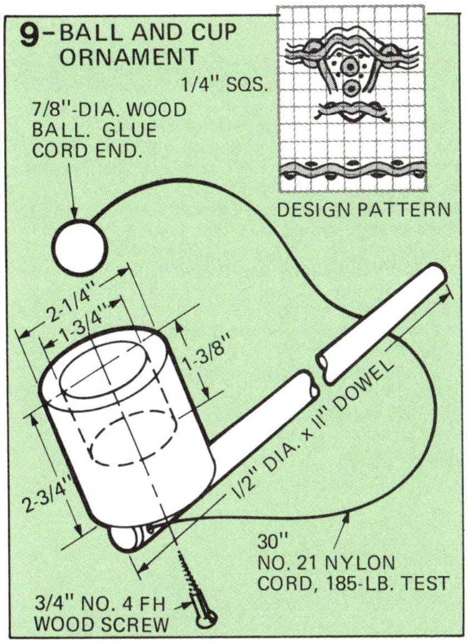

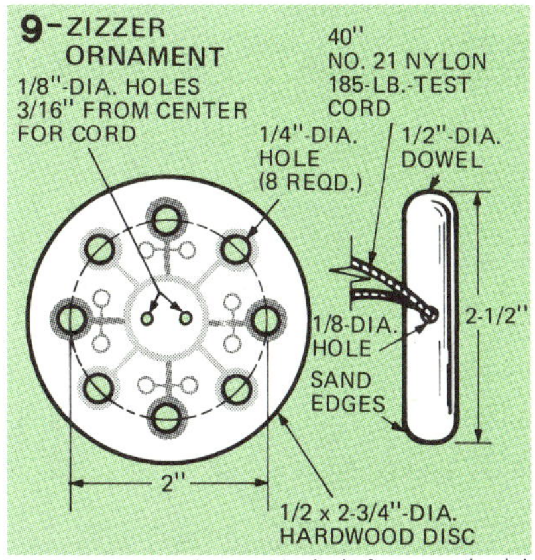

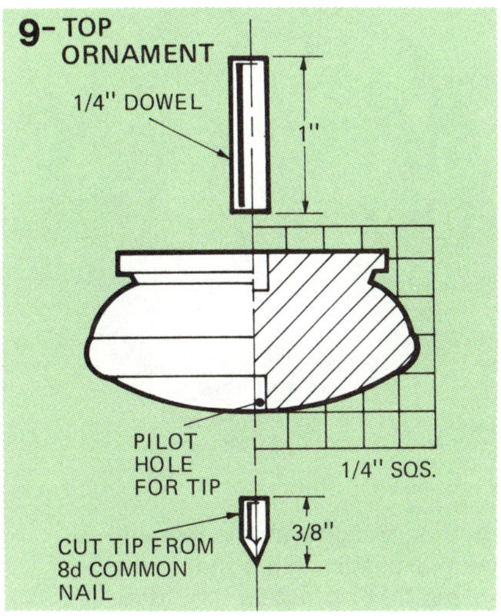

glue, allowing it to become tacky before pressing into position. Apply clamps or weights.

6. When panels are dry, carefully sand edges and apply several thin coats of spray lacquer.

7. Carefully paint edges and back of ornament and bore a 1/16-in. hole in each to hang.

9. Top ornament

Materials: 1-1/16x2½-in.-dia. hardwood top; 1x¼-in.-dia. dowel; white glue; ⅜-in. tip of 8d common nail; sealant; primer; spray enamel paint; plastic tape; enamel paints in jars.

1. Turn the top on a lathe.
2. Bore a dowel hole and insert with glue.
3. Bore bottom hole and insert nail tip with glue.
4. Seal, prime and spray paint.
5. Use thin strips of vinyl tape to make stripes. Hand paint the decorative designs, using enamel paints.

9. Ball and cup ornament

Materials: 2½x2½x2¾-in. hardwood block; ½-in.-dia.x11-in. dowel handle, ⅞-in.-dia. ball or macrame bead; No. 21 nylon twine, 185-lb. test, 30-in. long; ¾ in. No. 4 fh wood screw; white glue; sealant; primer; spray enamel paint and decorative enamel paints in jars.

1. Turn both ball and cup on a lathe from hardwood. Either use a faceplate to hollow out the cup or bore it out later. If you don't have a lathe, roughly bore out the inside of the cup, then smooth it with a drum-rasp drill attachment, followed by sandpaper.

2. Bore a pilot hole in dowel and cup. Also bore hole in dowel and ball for twine. Attach dowel and cup with screw.

3. Tie one end of the twine after threading it through the hole in the handle and glue the other end inside the ball.

4. Seal, prime and paint as previously noted. Draw, then handpaint decoration on cup.

9. Zizzer

Materials: ½x2¾-in.-dia. hardwood disc, ½-in.-dia.x2½-in. dowel handles; No. 21 nylon twine, 185-lb. test, 40 in. long; sealant, primer spray enamel and brush-applied decorative enamel.

1. Cut out the disc, sand edges and bore holes as needed.
2. Cut dowel handles, sand edges and bore center hole.
3. Seal, prime and spray paint. Hand-paint decorative designs.
4. Thread cord through center holes of disc and handles; tie knot securely.

10. Plastic tree ornaments

Materials: 3-in.-dia. clear or colored acrylic tubing cut into ½-in. rings; clear casting resin and catalyst; embedments such as dried flowers, pine cones and evergreen, hangers. For your nearest plastic supplier check the classified directory under *Plastics—Raw Materials—Powders, Liquids, Resins, Etc.* You'll also need a dowel or other stirring stick, 2-lb. coffee can or other container that can be discarded (or use a plastic bowl—dried resin will chip off it); medium and fine-grit sandpaper; aluminum foil; felt polishing pad and polishing wheel; polishing compound for plastics; cement used on plastics. Work in a well-ventilated area.

1. Cut tubing rings.
2. Spread aluminum foil on flat surface, and place clean, dry tubing rings on it.
3. Be sure coffee tin or other mixing container is clean and dry. Carefully measure out resin—use about ½ lb. for every two tubing molds. Carefully measure out the amount of catalyst noted in the manufacturer's directions and stir.
4. Fill the mold halfway with resin. Hold the mold with one hand while you pour. Let it cure. (Temperature may reach 150° during this time so be careful where you place it.)
5. After first layer has cured (it will take two hours to become sticky, but let it cure until completely hard), position embedments. Make pine cone flower by positioning petals individually in circle shape, overlapping in several layers.
6. Again mix resin and catalyst; fill molds to top—almost overflowing (steps 3 and 4). This layer will fill places where the first layer has shrunk away from the tubing.
7. After resin has cured, lift away from aluminum foil, sand and polish rough edges.
8. Bore a small hole at top for hanger and secure it with cement used on plastics.

11. Cookie cutter ornaments

Materials: ¾-in. pine stock for patterns; ¾-in.x18-in.-long tin-plated steel strips (check classified directory under *Tin plate*) solder with rosin-flux core.

1. Draw patterns on pine stock and cut out.
2. Cut tin strips to length.
3. Shape tin around patterns, pressing in place with three-square file to get sharp bends. Overlap ends ¼ in. and cut excess.
4. Hold with clothespins or clips while you solder at overlap.

12. Minitree centerpiece

Materials: ¼x10½x18-in. sheet acrylic and prismatic film. (For kit including punches, write Capro Craft, Box 18, Greenlawn, NY 11740.)

1. Trace outline of tree and cross brace onto sheet acrylic. Draw on the protective masking and don't remove it until all cutting and polishing is done.
2. Cut the outline with a fine-tooth blade in jig or sabre saw. Carefully cut the rectangular notches somewhat undersize and file them to size for an accurate slip fit.
3. Scrape out the saw ripples on the tree edges with a sharp knife blade or the back of a hacksaw blade with its back edge ground flat and corners sharp.
4. Sand the edges smooth using abrasive papers with grits up to 600.
5. Polish to a high gloss by hand using a damp cloth and polishing compound or with a power buffing wheel. If you polish by hand, hold the work firmly in a vise and work the cloth in the same manner as polishing a shoe. Finish off with some passes of a dry cloth. Remove paper.
6. Cut the film discs with scissors or, for speed and accuracy, with punches. Use saddler's punches, paper punch or clicker punches. Press discs into place.

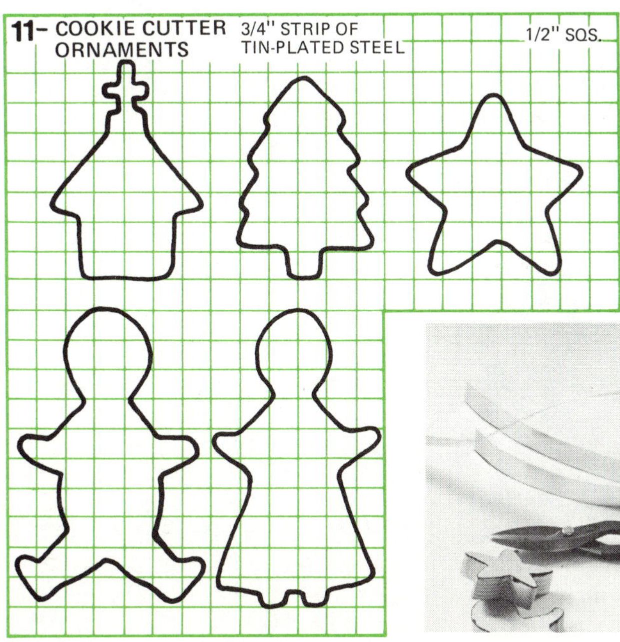

With a three-square file, mold a tin strip around a shape cut of ¾-in. stock. Overlap ends and cut. Secure with clothespins and solder. Hang ornaments on the tree with red cord or ribbon.

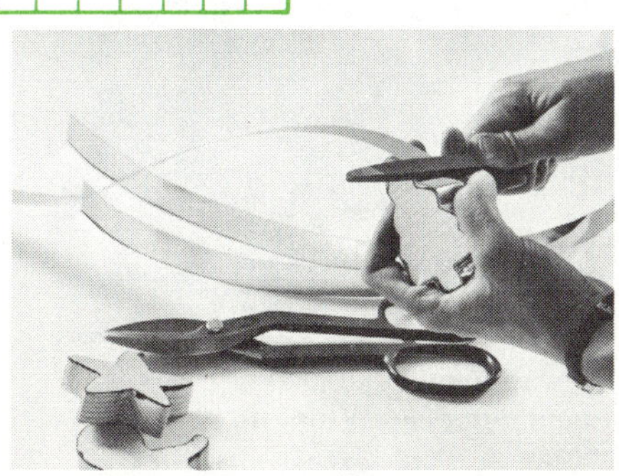

10. **Plastic tree ornaments are rings of plastic tubing with decorations embedded in resin poured inside.**

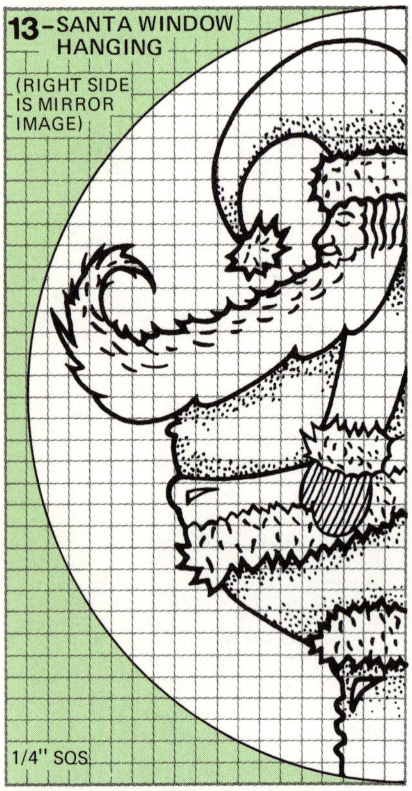

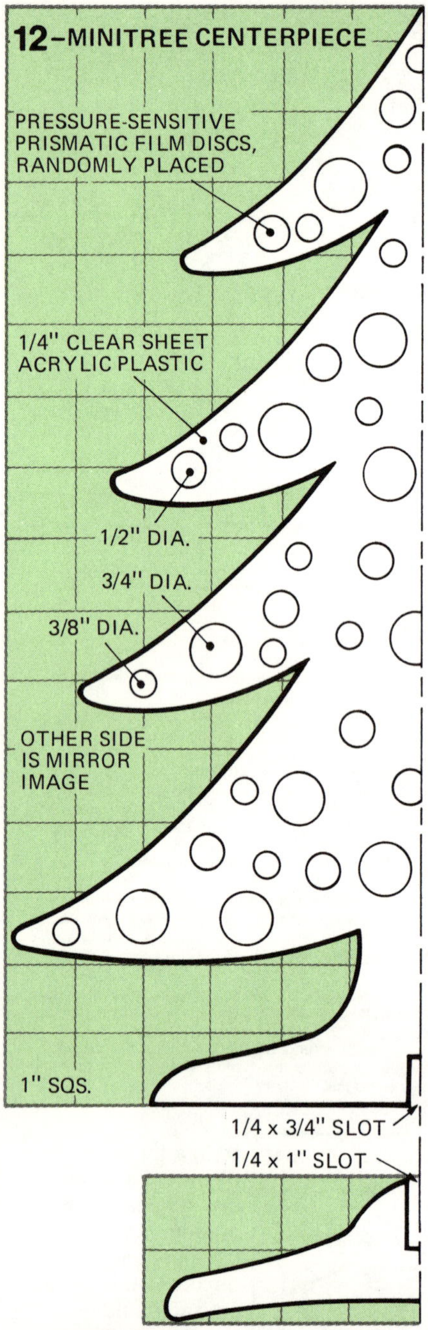

13. Santa Claus window hanging

Materials: ⅛x9-in.-dia. acrylic disc. (Have this cut by your supplier.) You'll also need a Dremel or other flexible-shaft tool with these attachments: Tungsten carbide cutter (No. 9909, 118 or equivalent) to cut outlines; small round engraving cutter (No. 107 or equivalent) for detail work; twist drill to bore hanging hole; plus an indelible-ink felt-tip pen to transfer drawing.

1. Enlarge design. Place it under the acrylic disc and draw design on disc with felt-tip pen.
2. With carbide cutter in Dremel tool, go over all lines as if retracing them.
3. Use same cutter and round engraving cutter to give texture where areas are darkened on plan.
4. Use twist drill accessory to bore hole for hanging.
5. Polish away pen markings with toothpaste on a soft cloth.

14. Wreath window hanging

Materials: clear casting resin and catalyst: embedments such as pine boughs, cone, dried flowers; hanger. You'll also need a frozen-pie tin; dowel stirring stick; coffee tin or bowl that can be discarded; Dremel or other flexible-shaft tool with tungsten carbide cutter (No. 9909 or equivalent). Work in a well-ventilated area.

1. Carefully pour about 2 lbs. resin into bowl and add catalyst according to directions on package; mix.
2. Pour half the mixture into the clean, dry pie tin.
3. Position the embedments in the resin.
4. Slowly, so as not to disturb the embedments, pour rest of resin in the tin. Use mixing stick to submerge the embedments if needed.
5. Allow the resin to cure (it may heat up to 150°, so use care in placing it). When it is hard and completely cured—it will be cool—remove it from the tin.
6. Sand off rough edges.
7. If you add a greeting, first mark it on the disc with an indelible felt-tip pen.
8. With a Dremel tool and tungsten cutter retrace the pen lines.
9. Remove excess pen marks with toothpaste and a soft cloth.
10. With twist-drill accessory in flexible-shaft tool, bore a small hole for the hanger on disc top. Cement hanger in place.

ADD wire handles to clicker punches and cut film discs. Work on hardboard.

14. Pine bough window hanging is made of casting resin that is molded in a pie tin to produce the attractive rippled edges.

Mix wood and oil?

I recently installed a wood-burning stove in my basement venting into the same flue as my oil burner. I'm told such venting is dangerous. Is this so, and will a stove vented this way affect draft control of my oil burner?—Joseph Filtz, Bangor, Me.

I hesitate to recommend this installation, because of potential hazard and reduced efficiency of both units. There is the perhaps remote possibility of inducing "blow-back" in the oil furnace owing to draft interference, and reduced efficiency of either unit or both will cost you fuel money. I think you would be wise to plan a means of venting the stove with its own flue.

A separate prefabricated chimney might serve the purpose.

Warping mantel

The mantel over my fireplace is an unfinished walnut plank, 3 in. x 7 in. x 10 ft., and it tends to warp, the center rising about ½ in. If we turn it over it levels temporarily, but warps again in time. What can correct this? Will finishing prevent warping? What finish?—Kenneth Hafner, Fowler, Mich.

You don't say how long the mantel has been installed, but insufficient air drying is a likely cause. Planks of this size usually stabilize when thoroughly dried to a low moisture content. Before taking any corrective action, such as planing the surface, I suggest you give the plank a little more time, as it might level of its own accord. Then it might be smoothed and given a clear finish such as used on bar tops.

'Mold' on plaster

What will remove what looks like mold from plastered walls? What paint should I use to refinish the walls?—Robert Woolsey, Salem, Ore.

I assume that the "mold" you refer to is mildew. Most any household cleanser in a strong solution will remove it. My preference is for trisodium phosphate, applied with a scrubbing brush. Be sure to wear rubber gloves and protect your eyes from spatters. But removal is only temporary unless you correct the conditions that produce the mildew. Usually it results from a lack of ventilation and excess moisture in room air. A ventilating fan installed in the kitchen or bath, or one in each, operated after meal preparation or bathing will help prevent new mildew. The wall can then be repainted with any interior wall coating, such as water-based paint.

Brick breakup

My brick-faced, two-flue chimney is only about 12 years old. The cap of cast concrete appears to be free of cracks. The bricks in the seventh course down from the cap are crumbling and "losing their faces," so to speak. What's the cause and remedy?—C.S., Kans.

I'll venture to say that the most probable cause is what is known as efflorescence—a breakdown of the masonry due to certain activated salts in the mortar, the bricks, or both. Such activation usually is due to the presence of moisture or of a continuing condition of dampness. There are other less likely causes, of course. Although the defect may show in only one course of brick, it's likely that courses immediately above and below also are affected. The only cure is to replace the defective bricks with new ones.

Usually, this is a job for a professional mason experienced in this type of repair. However, if you want to attempt this chore yourself, you'll need a ready-mixed mortar, such as Sakrete, a pointing trowel, hammer, chisel, a safe ladder and several sturdy supports. You'll also have to cut some props to wedge between the courses of bricks when you remove those which are found to be defective. Cut these from 1x1-in. strips so that they're a tight fit between courses.

As you remove each defective brick tap a prop into place. Be sure to chisel out *all* of the old bricks and old mortar. Then lay new mortar, "butter" the ends of each new brick and force mortar into the joint above each one, making sure the mortar is "packed" so that there are no voids to admit water. Strike the new mortar joints to match the old.

Usually it is best to dampen the old bricks that adjoin the work before inserting the new ones in place.

Chipped iron bathtub

Is there some way of repairing permanently chipped enamel on an iron bathtub?—P. Holmetoft, New Orleans

There are several commercial products made for this purpose, some of the consistency of a heavy enamel, others of a somewhat pastier material that can be putty-knifed into the recess formed by the break. Ask for porcelain enamel at your paint store. Before any of these products is used, the break must be thoroughly cleaned with a solvent such as is sold for cleaning typewriters, and it must be dry. Although these air-drying finishes are reasonably effective, none should be expected to equal the durability of the tub's original fired-on finish.

IN STEP 2 (above), press is opened to receive a bagful of apples that have been run through the grinder (in Step 1 below). Before pressing, apples are piled on grinder "rooftop." From there they are fed into the hopper. In Step 3, juice drains into a clean pail. For maximum portability, the press and the grinder rest on a pair of shop-built saw-horses. They're simply made from 1 x 6 stock.

SEE ALSO

**Airplane models . . . Bottle craft . . .
Cannon models . . . Hobby centers . . . Lapidary . . .
Modelmaking . . . Telescopes . . . Wood lathes**

Make your own cider with a homemade press

■ YOU CAN MAKE the most of a year's apple crop if you have your own cider press. The prototype shown on the facing page—which consists of a sprocket-wheel grinder and a clam-shell-design press—has yielded as much as 12 gallons of juice in an hour when operated by just one person. Using portable power tools and some careful craftsmanship, you can build your own press, grinder and sawhorse stand for about half the cost of manufactured units.

By KATHLEEN STILWELL and MARK JENSEN

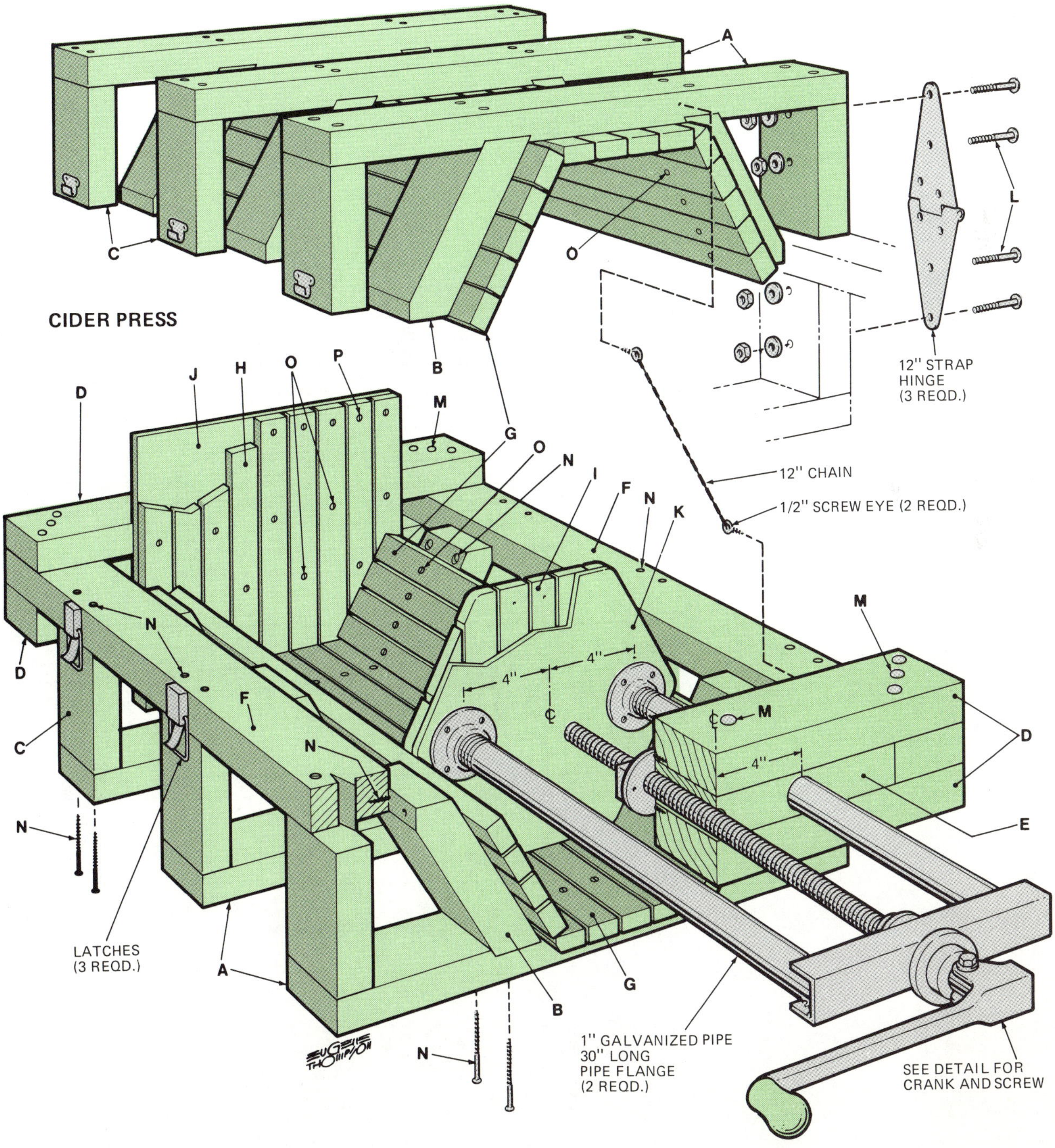

BACK VIEW of the closed cider press shows the three hefty strap hinges that hold the unit together.

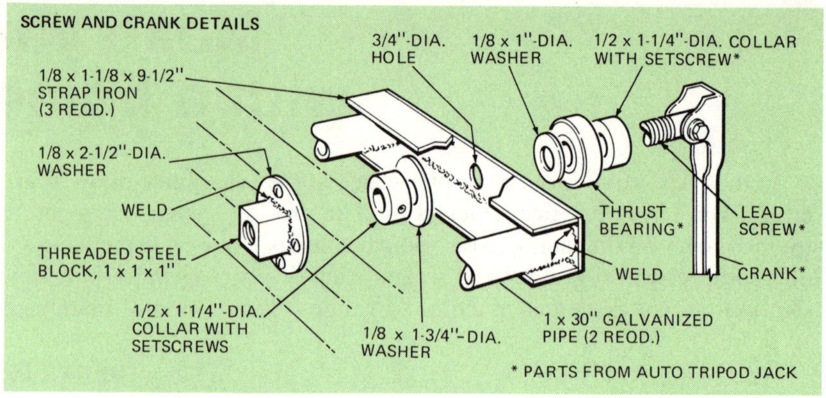

CIDER COLLECTION BOARD AND SPOUT DETAIL

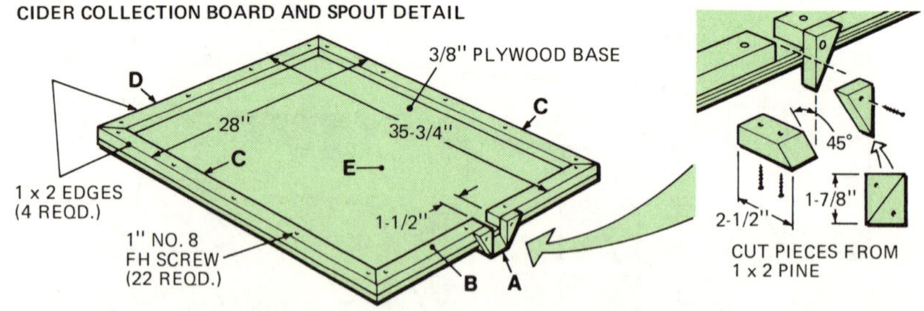

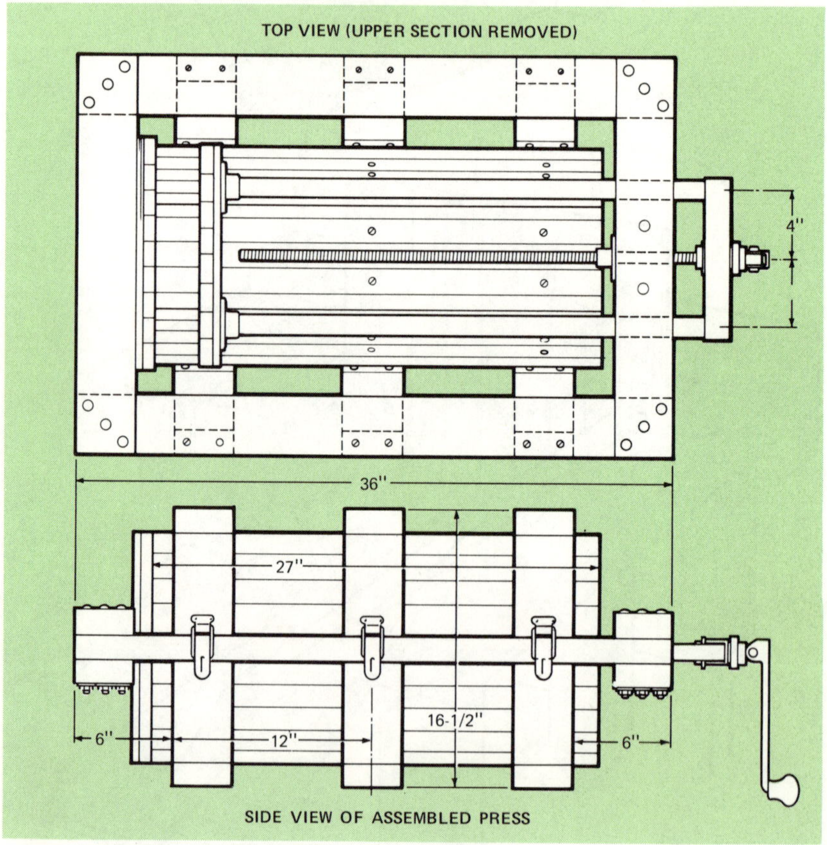

MATERIALS LIST— CIDER PRESS

Key	Pcs.	Size and description
A	6	1½ x 3½ x 23½" fir
B	12	1½ x 3½ x 9" fir
C	12	1½ x 3½ x 6" fir
D	4	1½ x 3½ x 23½" fir
E	1	1½ x 3½ x 14½" fir
F	2	1½ x 3½ x 36" fir
G	27	¾ x 1½ x 27" pine
H	9	¾ x 1½ x 13½" pine
I	8	¾ x 1½ x 12" pine
J	1	½ x 13½ x 14" plywood
K	1	½ x 12 x 12" plywood
L	12	3/16 x 2" rh machine screws, washers and nuts
M	14	¼ x 5" carriage bolts, washers and nuts
N	72	3" No. 10 fh screws
O	90	1½" No. 8 fh screws
P	36	1" No. 8 fh screws

Misc.: 3 latches, 2 pcs. 1" galvanized pipe x 30" with flanges, 3 pcs. ⅛ x 1⅛ x 9½" strap iron, ⅛ x 1¾"-dia. washer, ½ x 1¼"-dia. collar with setscrews, parts from auto tripod jack, 2 pcs. 1x30" galvanized pipe, 3 12"-long heavy strap hinges.

MATERIALS LIST—COLLECTION BOARD

Key	Pcs.	Size and description (use)
A	1	5" scrap 1x2 pine (spout)
B	3	¾ x 1½ x 13¼" pine
C	2	¾ x 1½ x 35¾" pine
D	1	¾ x 1½ x 28" pine
E	1	⅜ x 28 x 35¾" plywood

Misc.: 22 1" No. 8 fh screws, nontoxic white glue.

DETAIL OF PIECES A & B

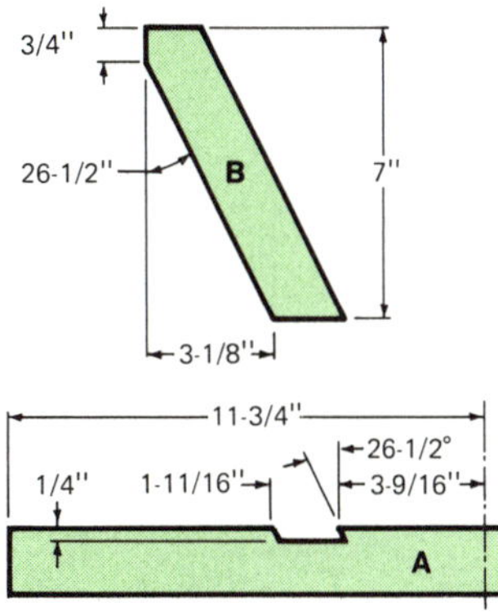

DETAIL OF PIECES K & I

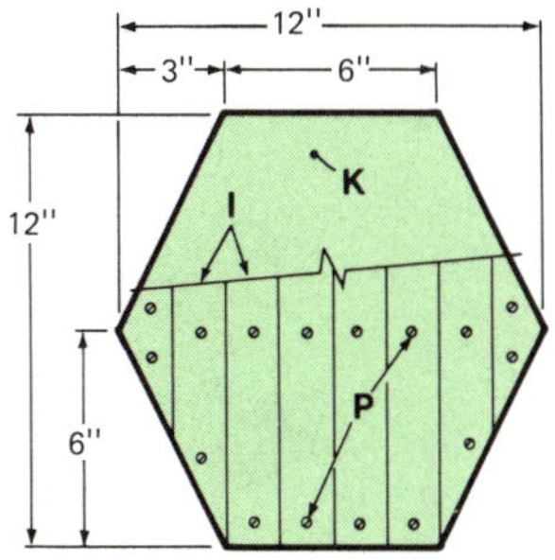

FRONT VIEW OF UPPER SECTION

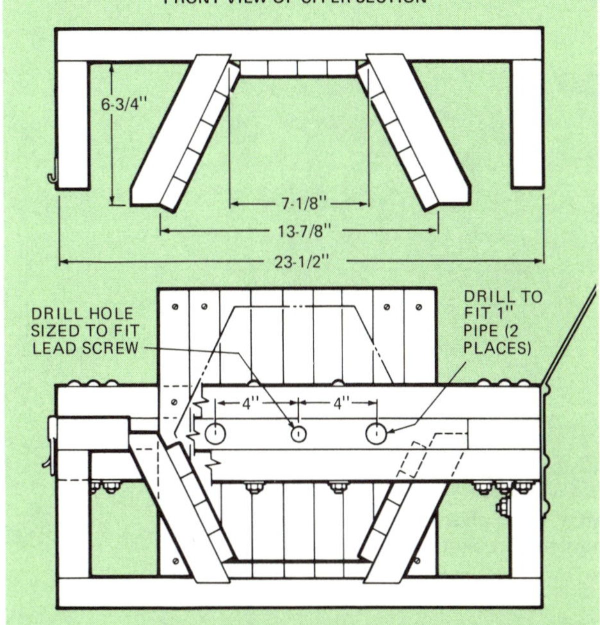

FRONT VIEW LOWER SECTION (LEAD SCREW AND CRANK OMITTED)

continued

GRINDER FOR CIDER PRESS

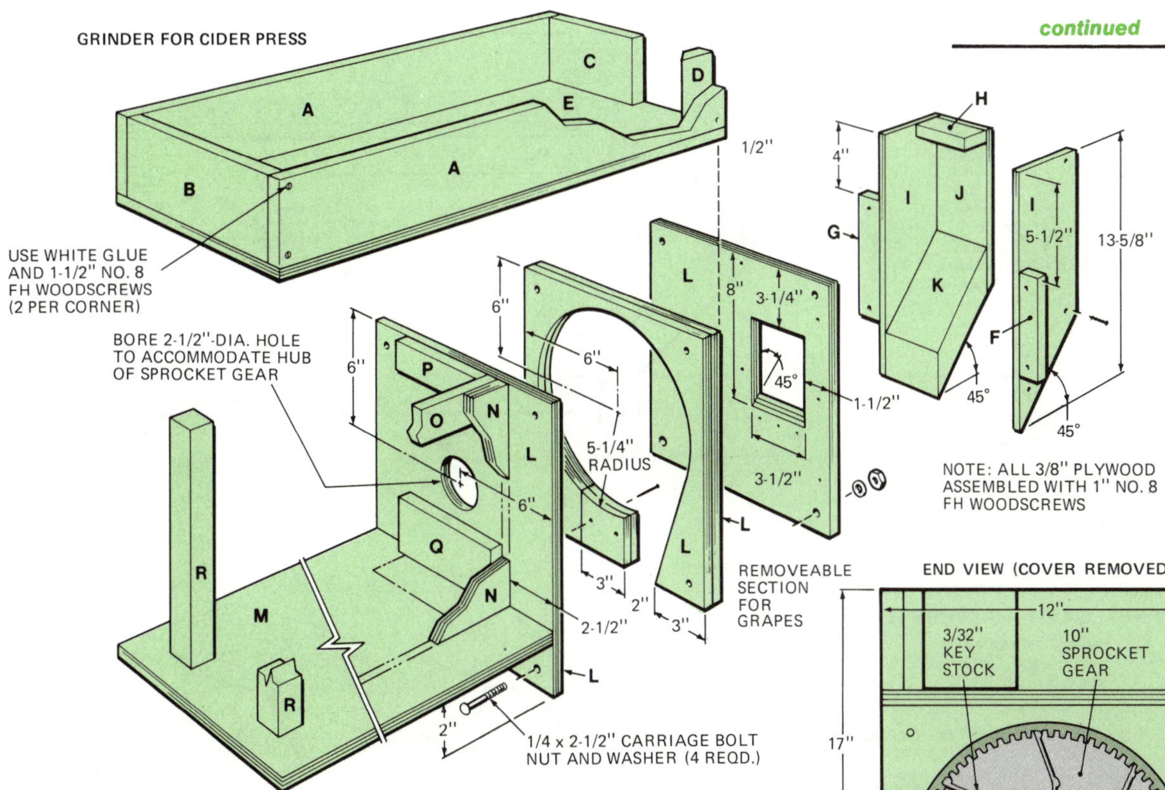

END VIEW (COVER REMOVED)

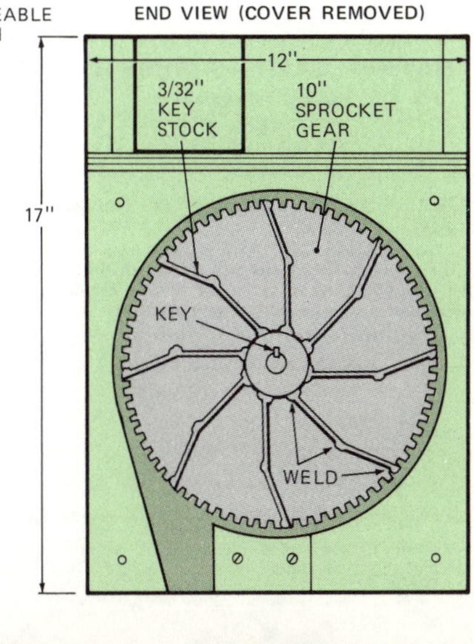

REMOVABLE plywood section permits access to sprocket wheel for cleaning.

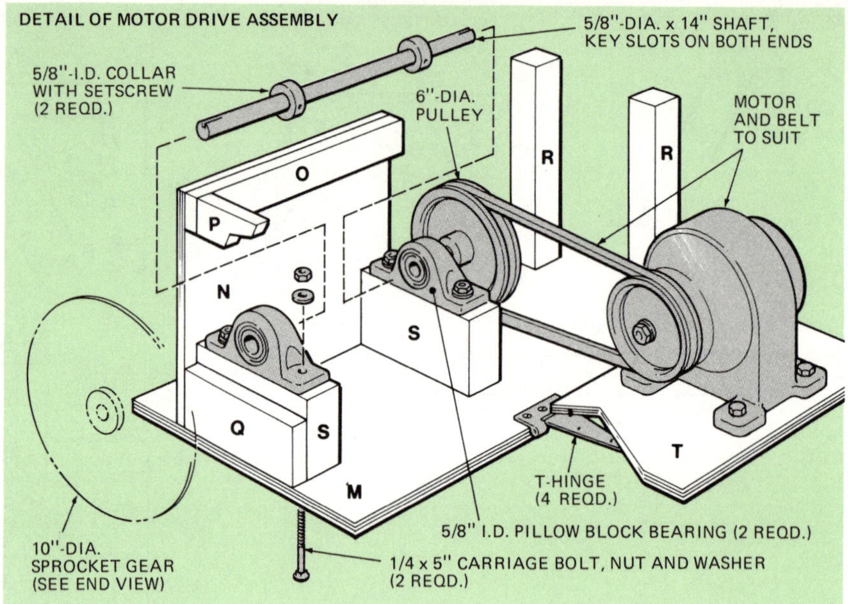

MATERIALS LIST— CIDER GRINDER

Key	Pcs.	Size and description
A	2	¾ x 3½ x 23½" pine
B	1	¾ x 3½ x 10½" pine
C	1	¾ x 3½ x 6¼" pine
D	1	¾ x 1½ x 3½" pine
E	1	⅜ x 12 x 23½" plywood
F	1	¾ x 1⅛ x 5½" pine
G	1	¾ x 1½ x 7" pine
H	1	¾ x 1½ x 3½" pine
I	2	⅜ x 4¾ x 13⅝" plywood
J	1	⅜ x 3½ x 9¼" plywood
K	1	1½ x 3½ x 8" fir
L	4	⅜ x 12 x 13" plywood
M	1	⅜ x 12 x 23½" plywood
N	1	⅜ x 10½ x 11" plywood
O	1	¾ x 1½ x 11" pine
P	1	¾ x 1½ x 6¾" pine
Q	1	¾ x 2½ x 6" pine
R	2	1½ x 1½ x 10½" fir
S	2	1½ x 3½ x 6" fir
T	1	⅜ x 7 x 12" plywood

Misc.: 4 ¼"-dia. x 2½" carriage bolts with nuts and washers, 1½" x No. 8 fh screws, 2 ⅝"-i.d. collars with setscrews, ⅝"-dia. x 14" steel rod, 6"-dia. pulley, 3" dia. pulley, No. 60 sprocket wheel (10" dia.), 3/32 x 3/32 x 32" key stock, 2 ⅝"-i.d. pillow-block bearings, ⅓-hp motor, 1 pr. heavy 6" T-hinges, 4 ¼ x 5" carriage bolts with nuts and washers.

GENERAL ARRANGEMENT (SIDE VIEW)

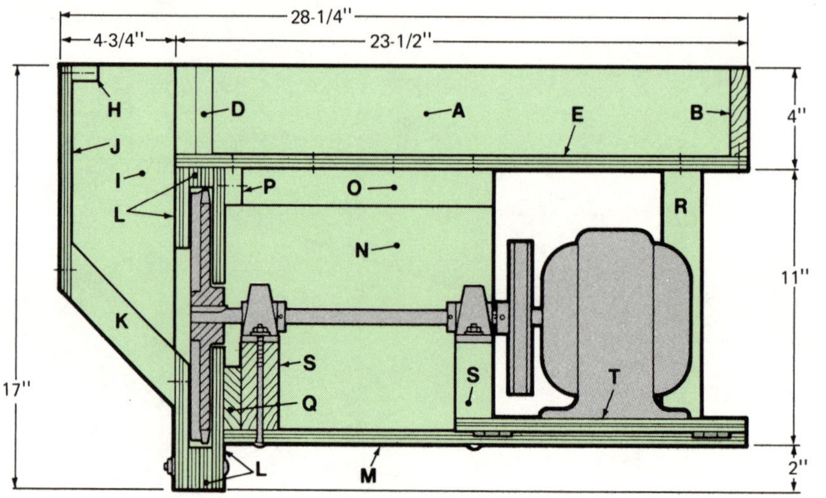

MATERIALS LIST—SAWHORSE

Key	Pcs.	Size and description
A	2	¾ x 5½ x 10" pine
B	1	¾ x 5⅜ x 32" pine
C	4	1½ x 2½ x 26⅛" fir

Misc.: 8 1¼" No. 8 fh screws, 8 3" No. 9 fh screws, white glue.

Note: The materials list above will make one sawhorse. Multiply the quantities listed above by the number of sawhorses you plan to build to hold the press and the grinder if desired.

SAWHORSE

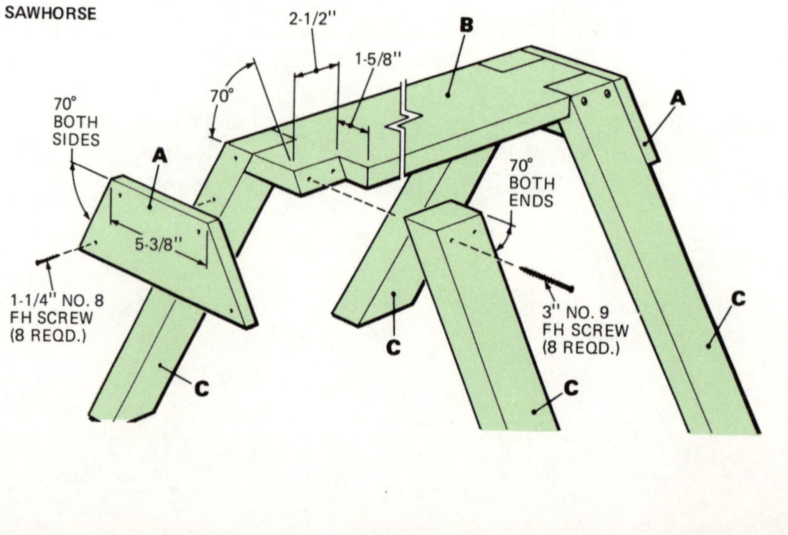

There's nothing quite like tangy, sweet cider as a family drink in the fall. Happily it's possible to freeze the juice for drinking later. (If you're planning to ferment it, remember that making hard cider is subject to the same restrictions as wine and beer making.)

After pressing for cider use the leftover apple pulp to make apple butter, or use it as garden compost. Bury the pulp rather than spreading it on top of the soil.

Begin work on the press by constructing the 24 x 36-in. rectangular frame made of 2 x 4s. Make six ribs. Nest the bottom three ribs in the frame. Then cut a 14-in.-square plate of plywood and nine 14-in. 1 x 2s to screw to the inside end of the frame. Fasten 13 sanded and rounded 1 x 2s into the bottom half with 1½-in. No. 8 wood screws. The corner 1 x 2s must be notched to fit the slant of the ribs. Attach the top 1 x 2s so the top ribs will align with the bottom three ribs. Hinge the top to the bottom with strap hinges at the back and catch locks at the front. A chain keeps the top from falling too far open.

When assembling the plunger, remember the action achieved will be a push-pull type. The jack, being cranked into a threaded block, will be pushing the pipe and plunger plate into the chamber.

To convert the car jack, remove the three leg standards. Replace the crank-handle rivet with a ⅜-in. bolt. Weld a crossbar made of 1⅛-in. strap iron to two 30-in. lengths of pipe. Insert the jack and clamp it with ⅝-in. set collars above the thrust bearing and below the crossbar. Screw on the pipe flange.

To maximize a tight fit, cut the plunger-plate slightly oversize. Cover it with lengths of 1 x 2s and trim. Assemble the plunger and plate after setting them inside the press.

For maximum squeezing pressure, you may consider wrapping a length of cable over the last rib. This is an extra security measure to guard against the wood screws not holding due to the great pressure created.

Make the cider collection board of plywood ½ x 28 x 35 in. Border it with 1 x 2s, allowing a 1½-in. break for a spout. Apply polyurethane varnish to all pieces.

building the grinder

Have a machinist mill keyways to engage sprocket wheel and pulley. Weld hub. Bend and weld the 3/32-in. key stock to the wheel. This key stock will be shredding the apples at grinding time.

Align and mount the pillow-block bearings on the grinder base. Mount the motor and second pulley on a board hinged to the base to provide a combination of gravity and torque which keeps the belt tight.

Cut four ⅜ x 12 x 13-in. plywood pieces (L in the main drawing on page 714), then cut out space indicated for the wheel and exit channel in the second and third pieces. The channel can have a removable section to make the exit large enough for treating fruits like coarse-stemmed grapes. Cut a 2½-in. hole in the fourth plywood piece for the sprocket-wheel hub. The first plywood piece will hold the front-side hopper. This plywood is removable for cleaning.

Now you can make and mount the rooftop bin and the hopper chute. The rooftop keeps handy the apples to be put in the hopper. The apples will need prodding into the hopper with a small board.

After construction is finished, polyurethane-varnish all wood pieces.

Attach hooks for holding prelaundered feed-bag-size burlap bags. When the apples are fed into the hopper the sprocket wheel behind the hopper shreds them and discharges the pulp into the burlap bag, ready to be squeezed in the press.

If you have a problem locating burlap bags, write to Commercial Bag Co., 119 Southwest Columbus, Des Moines, IA 50315.

The gusset-reinforced sawhorse is built to hold up under heavy loads and is ideal for supporting the cider press or grinder units. Cut gussets and top from 1 x 6 stock. Use screws and white glue to assemble.

MAKING CIDER ACROSS THE COUNTRY

Most cider makers agree that a blend of apple varieties makes the tastiest cider. A few crab-apples added to a batch of cider made from blander varieties can perk up its taste. In the northeastern states McIntosh, Jonathan, Red Delicious and Golden Delicious are among those varieties that make the best cider. In the middle and southern states the Red Delicious, Golden Delicious and Jonathan are also good choices; in the Appalachian area Stayman Winesaps are good. Red Delicious and Golden Delicious are favorites in the northwestern states. Experiment by blending varieties until you get one you like.

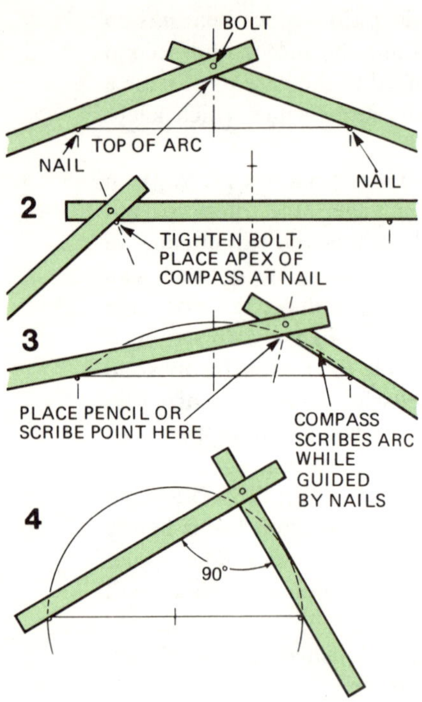

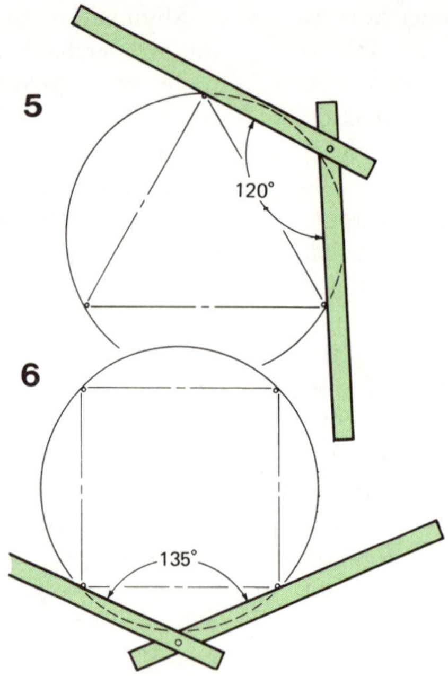

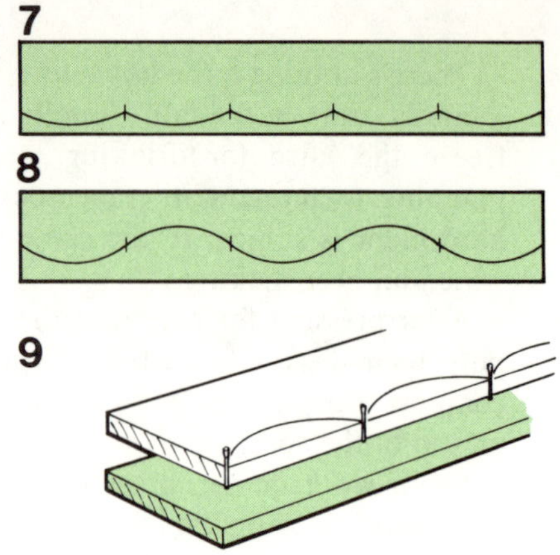

10

Easy way to scribe large circles

By BOB TOM

■ THE EASY-TO-MAKE compass lets you draw arcs that would be impossible with a conventional compass. It is constructed of two strips of wood hinged as shown with a nut and bolt. Each leg should be slightly longer than the distance from one end of the planned arc to the other.

1. To use the compass, put brads or nails where you want the arc's end points. Draw a straight line to connect them and mark the high point of the arc. Place bottom of the compass legs against the nails and adjust the compass until its apex is at the arc's high point. Tighten the bolt.

2. Place the apex at one of the nails

3. Hold a pencil at the apex and move compass legs across the nails, maintaining contact at all times.

SEE ALSO

Calipers . . . Combination squares . . . Joinery . . . Jointers . . . Lumber . . . Moldings . . . Nails . . . Scrapers . . . Scribers . . . Shop techniques . . . Shop tools . . . Woods

4. Compass legs can also be set at specific angles. Set at 90°, the compass will scribe perfect circles or semicircles.

5. By setting the compass at 120° and positioning the nails to make an equilateral triangle, it will scribe a complete circle if used on each pairing of nails successively.

6. Similarly, the compass set at 135° scribes a circle if four nails are positioned to form a square. The last two examples are useful when laying out a circle for a walk or driveway if an obstruction prevents the use of a center point. Using four nails (or stakes for large outdoor projects), as opposed to two or three, makes compass use easier since the compass legs can be made shorter.

7, 8. Other uses include the making of scalloped patterns and wavy lines. Be sure to place nails at equal intervals and in a straight line.

9. If the guide nails for a desired pattern need to be positioned on the workpiece edge, use a second board to hold the nails.

10. Decorative shapes can also be laid out.

Build a bench for your portable saw

By EMERY J. LOISELLE

COMPLETED TABLE boasts miter gauge, fence and a sawdust clean-out drawer. It can be easily carried to job site (above). Following photos show how to build it.

■ GET TWICE as much work from your portable circular saw by building this table that lets you convert it for use as a stationary unit. With the aid of an adjustable fence and miter gauge you make, this rig lets you make accurate rips and angled crosscuts quickly. When you have

SEE ALSO

Bench saws . . . Blades, carbide . . .
Circular saw blades . . . Circular saws, portable . . .
Motors, shop . . . Power-tool maintenance . . .
Power-tool stands . . . Saws, bench . . .
Shop techniques . . . Stands, bench saw

TO MAKE cutouts in the plywood for various bench parts, drill holes at corners and then use a sabre saw guided by a tacked-down straightedge.

USE GLUE and 1½-in. finishing nails to assemble the sides. Be sure to check for squareness. Set the nails with a nailset and then fill the holes.

POSITION SAW on table underside using a straightedge along side of blade. It should be parallel to table sides and perpendicular to front.

CUT TABLE INSERT recess using a router and mortising bit. Wood strips tacked to the plywood act as a guide for the base of the router.

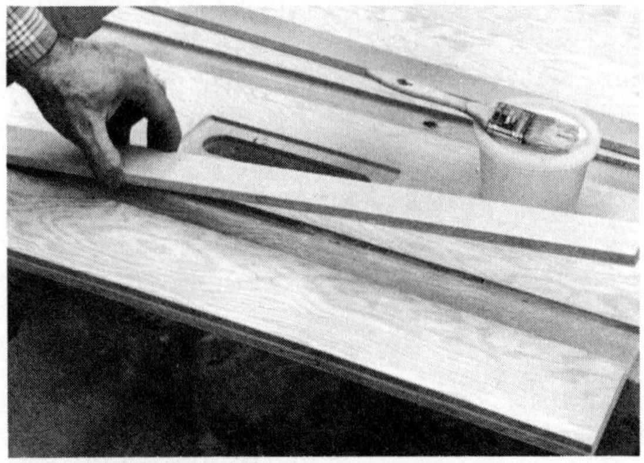

FOR LONG-WEARING miter-gauge grooves, glue maple inserts (U) in table recesses. Use a router with a mortising bit to cut these grooves.

DEPENDING on the angle or range of angles required to cut a particular bevel, one of four inserts is used to reduce the cutout width.

need for a portable saw, simply detach it from the table underside.

The on-off switch is mounted on the table front to let you control the saw from the operating position. Use a length of wire or electrician's tape wrapped around the saw's trigger and handle grip to secure it in the ON position.

The main design problem for any portable saw table is providing enough clearance for the saw to tilt and cut bevels—without making the cutout opening for the blade and guard so wide that it would pose a hazard when cutting small pieces of wood. The problem is solved here by making a series of four blade inserts of ¼-in. plywood. The

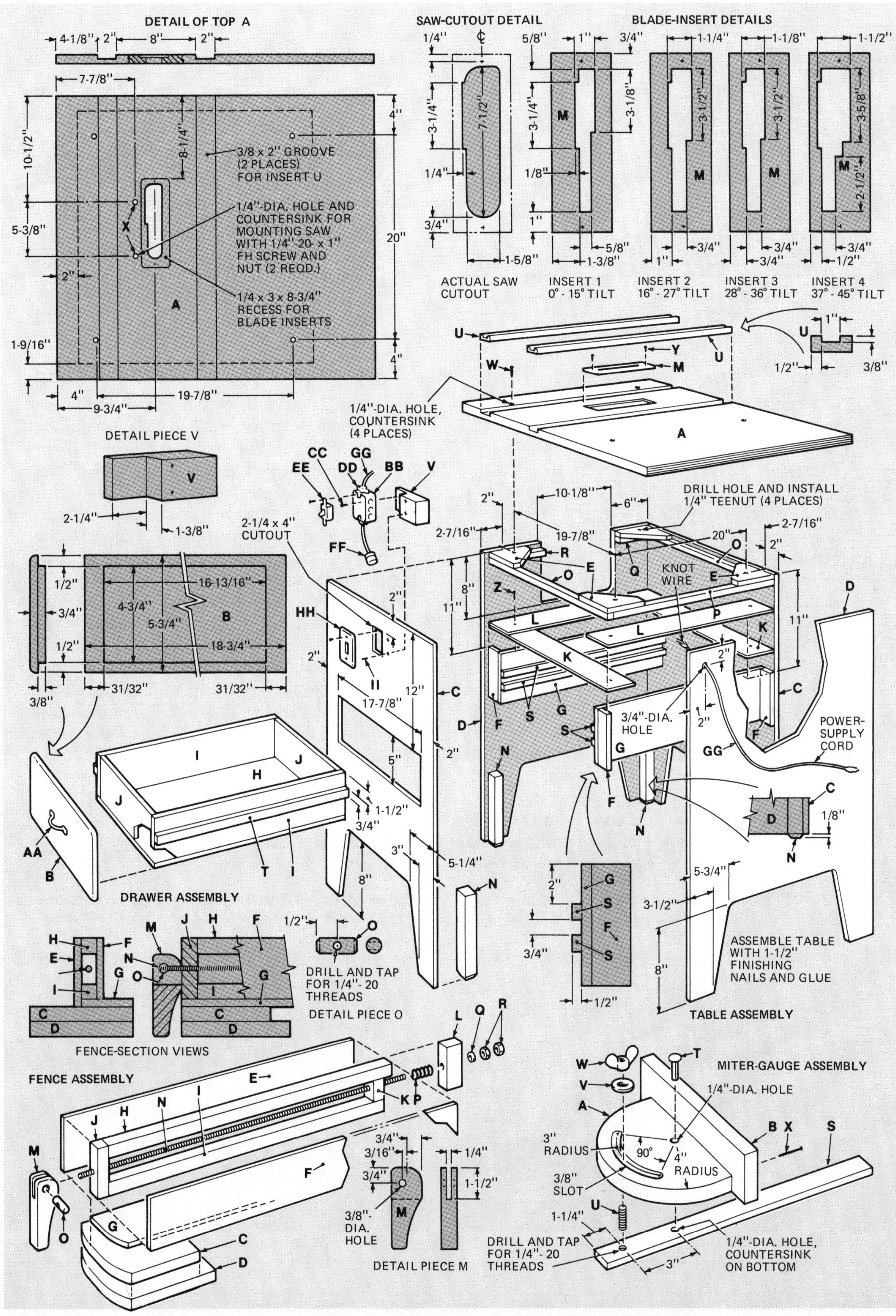
DETAIL OF TOP A
3/8 x 2" GROOVE (2 PLACES) FOR INSERT U
1/4"-DIA. HOLE AND COUNTERSINK FOR MOUNTING SAW WITH 1/4"-20- x 1" FH SCREW AND NUT (2 REQD.)
1/4 x 3 x 8-3/4" RECESS FOR BLADE INSERTS
SAW-CUTOUT DETAIL
BLADE-INSERT DETAILS
ACTUAL SAW CUTOUT
INSERT 1 0° - 15° TILT
INSERT 2 16° - 27° TILT
INSERT 3 28° - 36° TILT
INSERT 4 37° - 45° TILT
1/4"-DIA. HOLE, COUNTERSINK (4 PLACES)
DETAIL PIECE V
DRILL HOLE AND INSTALL 1/4" TEENUT (4 PLACES)
2-1/4 x 4" CUTOUT
KNOT WIRE
3/4"-DIA. HOLE
POWER-SUPPLY CORD
DRAWER ASSEMBLY
TABLE ASSEMBLY
ASSEMBLE TABLE WITH 1-1/2" FINISHING NAILS AND GLUE
DRILL AND TAP FOR 1/4"- 20 THREADS
DETAIL PIECE O
FENCE-SECTION VIEWS
FENCE ASSEMBLY
3/8"-DIA. HOLE
DETAIL PIECE M
MITER-GAUGE ASSEMBLY
1/4"-DIA. HOLE
3" RADIUS
4" RADIUS
3/8" SLOT
DRILL AND TAP FOR 1/4"- 20 THREADS
1/4"-DIA. HOLE, COUNTERSINK ON BOTTOM

MATERIALS LIST—SAW TABLE

Key	No.	Size and description (use)
A	1	¾ × 28 × 36″ plywood (top)
B	1	¾ × 5¾ × 18¾″ plywood (drawer face)
C	2	½ × 22⅞ × 34″ plywood (front, back)
D	2	½ × 24⅞ × 34″ plywood (side)
E	4	½ × 5½ × 5½″ plywood (corner blocks)
F	4	½ × 2 × 6″ plywood (drawer supports)
G	2	½ × 6 × 23⅞″ plywood (drawer supports)
H	1	⅜ × 16 13/16 × 23½″ plywood (drawer bottom)
I	2	⅜ × 4⅜ × 23½″ plywood (drawer sides)
J	2	⅜ × 4⅜ × 16 1/16″ plywood (drawer ends)
K	2	¼ × 4¼ × 22⅞″ plywood (sawdust-shield ends)
L	2	¼ × 4¼ × 23⅞″ plywood (sawdust-shield sides)
M	4	¼ × 3 × 8¾″ lauan plywood (blade inserts)
N	4	1½ × 1½ × 8″ fir (glue blocks)
O	2	¾ × ¾ × 22⅞″ pine (cleats)
P	1	¾ × ¾ × 23⅛″ pine (cleat)
Q	1	¾ × ¾ × 4¾″ pine (cleat)
R	1	¾ × ¾ × 8″ pine (cleat)
S	4	½ × ¾ × 23⅞″ pine (drawer guide)
T	2	½ × ¾ × 23½″ pine (drawer guide)
U	2	⅜ × 2 × 28″ maple (tabletop inserts)
V	1	2⅛ × 3¼ × 6″ fir (outlet-box support block)
W	4	¼″-20 × 1½″ fh machine screw and Teenut
X	2	¼″-dia. × 1″ fh machine screw
Y	2	¾″ No. 6 fh screw
Z	4	1″ brad
AA	1	drawer pull
BB	1	outlet box
CC	2	½″ No. 8 fh screw
DD	2	cable clamp
EE	1	single-pole switch
FF	1	single receptacle and short length of No. 12 wire with ground
GG	1	6′ or to suit, 3′ lead wire and male plug
HH	1	switch plate
II	2	1½″ No. 10 fh screw

Misc.: 1½″ finishing nails and glue as required.

MATERIALS LIST—FENCE MITER GAUGE

Key	No.	Size and description (use)
A	1	¾ × 5 × 8″ plywood (miter quadrant)
B	1	¾ × 2½ × 10″ plywood (miter-gauge face)
C	1	¾ × 4½ × 5¼″ plywood (fence head)
D	1	¾ × 5¼ × 5½″ plywood (fence head)
E	1	⅜ × 3⅜ × 33½″ plywood (fence face)
F	1	⅜ × 3 × 33½″ plywood (fence back)
G	1	⅜ × 3 × 31¾″ plywood (fence bottom)
H	1	¾ × ¾ × 31¼″ pine (fence core)
I	1	¾ × ¾ × 31″ pine (fence core)
J	1	¾ × ¾ × 3″ pine (fence core)
K	1	¾ × ¾ × 1½″ pine (fence core)
L	1	¾ × 1½ × 4½″ pine (fence clamping toe)
M	1	¾ × 1½ × 4″ pine (fence clamping cam)
N	1	¼″-20 × 34¾″ threaded rod (fence hardware)
O	1	⅜″ dia. × 1″ steel rod (fence hardware)
P	1	11/16″ dia. × 1¼″ compression spring (fence)
Q	1	¼″ I.D. rubber grommet (fence hardware)
R	2	¼″-20 nut
S	1	¼ × 1 × 16″ aluminum bar (miter-guage hardware)
T	1	¼″ dia. × 1″ aluminum rivet (miter-gauge)
U	1	¼″-20 x 1¼″ threaded rod (miter-gauge)
V	1	¼″ I.D., ¾″ O.D. flat washer (miter-gauge)
W	1	¼″-20 wingnut (miter-gauge hardware)
X	2	¾″ no. 10 fh screw

Misc.: 1″ brads and glue as required.

odd configuration of the inserts is due to changing blade-guard positions at various blade heights and tilt combinations. See details on page 719.

This portable saw table was dimensioned for a J. C. Penney Model 1125 7¼-in. saw. If you have a different model, change inserts to suit. Make cardboard patterns to work out shapes.

The easiest way to build the table is to cut all parts and then preassemble the sawdust clean-out drawer supports (F, G and S). After assembling the sides, install drawer supports by nailing from the outside.

Four corner blocks (E) are used to anchor the tabletop to the sides. They should be temporarily nailed to the supporting cleats so mounting holes can be bored through top (A) and blocks (B) simultaneously. Remove the blocks to install Teenuts before gluing them permanently.

Aligning the saw with the table is critical. After making the cutout in A, locate the saw mounting holes to correspond to those provided on your saw shoe. If holes are not provided, you will have to drill them. Align the blade with the sides of the squared table; do not use the edge of the saw shoe. Then mark and bore holes for ¼-20 fh machine screws. Countersink for screwheads.

Note that the stepped patterns on the right sides of the inserts are important. They hold the guard partly raised and let it be pushed back as work is fed toward blade.

One fence-assembly step that may give you trouble is attaching the fence's cam lock (M) to the threaded rod (N). To attach, bore a hole in a length of ⅜-in. steel rod using a drill press and clamp to hold the work. Tap ¼-in.-20 threads in the hole and cut the rod to size. Insert the piece (O) through holes in sides of cam lock and screw in the rod (H).

When the table is complete, the base may be painted. The top should be finished with two coats of satin varnish, lightly rubbed with 000 steel wool and coated with silicone lubricant or wax.

SINGLE-POLE switch is connected between power-supply cord (CG) and pigtail (FF). Saw plugs into receptacle.

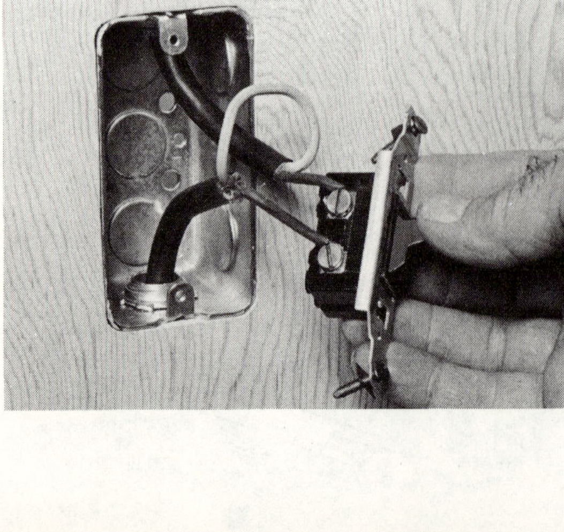

CAREFUL CONSTRUCTION of fence (part E removed to show assembly) and miter gauge assures accurate cuts.

A MITERBOX can be held rock-steady in a bench vise whenever needed with a length of angle iron screwed to its bottom. This way it is not in the way as a permanently bench-mounted one would be.—*Ken Patterson, Regina, Sask.*

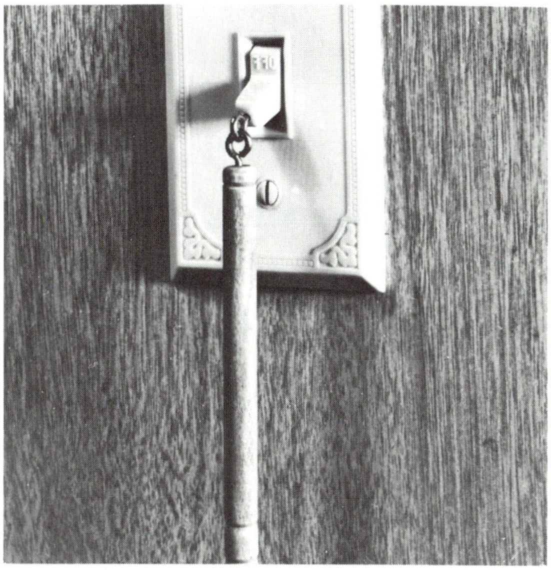

A LIGHT SWITCH too high for a youngster to reach can be made accessible with a dowel and linked screw eyes. Drill a hole in the switch toggle to the exact size or the screw eye will crack it.—*Robert Gentry, Waco, TX.*

WELL-MADE LEATHER and plastic cases for photo gear often outlive the equipment for which they were intended, and are sold at low prices. They are excellent for protective storage of precision tools. Fitting is not necessary because of the variety of sizes and shapes of cases available.—*Walter E. Burton, Akron, OH.*

TO HOLD THIN-WALL TUBING in a vise for slitting, insert it into a hardwood block drilled for a tight friction fit, with the line of cut scribed lengthwise, center-to-center, on the side. Drilling the hole about 1/8 in. from the side of the block allows accurate starting of the cut with a fine hacksaw blade.—*Edwin W. Fuerst, Colrain, MA.*

Use the right saw blade

SEE ALSO
**Bandsaws . . . Bench saws . . .
Circular saws, portable . . . Cutoff machines . . .
Discs, wood . . . Power hacksaws . . .
Radial-arm saws . . . Sabre saws . . . Table saws . . .
Workshops**

WHEN ONE TYPE of saw blade is used to cut all kinds of material, it's almost like using one size nail to build a house. Only when a plywood blade is used to cut plywood, or a hardboard blade is used to cut hardboard, for example, can you turn out the best work and get the most from your bench saw or portable power saw.

That's why a selection of blades having a wide range of tooth patterns is available, each designed to cut a specific material in the best, fastest and smoothest way.

For general-purpose cutting, both with and across grain, a flat combination blade is your best bet, but, again, it won't match the extra-smooth cut you get with a hollow-ground planer blade. Thus it's important to keep several types of saw blades on hand so you can switch from one to the other, whatever your cutting requirements.

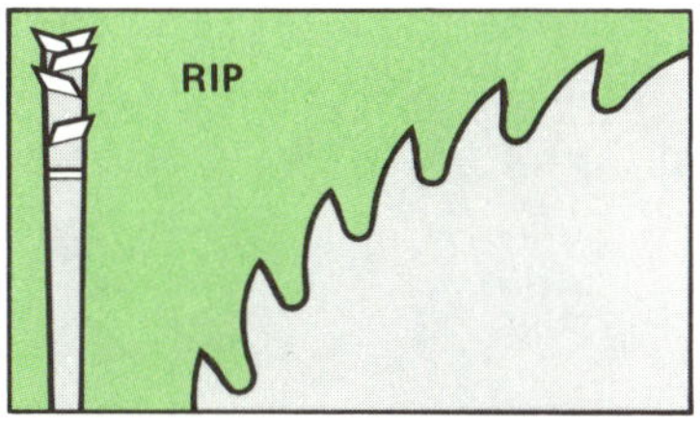

FOR RIPPING all hardwoods and softwoods. Has heavy hub and is taper-ground for extra clearance.

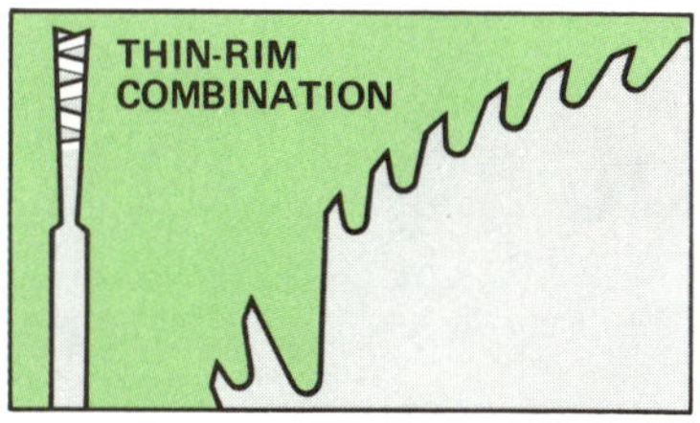

FINEST combination blade for fine trim and finish work. Use it to rip, crosscut or miter.

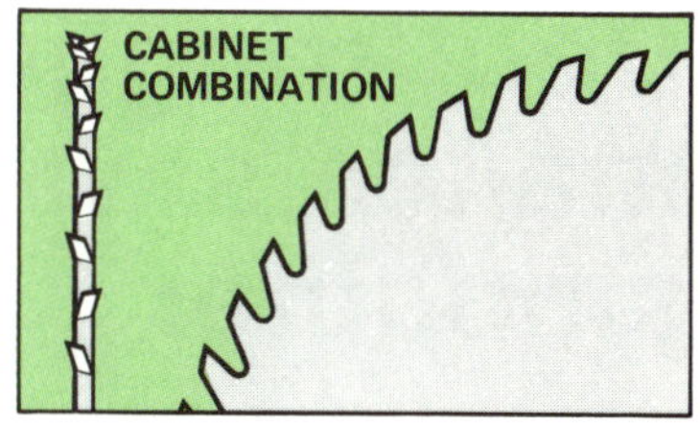

CABINETMAKER'S combination blade cuts in any direction through either hardwoods or softwoods.

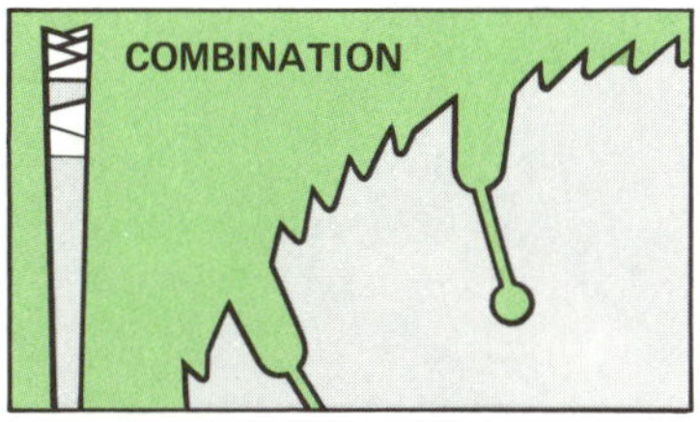

CABINETMAKER'S blade. Produces smooth and accurate cuts in any direction in hardwoods.

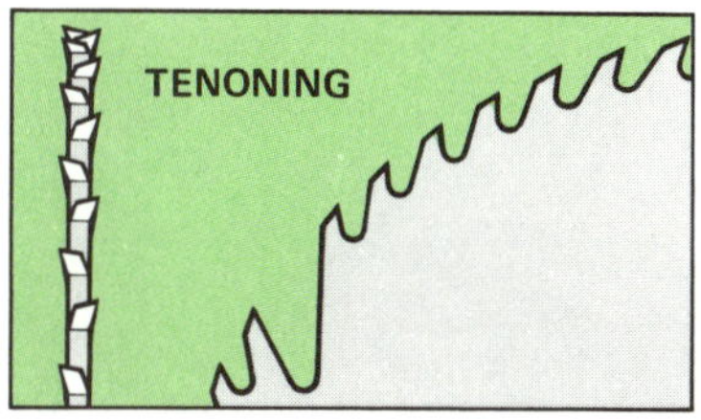

ALL-PURPOSE blade is wide-kerfed for cutting tenons and splines in all hardwoods and softwoods.

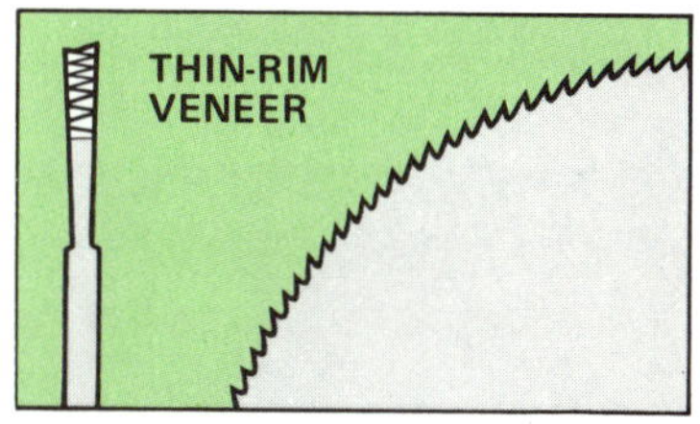

FOR SATIN-SMOOTH finish cuts in either plywood or thin veneers without splintering.

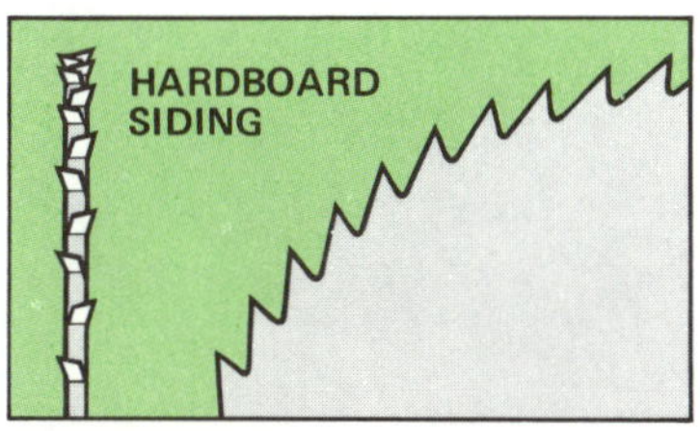

BEST BLADE for cutting tempered hardboard underlayment, siding and perforated board.

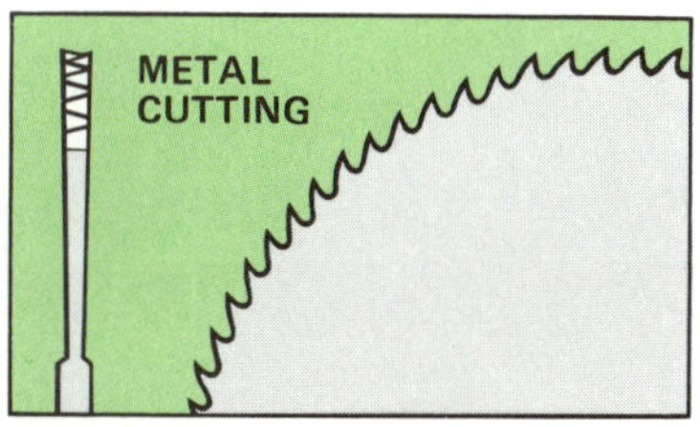

INTENDED for aluminum, brass, bronze, copper, zinc and lead. A truly professional blade.

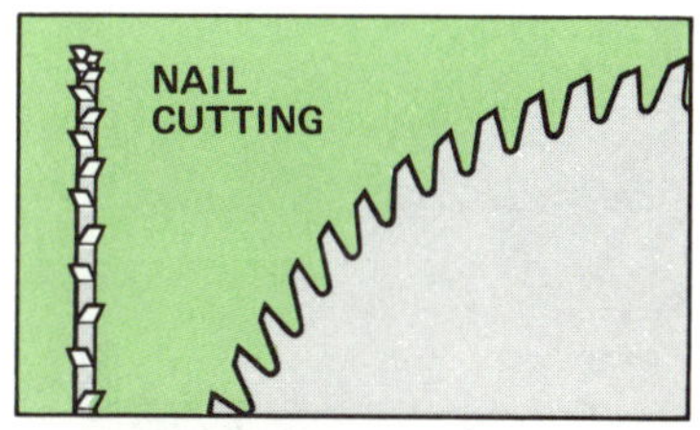

FOR ROUGH-CUTTING (rip and crosscut) through all woods that have an occasional nail.

EXCELLENT FOR WOOD, but can also be used on hardboard siding. Its 32 teeth cut fast and straight.

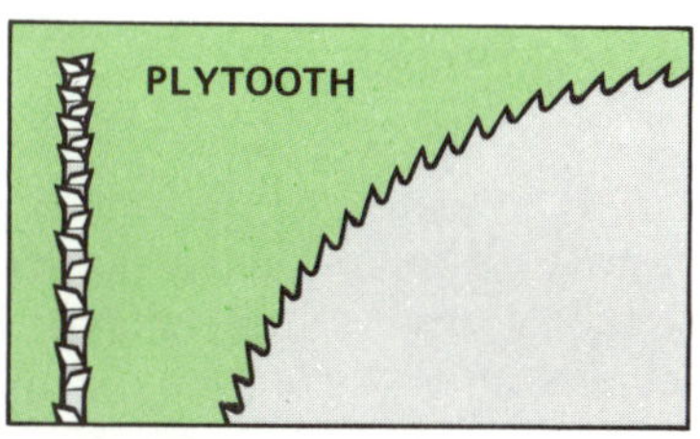

FINE-TOOTH, smooth-cutting blade for plywood, composition board, softboard and the like.

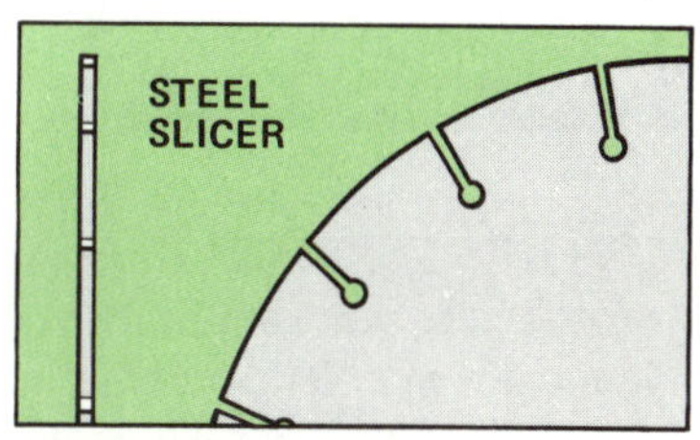

FOR LIGHT-GAUGE sheet steel, roofing, guttering and downspouts, up to 1/16-in. thick.

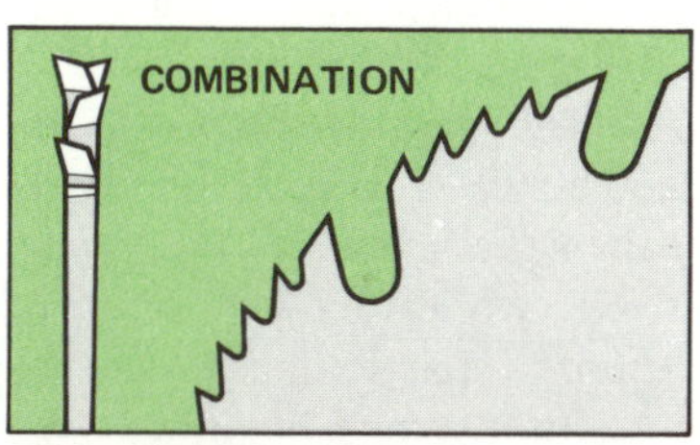

GOOD FOR RIPPING, crosscutting and mitering on all hardwoods and softwoods. Comes taper-ground.

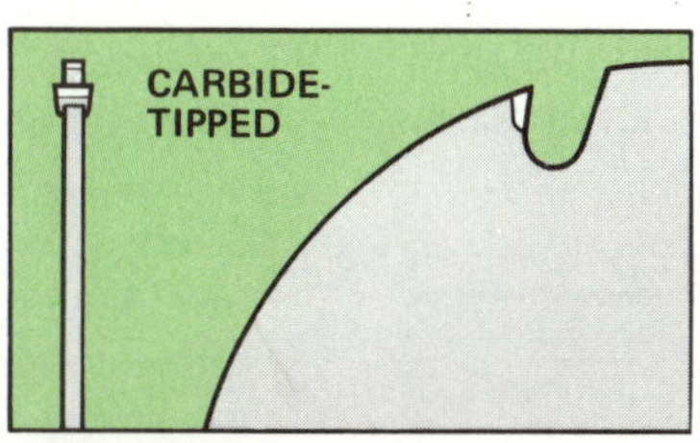

CARBIDE-TIPPED combination blade for long cutting life; ideal for abrasive materials.

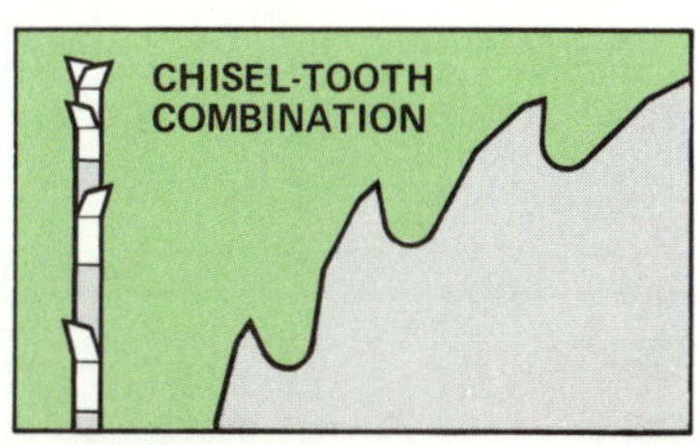

ALL-PURPOSE, fast-cutting blade for all woods. An excellent contractor's framing blade.

Deburring jig makes saw cut smoother

By E. A. FRANKS

YOU'RE PROBABLY NOT getting the smooth cuts you should from your circular-saw blades. Even a blade that has just been ground or filed properly has a residual burr that chews up edges and leaves a rough-cut surface. This burr can be eliminated with a jig like the one I made to give my saw blades a final dressing. Dimensions must suit the saw-blade diameter you use.

Blades must be absolutely free of gum and pitch before deburring. The stones are not oiled. The jig is intended for use only with blades that have no set (those with a set do not require deburring); I have found it produces excellent results with plywood blades and combination blades.

It's essential to use a regular (commercial) saw arbor, which must be mounted so that it is at exactly 90° to the stone-carrying slide, in both horizontal and vertical planes. The arbor is secured with a blunt-tipped Phillips-head screw, turned just snug, as a setscrew; the cap atop the post hides the screwhead. A suitable handle is attached to the rear of the arbor.

Bevel natural stones to allow easy insertion of blades between them. I particularly like the stones supplied by Hindostan Whetstone Co., Bedford, IN 47421. Use glue sparingly when attaching the stones. Allow complete drying between gluing operations to keep foam spongy.

SEE ALSO
Bandsaws . . . Bench saws . . .
Circular saws, portable . . . Motors, shop . . .
Power hacksaws . . . Radial-arm saws . . .
Sharpening, tool . . . Table saws . . . Workshops

CHISEL TOOL separates foam-sprung stones for insertion of saw blade, is kept in the spool at rear of jig.

SLIDE IS PINNED into place with blade between stones. Pin is mounted in cutoff thread spool attached with cord keeper.

BLADE gets five or six turns between soft stones first, in direction *counter* to that in which it normally cuts.

AFTER ANOTHER half-dozen turns between hard stones, blade is turned against paper on block to test for smoothness.

CUTTING OR SCRATCHES on paper surface indicate that deburring is incomplete and that process must be repeated.

STONES MEASURE 3/8 x 7/8 x 3 in., are lightly glued to 3/8-in. polyurethane foam blocks lightly glued to slide.

HARD STONES GRIP BLADE for second stage of deburring. Three-quarter view shows fitting of slide to rail and spool holder for stone-opening chisel tool.

WINGNUTS FASTEN REAR FACE of slide in place, so it can be removed when stones must be replaced. Front face attaches to center piece with three Phillips-head screws.

Circular saw know-how

By HARRY WICKS

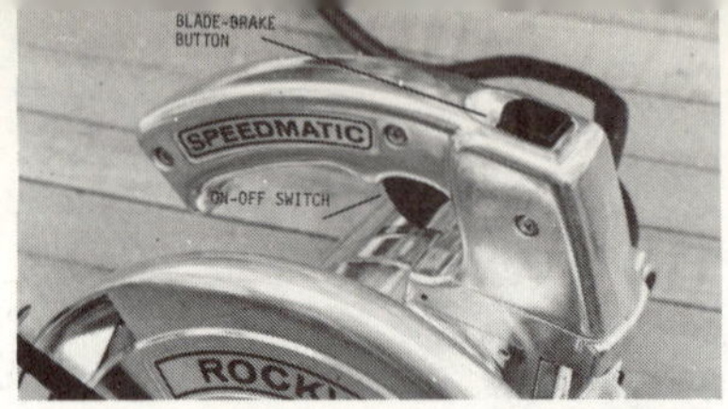

GOOD SAFETY feature on a Rockwell saw—a thumb-operated blade brake.

TO ADJUST cutting depth, raise or lower saw body, lock it in place.

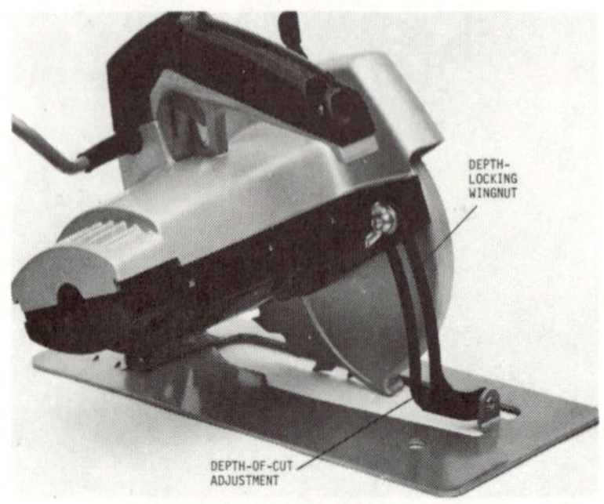

OTHER METHOD is to change depth by pivoting, as this Skil saw does.

TYPICAL CIRCULAR saw (above, left) includes a rip guide and blade wrench. Various makers use different methods for setting and locking blade at desired depth as shown above.

IT DOESN'T TAKE very long for anyone interested in do-it-yourself jobs to realize that a portable circular saw is a "must-have" tool. With a power saw, you will be able to do your cutting a lot faster with considerably less effort than ever before. What is often surprising to a first-time saw owner is just how much a circular saw—used properly—will upgrade craftsmanship.

Be aware there is a certain hazard involved when cutting with a portable saw. As with most tools—hand and power—common sense plays a very important role when it comes to safety. Once you understand the tool and how to handle it correctly, you will wonder how you ever got along without it.

As you view a circular saw from its right side, the spinning blade rotates in a counterclockwise direction. This means that the blade does its cutting on the "upstroke." For this reason,

SEE ALSO

Circular saw blades . . . Cutoff machines . . . Drills, portable . . . Motors, shop . . . Plywood . . . Power-tool stands . . . Sanding

Getting the saw ready and using it properly

HOLDING BLADE against wood prevents movement as arbor nut is tightened.

whenever it makes a difference the cutting is always done with the "good," or "decorative," side down.

Circular saws are generally described by size: for example, 7-incher, 7¼-in. and the like. This size denotes the maximum-diameter blade that the saw will accommodate. A 7¼-in. saw is generally considered most desirable by do-it-yourselfers. Larger-diameter, more expensive saws are available, but these are intended primarily for builders.

With a 7¼-in. saw you can cut through 2-in. stock effortlessly—even when the saw is set to cut at a 45° bevel. When you must cut heavier stock such as a 4x4, you can do it with two passes.

Most circular-saw motors are of the universal type that operate at voltages within 5 percent above or below that indicated on the tool's specification plate. Also check the plate for the type of power circuit on which it is designed to operate. Many saws can be used on both a.c. and a.c.-d.c.

To protect yourself from electric shock, work only with a tool that is either grounded or double-insulated. If not of the double-insulated variety, your saw should come with a three-prong grounding plug. If you must use an extension cord, use only a three-conductor type so a continuous grounding circuit is provided. Also, make certain that the conductor size of the cord is large enough to prevent an excessive voltage drop.

All circular saws have retractable blade guards. As the saw is pushed into the work the guard retracts into the saw's upper blade housing—leaving the portion of the blade below the workpiece exposed. Develop the habit of making certain that the blade guard is operational before starting the saw—*every time*. You want to be certain that the guard snaps back to its lower position before setting down with a spinning blade. *Never, under any circumstances, remove the blade guard from your saw.*

Always keep the saw away from your body when the blade is spinning, and *never* walk away from the tool while the blade is still in motion. And don't forget this (very) basic rule—always disconnect power before changing blades.

Finally, read the manufacturer's manual before using the tool.

In broadest terms, three factors will affect your decision when picking a saw; materials, comfort and cost.

Materials. Obviously, you need a saw with extra power if you intend to use it primarily to

SAWS GROUPED here were used for how-to photos on these pages.
1. Skil model No. 537
2. Rockwell No. 597 AK
3. Shopmate 1875
4. Stanley No. 80278
5. Sears Craftsman No. 9 H 1182
6. Black & Decker No. 7310
Some saws are available in what manufacturers call "kits"; this simply means the saw comes in a fitted box for storage and carrying convenience. For most users, the kit makes sense.

TO DETERMINE blade depth, place saw on stock; use minimal projection.

FOR SAFETY, saw weight should be on workpiece, not cutoff.

GOOD JOB TABLE: Two sawhorses and three 2x3s. Cutoff is over a single 2x3.

Basic cutting techniques

CORRECT SAW-HOLDING technique is to clamp work and use both hands.

IMPROMPTU RIP GUIDE—thumb and finger squeeze saw shoe, travel board edge.

TO RIP narrow piece accurately, lock the rip guide, make it ride work edge.

SOME MITER guides are adjustable for angle-cutting. When possible, clamp guide.

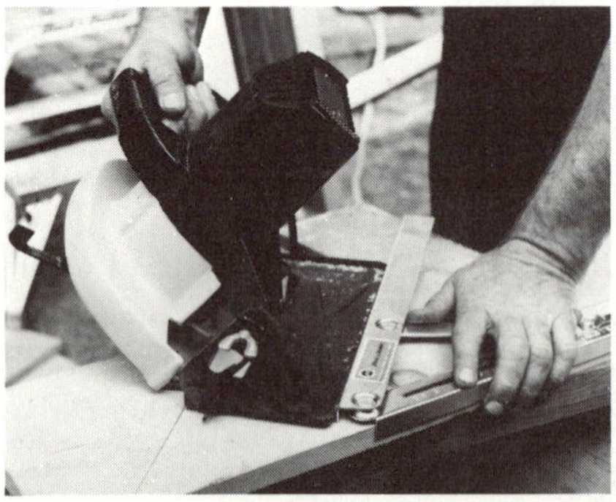

COMPOUND-ANGLE cut is made by setting saw at desired bevel, using miter guide.

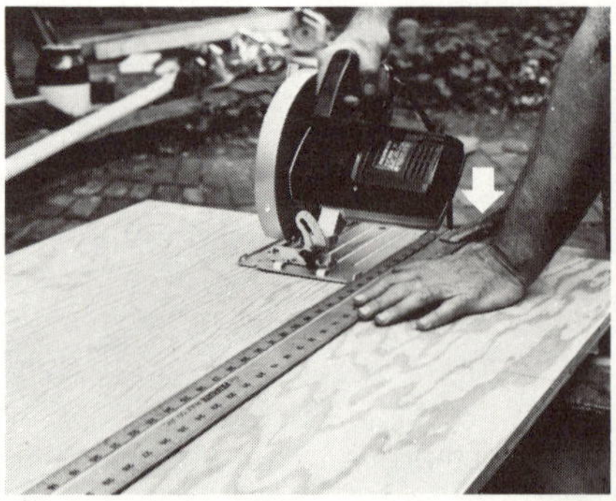

TO CUT plywood sheets, you can use a 4-ft. T-square clamped to the workpiece.

Plywood blades

Sears' ply-tooth

Skil's plywood

Rockwell's plywood

Other cuts you can make

TO JOIN boards at angle, tack boards together and cut them simultaneously.

CUT THIS way, boards fit perfectly, even if you stray from cutting line.

TWO GROOVING techniques (above and right): Make overlapping passes . . .

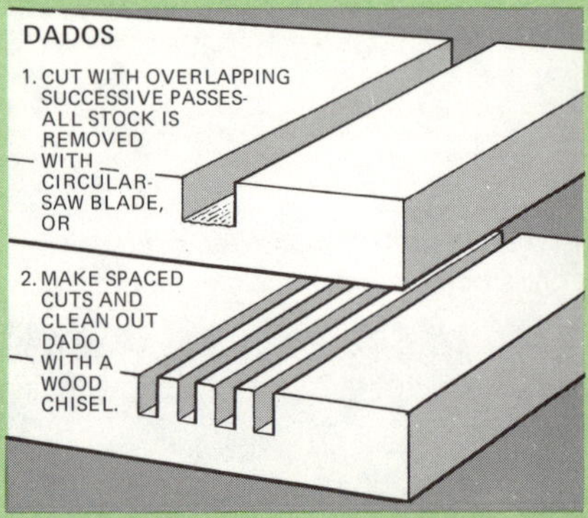

OR ROUGH OUT dado with spaced kerfs, finish groove by cleaning with a chisel.

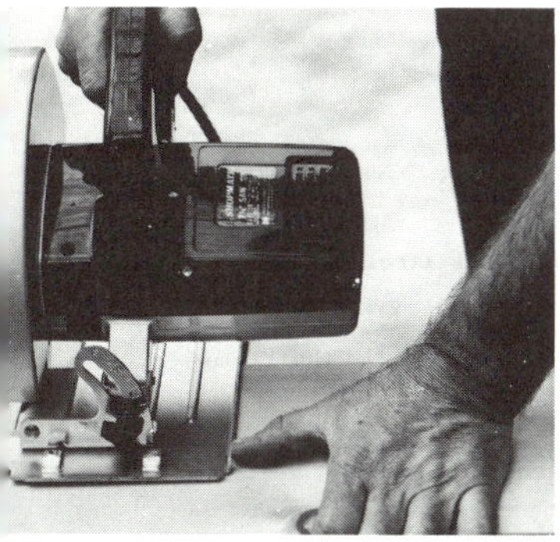

WHEN YOU crosscut rough work, a positioned thumb can be a guide.

IF NEATNESS is important, always use a miter guide.

BE SURE of accuracy on long cuts with a tacked-on guide.

USE A SLOW feed for bevel cutting because the saw tends to drift.

cut concrete or steel. But there's no need to pay for all that power if your work will be confined mostly to wood.

Comfort. The tool has to feel good to *you*—you're the one who will use it. Never buy a tool without some type of personal-use test—even if it is strictly a simulation-use in the store.

Cost. Make no mistake about the fact that you get what you pay for. A $20 saw, for example, will indeed cut 2x4s, but don't expect it to do this all day and survive. A $75 tool will.

Once you own a saw, get to know it. Be aware that the saw must always be firmly held, and that a two-hand grip is best. If you must use one hand to hold the work, keep that hand well away from the cutting line.

Also, keep your body to the side of the cutting line. Set the blade to project about ⅛-in. or so below the work. For a good worktable setup, use two sawhorses, and three lengths of two-by stock.

Rate of feed is important: Never push the saw so there is a strain on its motor. The density of material being cut and the type of blade used dictate the feed rate.

TO CUT edge rabbet, make the first pass with a guide temporarily nailed to work.

THEN CLAMP work in vise and tack guide to workbench top for the second pass.

HEFTY WORKPIECE can be cut by making passes from opposite sides of the board.

IF SAW MUST ride cutoff position, clamp work, hold tool with two hands.

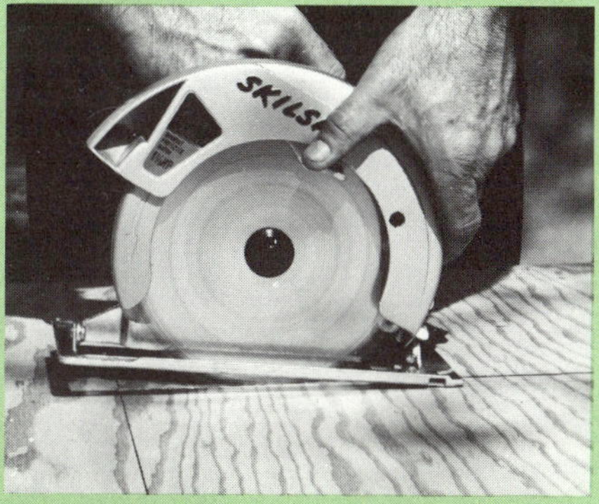

PLUNGE CUT is made by slowly lowering the spinning blade into workpiece.

BEFORE CUTTING fourth line, tack support strip to keep blade from binding.

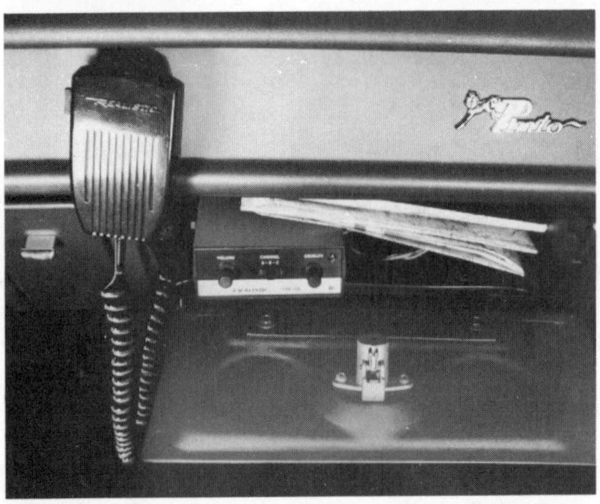

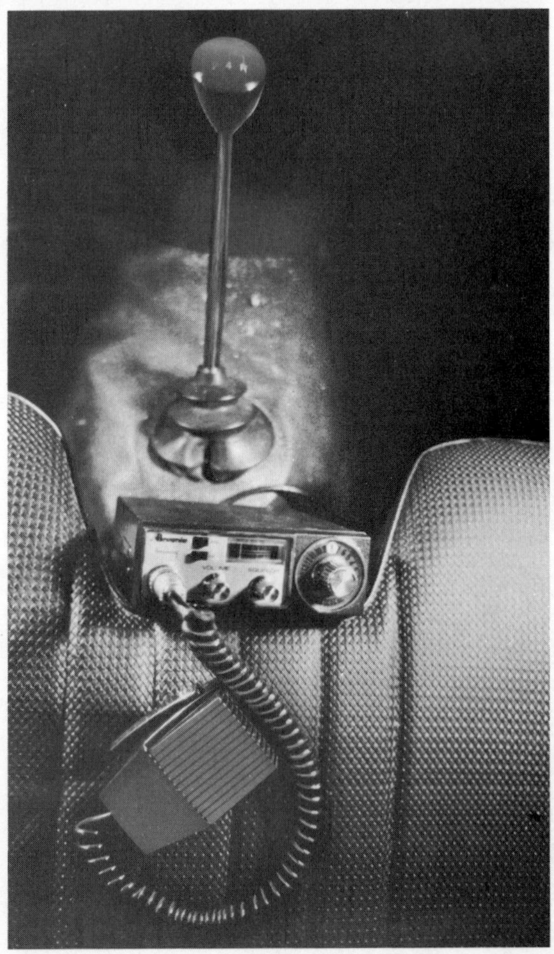

INTERESTING CB installations include a center-mounted set with a telephone-type handset hooked handily over the rim of the dashboard padding (top); a set hidden in the glove compartment (above) to elude thieves (but don't leave a microphone clip nearby as a tip-off; this mike is magnetically mounted); a small set in the shift-lever notch (right) of a mini-truck (but make sure to leave enough room to shift easily)

The best spot for your CB

By ANTHONY R. CURTIS

■ BIG BOPPER, a Pennsylvania CBer whose wife goes by the name of Chantilly Lace, goofed when he mounted a Citizens Band radio in his car. Figuring his wife would like to talk on the radio from her side of the front seat, he placed the set under the dash on the passenger side. But one snowy day last winter, when Bopper was driving alone, he reached over to twist the channel selector and didn't see a car blocking his way. There was just time to avoid it by skidding to a stop against a hillside—and losing a tooth on the steering wheel.

The moral? Safety and convenience, *in that order*, are the main considerations when you're placing a CB transceiver in your car. The set has to be where you can operate it without looking away from the highway, and where you won't bang your head or knees on it when getting in and out or in a sudden stop. But since safety usually means making life convenient for the driver, there's little conflict between the two goals.

MOUNT YOUR set where the driver can reach it as in the homemade, overhead-van console above, or under the dash near the center (other photos here). Where both a scanner and a CB set are used (upper left), the CB should be near the driver, since its controls need more attention. Microphone hangers can be attached to the CB set's mounting bracket, as shown above, or wherever else on the dash you find convenient. The most important things to keep in mind when mounting your CB are the safety and convenience of the driver.

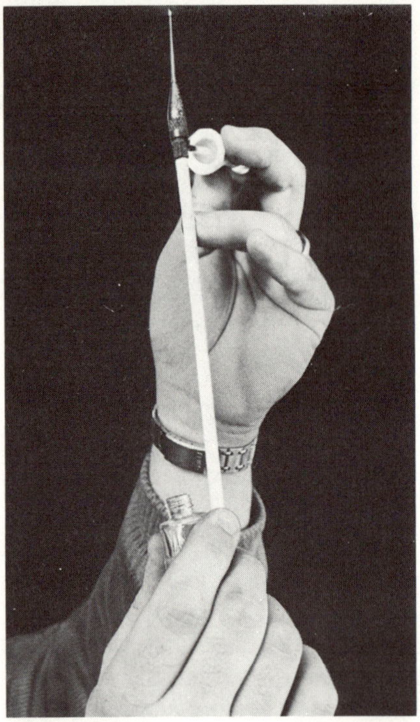

TO PROTECT your set, you can mount it in a sturdy, strongly installed locking device (above right) with a strong padlock to secure it. Use cardboard to protect it against scratches during installation (right), and cover exposed metal parts of your antenna with colorless nail polish to prevent weather damage. Check periodically, and if the polish is worn, apply a fresh coat to the antenna

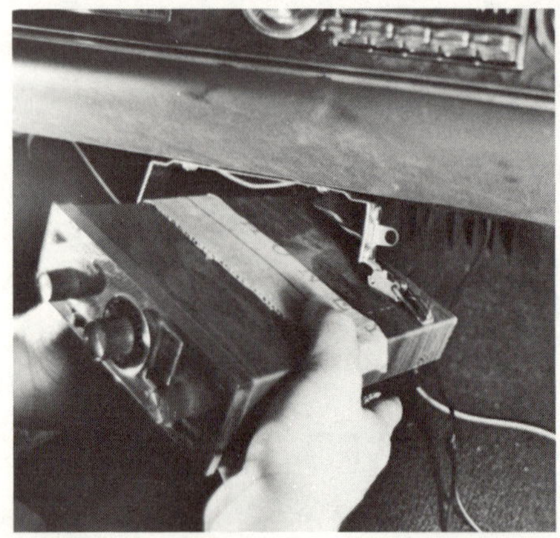

Mobile radios have been mounted in every conceivable corner of a car. For example:

- Behind the front seat in the rear passenger compartment.
- Sitting loosely on the seat or dash.
- In the glove compartment.
- Under the front seats.
- Between driver and front passenger seats.
- Above the windshield.
- Above, on, in or under the dashboard.

Let's compare them, one by one.

In the rear-seat area might be a good location in a chauffeured limousine, where only the passengers would use the set. If the driver is going to use it, though, a radio mounted in back of the seat, with the microphone cord snaked around to the front, may look classy, but it can hardly be safe when you turn around to change channels.

Unattached radios sitting on the front seat, tunnel hump or dash will slip around as you maneuver the car or adjust the radio controls. Such units can distract the driver and possibly become flying hazards in a panic stop or collision.

"Invisible" locations in the glove compartment or under the seat are awkward for the driver to reach, as Big Bopper found out. They're not that theftproof, either, since thieves can guess there's a CB somewhere as long as you leave your antenna on the car.

Between the front seats, all controls are easily within the driver's reach—but since he can't see the dial without twisting half-way around in his seat, he'll have to select channels by counting the clicks. (It might help to cement markers of different shapes at the most commonly used channel positions.)

Above the windshield is where you find many CB sets in vans or trucks (cars usually lack sufficient headroom for this). This is actually a variant of a dashboard mounting; it turns the over-windshield area into a second dash.

Both driver and passenger can have easy access to an overhead set, depending on how far across the car you put it. And if you don't want to build your own roof-mounted console, you can buy ready-made mounts. But be sure the mike cord doesn't dangle in the driver's line of sight or jiggle distractingly in the corner of his eye. And since a sharp-cornered radio can be a hazard in a crash, make sure it's above head level and that everyone's well belted in.

Another roof-mount technique is to hang the set from a van's roof right behind the front seats. This makes the controls more accessible to the driver than hanging it from the back of his seat, but still means that he'll have to tune by touch—or turn away from the road to find his channel. And with controls facing forward, the rear passengers have no access to them.

The dashboard is the best and most common mounting point. Here, the radio can be visible and accessible to both driver and front-seat passenger, there is easy access to 12-volt power and the connections can be inconspicuous.

A few CB sets, mostly combinations that include commercial broadcast radio and/or tape, fit in the dash, like factory-installed car radios. The location is convenient, and an in-dash set is hard to steal; but it's hardest to install, too.

Atop the dash is where the tuning dial is easiest to read and the controls are often nearest at hand. But a radio here can also block the driver's view ahead, or cause head injuries in an accident. And holes that are cut into the top of its dashboard may reduce a car's resale value. Also, since the speakers are located at the bottom of most CB-set cabinets, an on-dash mounting may muffle the sound somewhat.

So most sets are slung beneath the dash, using the brackets that come with them. For increased rip-off protection, you can substitute a locking bracket (make sure the lock is hefty and the bracket's mountings strong and solid) or a slip-on bracket that lets you remove the set without having to undo all its connections individually.

Connect your set's power line to a handy 12-volt source and snake the coaxial cable lead-in from the antenna to the radio or vice versa, depending on which end of the wire has the thinner plug.

Antennas mounted in the front cowl or fender have shorter cables that can be passed through the firewall directly into the dash area.

Make sure the plug at the radio end of the antenna cable matches the radio's antenna socket. If not, you can cut off the old plug (as close to the cable's end as possible) and mount a new one; but since coax connectors are no fun to install, you may prefer to buy a ready-made cable with connectors attached if your antenna's cable is removable.

When all connections have been made, and the bracket mounted, you're ready for the last two steps. Stick on your radio the FCC-required Transmitter Identification Card (FCC form 452-C, usually supplied with your radio) with your name, address and call sign.

You may also wish to engrave your driver's license number and state inside the cabinet, to help you recover your set should it be stolen. (Social Security numbers aren't as good, since federal privacy laws make them harder to trace.)

The other necessary step is to mount the microphone hanger. Most radios are supplied with hangers that are designed to be screwed to the dash or the radio's bracket (which may have pretapped holes to hold it in place).

Where to get your CB's 12-volt power

Before looking for a power source for your mobile CB, consider whether you want to use a circuit that's always on (so the set is always available, should an emergency arise), or one that's switched off when you turn off the ignition (so there's no chance of accidental battery drain if you leave the set on, and to prevent unauthorized use).

Both kinds of circuits are available under the dash and at the fuse block (which may be under the dash, on the firewall, or in the engine compartment).

Unless it's hard to reach, the fuse block is your best power source because it lets you wire your set to the battery side of the fuse where it won't add to the load of the car's fuse is already carrying (your set has its own fuse, either on its back panel or in its power cord). A ring, spade or hook-tongue connector soldered or crimped to your power cord will help you make a solid, secure connection to the fuse block; if its wires are buried, you can also push the tongue of a spade lug into the clip that holds the fuse.

Make sure your polarity is correct: Hot wire (usually red) to the positive (+) side of the line, ground wire (usually black) to the negative (−) side—even if the car's ground is positive. If your car has positive ground, you may also have to insulate your CB set from its mounting bracket.

CB can make your vacation better

By IVAN BERGER

DRIVE down those old, familiar roads, and you know just when and where to expect traffic, where to find good coffee while you wait the jams out, which gas stations honor your credit cards and which stay open late. And of course you know where all those roads are going.

But pile the family into your car to head off for a vacation somewhere new, and you're on your own again, a stranger. Ever ride down a back-country highway in the dusk looking for gas, a place to eat or someone to give directions?

With CB though, you're not a stranger any more. Pick up the microphone, ask for help or informtion and pretty soon some good buddy or another will provide. Last we heard, about half the trucks in the United States have CB rigs, and about one in every 20 cars. Those numbers are rising rapidly, too. And the more time a vehicle spends on the road, the more likely it is to be CB-equipped—and to help you.

Not only can you get help, you can be a good

SEE ALSO
**Amplifiers . . . Cassette recorders . . .
Cassette tapes . . . Mixers, audio . . .
Security, home . . . Soldering . . . Speakers . . .
Television antennas**

A MOBILE CB unit in your camper, and a walkie-talkie model outside, can help keep the family in touch with each other and their roving home base when parked at campsites—or even more important, when various members of the family are wandering around at roadside stops.

Samaritan yourself, passing on information about traffic jams, calling in if you see a roadside emergency, even relaying messages to travelers farther down the road (it's legal as long as CB messages travel no more than 150 miles).

And it does, thank goodness, take your mind off what the kids are doing in the back seat.

It's educational, too. Listen as you drive your way cross-country and you'll hear the constant shift of accents from one region to another, the differences not polished down as they are on commercial radio stations. You'll learn a bit about what life's like in each area, too, as your lakeside and riverside travels put you in contact with small boats, or your rural roamings let you talk to farmers—yes, even tractors are being CB-equipped.

Then there are those psychological puzzles. What do those handles—CB nicknames—mean, and how did their owners pick them? Is that guy on the air to convey real information, or just for an excuse to talk? And is that resonant, self-assured, rich-sounding voice coming from the sleek, expensive Porsche ahead, or from the rattletrap old Chevy right behind you?

A few hundred miles of that, and you should be ready to settle in somewhere for the night. CB will help there, too. Talking to other travelers can help you find a good place to bunk down. And if you need to make a reservation, confirm one

HOW'S THE FOOD at this truck-stop—or the next one down the line? There's a trucker somewhere on your road who can tell you—via CB. The scale's too small to show it, but virtually every truck in this photo sports CB "ears."

PORTABILITY can range from walkie-talkies like the ones in the child's hand above or the fisherman's at right, to magnet-mount antennas that can be shifted from one car to another.

IF YOU RENT your vacation car, carry a CB in a suitcase and plug it into the lighter socket.

you've already made, or let a motel know you've been delayed so they'll still honor your reservation, get on your CB. Chances are you'll be able to find some CBer with a base station who'll pick up the phone and make a call for you. Possibly, you may even reach your goal directly: Quite a few campgrounds (and many marinas, if you're vacationing by boat) already monitor CB channels, and I wouldn't be surprised if some motels did, too.

Garages, especially on or near interstate highways, often monitor CB, which can be a godsend if you break down on the road. I've even heard of one motor-home owner who, with his tank nearly dry, managed to catch a gas-station operator who was just about to close up and go home. The station stayed open another 10 minutes, and the RV filled his tank and sped off into the night.

If you have kids, CB can be a big help. Use it to find out which campgrounds have playgrounds or pools, and you can assure yourself a few quiet moments while your kids are burning off the energy you don't want them trying to burn off in the back seat tomorrow. If they're homesick, see if you can find a base station with a phone patch and the willingness to put through a call to their friends back home. By the time they've finished telling what a good time they're having on the trip, they may even believe it themselves.

CB is also a handy way to check out those little-known tourist sites printed in tiny type on road maps. Some of them are rather dull—I've used CB to tell one inquisitive tourist that an historical marker he was searching for was not worth breaking his way through a scrubby New England woods to see.

CB LINGO—IT'S ENGLISH, SORT OF

Three things you're never supposed to say on CB are swear words, your real name or ordinary English. Here's some of what you do say:

COMMON 10-CODES FROM THE ASSOCIATED PUBLIC SAFETY COMMUNICATIONS OFFICERS, INC CODE

10-4: Okay, affirmative, I got it.
10-10: Transmission complete, standing by.
10-13: Advise weather, road and traffic conditions.
10-20: What's your location?
10-34: Correct time (also 10-36).

CB SLANG

Back: Over. Back to you.
Back door: Rear of vehicle, or last vehicle of group.
Back down: Drive slower.
Back out: Stop transmitting.
Bad scene: Crowded channel.
Ballet dancer: Swaying antenna.
Barefoot: Using legal power.
Beam: Directional antenna.
Big Daddy: The FCC.
Big 10-4: Enthusiastic okay.
Bleeding: Interference from next channel.
Bodacious: Shamelessly strong.
Boulevard: Interstate highway.
Break: Let me talk.
Camera: Police radar.
Catch: Talk to.
Channel 25: The telephone.
Charlie: The FCC.
Chopped top: Short antenna.
Clean: No bears (police) in sight.
Clear: Done talking.
Come again: Repeat, please.
Come back: Return call.
Come on: Go ahead and talk.
Copy: Hear, understand.
Covered up: Blocked by interference.
Cut out: Leave the channel.
Drop the hammer: Step on the gas.
Ears: CB set.
18-wheeler: Truck, semi-trailer.
Eights: Warm goodby.
Eyeball: Face-to-face meeting.
Feed the bears: Get or pay a ticket.
Final: Last transmission.
Five-five: 55 mph (speed limit).
Flip-flop: return trip.
Four: OK (as in "10-4").
Four-wheeler: Automobile.
Front door: First vehicle in a group.
Getting out: Transmission being heard.
Gone: My last transmission on this channel.
Green stamps: Dollars: tolls or fines.
Hammer: Accelerator.
Handle: CB nickname.
Holler: Call.
How about . . .? Calling . . .
Linear: Illegal signal booster.
Mail: Overheard CB conversation.
Momma bear: Female police officer.
Mercy sakes: CB substitute for swearing.
Modulate: Talk with.
Negative: No.
Negative copy: Couldn't understand.
Negatory: No; emphatic no.
One time: For a short contact.
Over your shoulder: Behind you.
Overmodulating: Too loud, distorted.
Peanut butter in ears: Not listening to CB.
Pedal to the metal: Accelerator to the floor.
Picture taker: Police radar.
Piggy bank: Toll booth.
Ratchet jaw: Nonstop talker.
Radio check: Reception report.
Read: Hear, understand.
RFI: Radio frequency interference.
Rockin' chair: Middle vehicle of group.
Roger: I acknowledge.
Roller skate: Small car.
Seventy-three: Best regards.
Shout: Call.
Smokey Bear: Highway patrol.
Stepped on: Blocked by another's transmission.
Tijuana taxi: Well-marked police car.
Threes: Seventy-threes, regards.
Throwing: Transmitting.
TVI: Television interference.
Twenty: Location (see 10-20).
Walked over: Overpowered by a stronger signal.
Wall-to-wall: Loud and clear.
Wrapper: Color of car.
X-ray machine: Police radar.

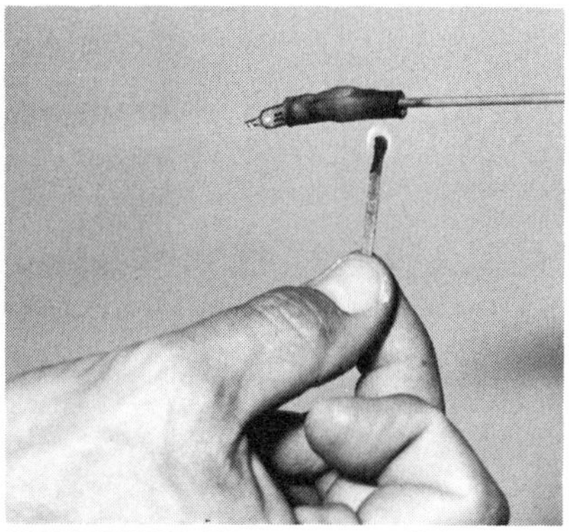

WANT YOUR CB antenna to light up when you transmit? All it takes is one neon bulb and a piece of heat-shrink tubing costing less than a dollar. The bulb, at the tip of your antenna, will blink on and off as you talk.

Tell the world you're on the air

By JOSEPH P. GREEVES

■ I DON'T EVEN KNOW how this flashing antenna light works. But it sure is fun and it's a cinch to make. It uses only a small neon bulb mounted on top of the antenna. It needs no electrical power because it's activated by radio waves when you transmit. The bulb is the kind you find glowing in household voltage testers. The bulbs I bought from Radio Shack came two on a card and cost about 50 cents. I also purchased the "shrink tubing" used to keep the light in place on top of the antenna.

The modification couldn't be simpler. The first step is to try the bulb in place to make sure you have the right kind. Just wrap *one* of the wires from the bulb (not two) around the antenna and stick some masking tape over it. Key the mike with the radio on and the light should glow. If it does, clip the second wire off and get ready to mount it. If it doesn't, continue your search for the right type of neon bulb. Remember, the kind with a filament won't work.

After you've checked out the bulb, position it at the very top of the antenna and tape it in place. Double check by keying the mike and, if the bulb lights, position the shrink tubing so that it covers the bottom part of the bulb and the end of the antenna. Hold a match near the tubing and carefully shrink the tubing so that it grips the bulb and the end of the antenna.

The final step, of course, is to check your signal-strength meter. Since the length of the antenna has been changed slightly, you may need an adjustment. If so, it is a five-minute operation any CB technician can perform. You should have this done every six months or so anyway in order to maintain maximum performance from your set.

The rest is all fun. Several members of the local van club have added antenna lights, and it's fascinating to watch a convoy of 10 or 12 vans, going down a long, dark highway, twinkling back and forth to each other. The bulb blinks on and off as your voice peaks the power output from your transmitter. Make sure, though, that everything you do about your rig is legal because "Uncle Charley" will now know who is transmitting, for certain, Good Buddy. 10-4?

SEE ALSO

Amplifiers . . . Cassette recorders . . . Cassette tapes . . . Mixers, audio . . . Security, home . . . Soldering . . . Speakers . . . Television antennas

THE PROPER clamps and a few blocks of wood make even the most difficult-to-hold joints, such as these curves, easy to glue.

By JOHN BURROUGHS

Choose the right clamp

Only after you've collected a good assortment of the three basic general-purpose clamps should you consider buying some of the special-use clamps. And then you should select carefully, based on need

SEE ALSO

Abrasives . . . Adhesives . . . Calipers . . . Joinery . . . Moldings . . . Sanding . . . Veneering . . . Wood bending . . . Woods

WHETHER IT'S ACTUATED by a screw, toggle or cam mechanism, a clamp has one prime function—to squeeze. Keep this in mind when searching among the clamps available commercially, and you'll find that the selection of the right clamp for your shop or the job at hand will depend upon the size and the type of material to be squeezed or compressed.

Compression has three common uses in shopwork. Clamping glued joints is one. Securing stock to be worked with power tools is another. The third is the clamping together of temporarily assembled jigs and fixtures.

For all these jobs, compression in the range of 100 to 200 lbs. is required. This is the optimum clamping pressure for glued joints. It's sufficient pressure to hold clamped-down work firmly and safely, and to keep jigs from slipping or sliding.

general purpose clamps, special clamps

The many different shop clamps used to apply this compression—without damaging or marring the work—can be grouped into two classes: general-purpose clamps for most jobs and special clamps for specific jobs.

C-clamps, handscrews and short-bar clamps are three useful general-purpose clamps that you should have in your shop. C-clamps (termed G-clamps in England) are so useful in everyday shopwork that they are considered basic hand tools. With enough of them—together with lengths of scrap lumber, blocks and wedges—you can easily improvise clamping setups for just about any job.

MAPLE-JAW handscrews offer the inherent advantage of distributing clamping pressure over a broad area.

Most moderately-priced C-clamps have frames of malleable iron, while top-quality clamps have frames of drop-forged steel, heat-treated Acme-threaded screws and smoothly machined ball-swivel pads for the greatest strength and performance.

Frame patterns also differ. Standard-pattern clamps are fine for many jobs, but have a limited depth-of-throat. Both malleable iron and forged steel clamps are available in deep-throat patterns that will prove well worth their extra cost.

Large C-clamps can apply considerable pressure, but because the pressure is applied in one spot, you should always use strips of scrap wood to distribute the pressure evenly. If you're clamping wood, this will prevent the clamp pads from compressing and denting the surface.

Handscrews, for centuries the clamps preferred by fine-furniture craftsmen, have parallel jaws made of straight-grain hard maple. When properly adjusted, the oil-finished jaws apply the pressure evenly over a broad area to grip tightly without marring the work. After you've caught the knack, you'll find that you can adjust a handscrew very quickly by grasping the handles and swinging the jaws around the spindles. Screwing the outer spindle develops leverage and tightens

SHORT-BAR CLAMP with disc-clutch sliding head is modern descendant of the old-time iron ratchet clamp.

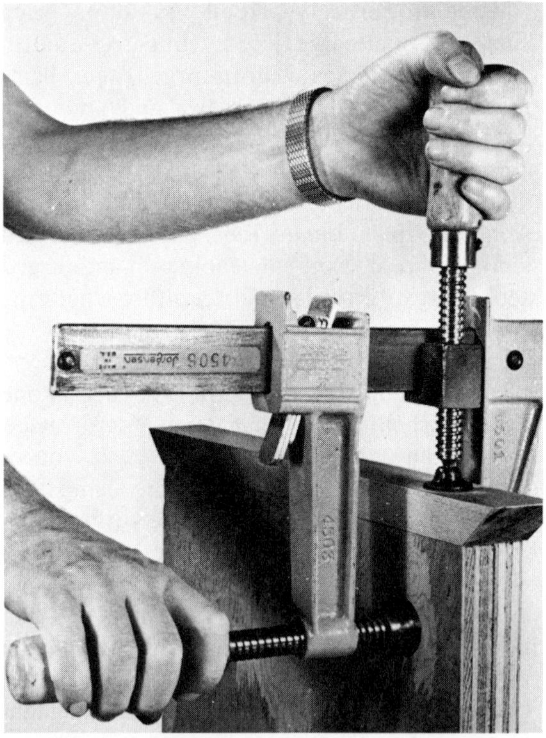

EDGE-CLAMP FIXTURES are auxiliary screws that attach to bar clamps, apply pressure at a right angle.

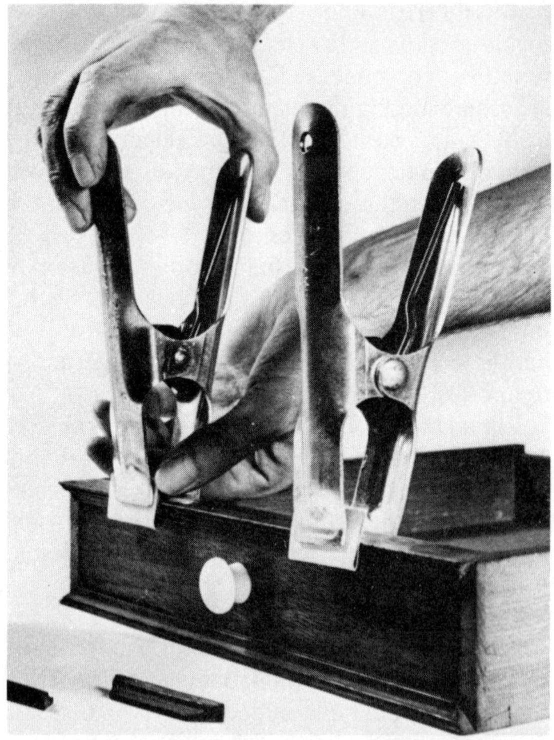

CLOTHESPIN-TYPE SPRING clamps apply adequate pressure for small gluing jobs, positioning of parts.

LONG CLAMPS for edge-gluing strips of lumber can be made of ¾-in. pipe and commercial clamp fixtures.

ALUMINUM-ALLOY corner clamps are handy for gluing mitered joints in frames made of light stock.

UNIVERSAL MITER clamp has two screws that grip halves of miter joint and a third screw to tighten the joint.

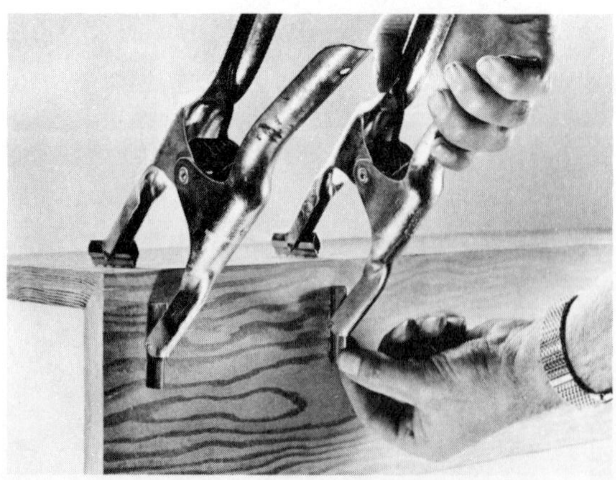

SPRING CLAMP has pivoting jaws, needle-sharp teeth to grip wood. Masking tape minimizes tooth marks.

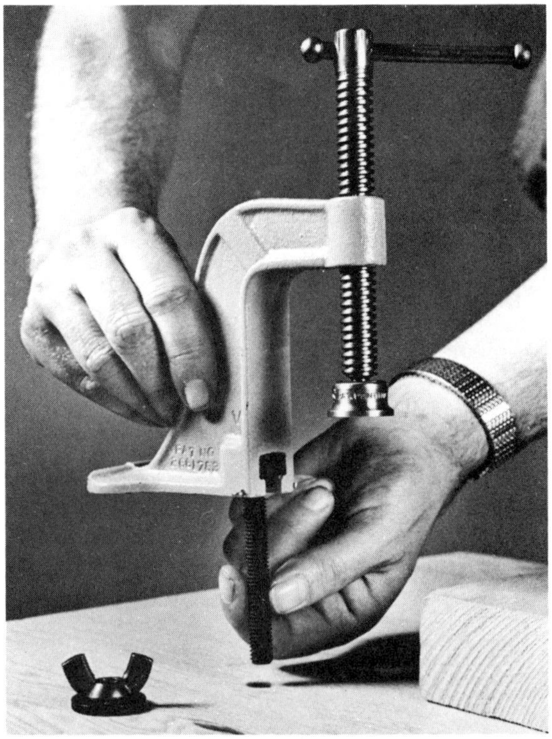

HOLD-DOWN CLAMP for benchtop requires drilling hole in top, inserting clamp and tightening the wingnut.

BLOCK-AND-WEDGE JIG is easy setup for gluing 90° joints. Nail blocks to scrap plywood, tap in wedges.

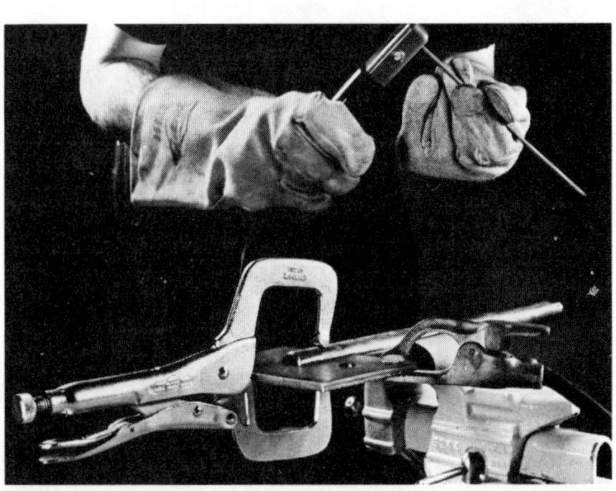

TOGGLE CLAMPS grip tightly without twisting work. Quick-release model above aids in welding, brazing.

TRIGGER-RELEASE CLAMP is handy for securing metal stock to be worked safely with portable power tools.

the jaws which, in turn, should always grip the work squarely.

A handscrew's depth-of-throat is half its jaw length. Commonly available are handscrews with jaws 4 to 24 in. long. Most cabinetmakers find that the 12-in. size (No. 2) ordinarily is the most useful.

Short-bar clamps, which essentially are quick-adjusting C-clamps, are also excellent general-woodworking clamps. The newer types have disc-clutch screwheads that slide on heavy spring-steel bars. Top-quality models have a depth-of-throat of 5 in. and capacities beginning at 6 in.

These three standbys—C-clamps, handscrews, and short-bar clamps—will take care of almost any common clamping job you're likely to encounter, provided you use enough of them. Clamping generally requires the application of evenly distributed pressure over the entire gluing surface. Thus, because you'll need a clamp every 8 to 12 in. along a long joint, a number of clamps should be kept in your shop. You just can't have too many.

other woodworking clamps

There are three other clamps you might find useful for common woodworking jobs. The first is a long-bar clamp, especially useful for edge-gluing and cabinet assembly. The second is a half-C-clamp that bolts through a benchtop to hold down work firmly. The third is a short-bar clamp with a hinged foot that screws under the edge of a benchtop.

A SCREW or wedge can easily apply enough clamping force to hold a machine vise; flat pieces of stock;wide or odd-shaped sections that are too awkward for the vise alone. When holding flat work, shims usually are necessary.

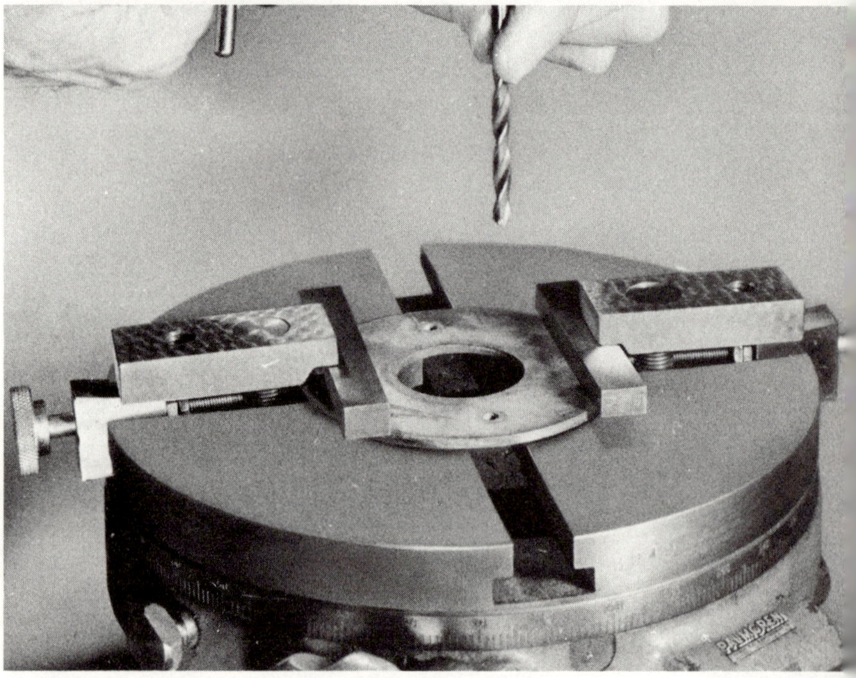

Are you looking for a way to hold a drill-press vise on a T-slotted table without disturbing the project held in the jaws? There's an easy answer to this problem

Make a machine- vise clamp

By WALTER E. BURTON

SEE ALSO
Angles, drilling . . . Drill press techniques . . . Lifters, drill press . . . Motors, shop . . . Shop techniques . . . Twist drills

■ HERE'S AN EASY way to clamp a drill-press vise on a T-slotted table without interfering with the work in the vise jaws. It's called a two-way machine-vise clamp and is operated either by a simple screw or a screw-operated wedge that's quick acting and requires no wrench.

The essential clamp components include the steel block that acts as a lever; a ½-20 bolt that serves as the fulcrum; a sliding wedge, and a lathe-turned T-nut threaded on the ½-20 bolt. The wedge slides along the bottom of the table slot and is applied or retracted by turning the long threaded rod engaging the threaded hole

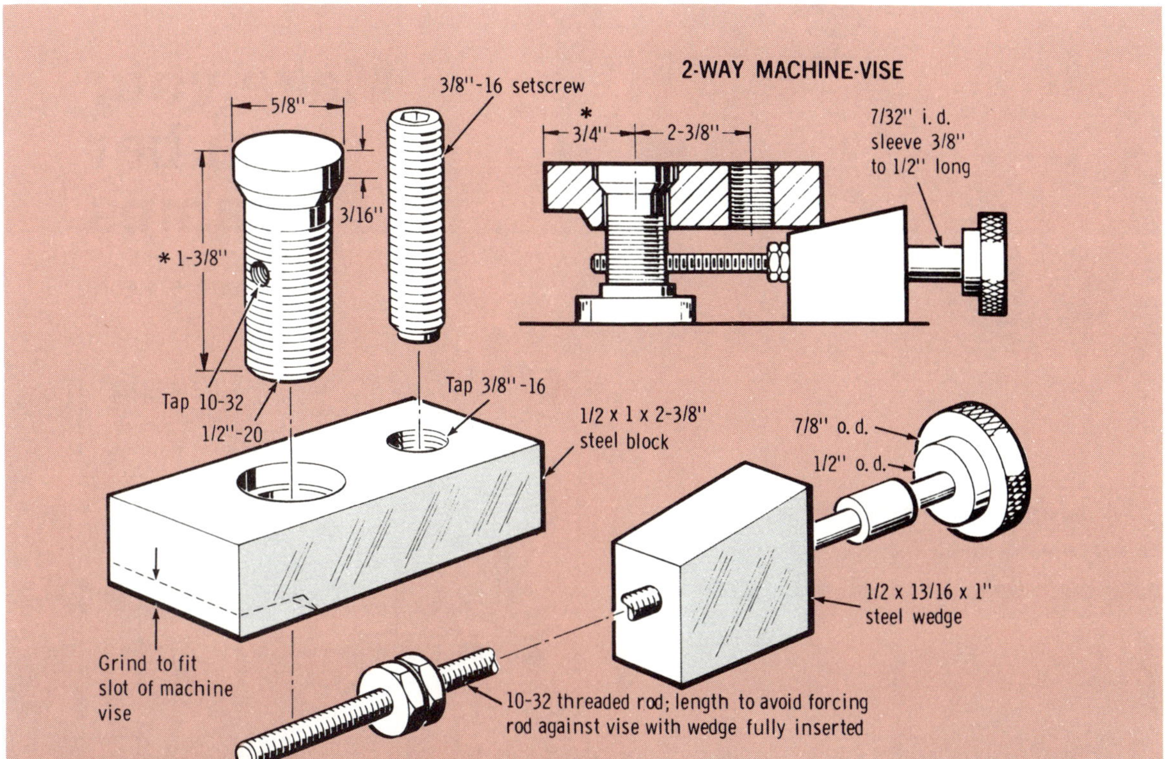

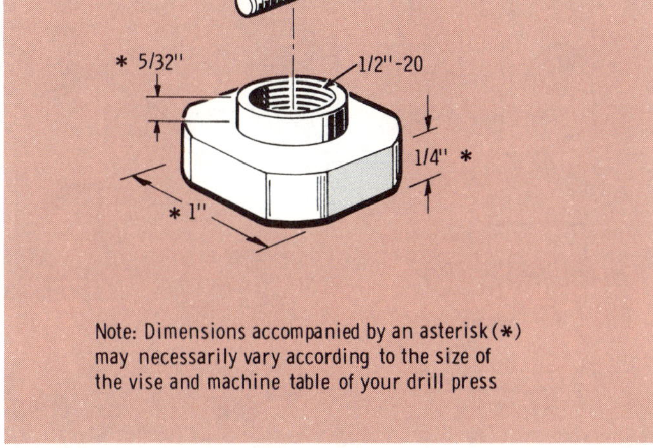

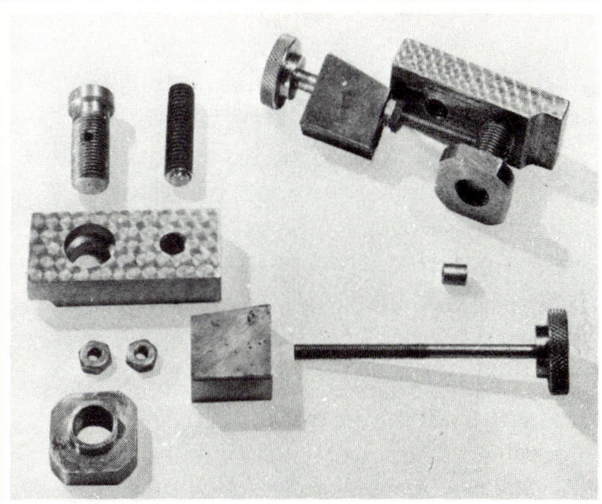

MAKE TWO of each piece to produce a pair of these clamps. Above, they're ready for assembly.

through the ½-20 bolt. The collar between the knurled knob and the wedge serves to position the knob so it falls outside the table slot.

For these parts, you can use either hardenable tool steel or cold-rolled steel, case-hardened where maximum wear resistance is required. The head of the ½-20 bolt should be turned so it is a loose fit in the counterbored hole in the steel block. Similarly, the hole for the long threaded rod through the sliding wedge should be large enough to pass the rod freely. The two locknuts on this rod serve to withdraw the wedge when the rod is backed out of its hole in the ½-20 bolt.

The alternate method of applying the clamping force requires an additional threaded hole (⅜-16) in the steel block. Through this extends a matching bolt long enough to press against the bottom of the table slot, but short enough to keep from projecting above the top of the block. This arrangement is compact and provides good clamping force—but a wrench is required to tighten or loosen the clamp, and the hollow-head screw will tend to fill with metal chips that interfere with the wrench.

As noted, the specific dimensions in the drawing are for the clamps shown.

Make your own bar clamps

By R. S. HEDIN

A clever toggle linkage is used to exert the force with these clamps. You can make them up to 10 ft., using conduit

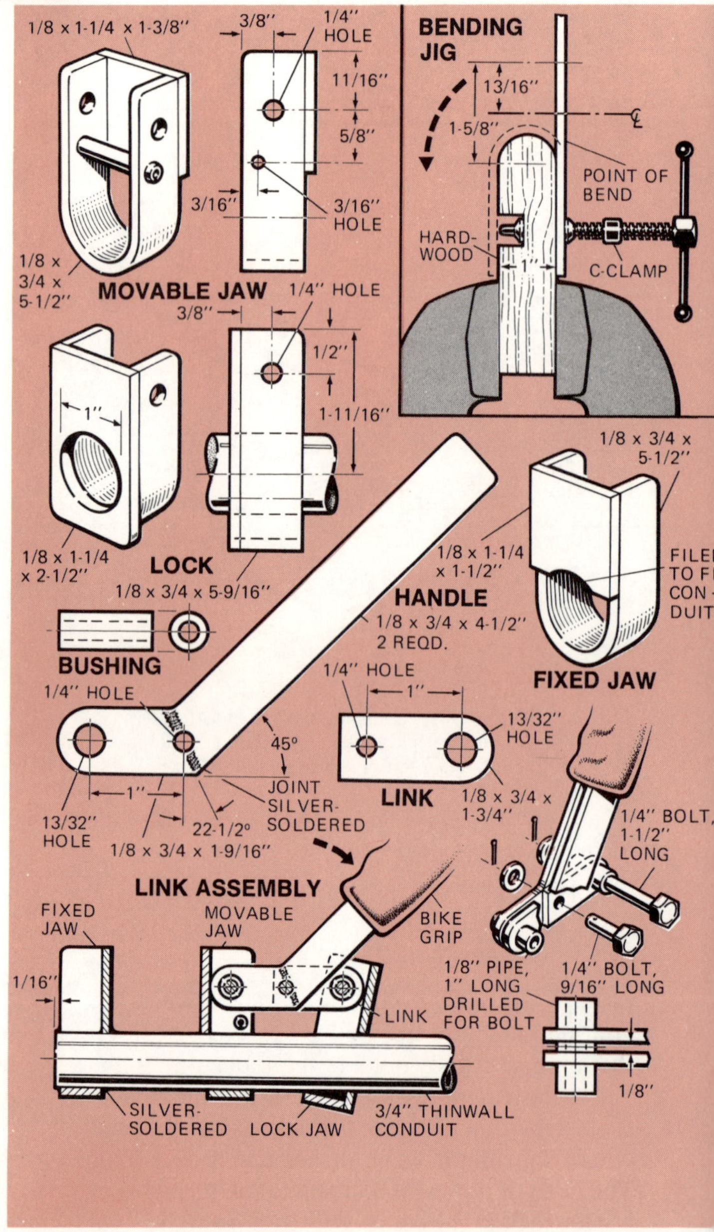

■ THESE LIGHTWEIGHT, quick-acting bar clamps are ideal for woodworking where only moderate pressure is needed to hold the joint. The clamping action is produced by a toggle linkage which snaps past center to exert force. To operate the clamp you bring the handle forward and slide the movable jaw against the work. Then you pull the handle back with one hand and adjust the locking jaw with the other until sufficient force is applied to the work. Finally, you pull the handle all the way back to lock the clamp. This causes the locking jaw to bite into the bar.

The three jaws required for each clamp (movable, fixed and locking) are formed from hot-rolled strip steel and are bent around a hardwood form clamped in a vise. The steel strip is clamped to the block with a C-clamp and bent by hand around the end. Notice that the bending point is 1⅝ in. from the center point of the strip. I used a tension pin in the movable jaw, but a No. 10 machine screw will do. I also silversoldered the parts with a butane torch, but they could be welded.

Common ¾-in. thinwall conduit is used for the bars and they can be made any length you want up to 10 ft. The fixed jaw is silver-soldered to the end of the bar, while the others are free to slide along it. Bike handlebar grips can be added to the clamp handles.

SEE ALSO

Adhesives . . . Joinery . . . Lumber . . . Wood bending . . . Woods

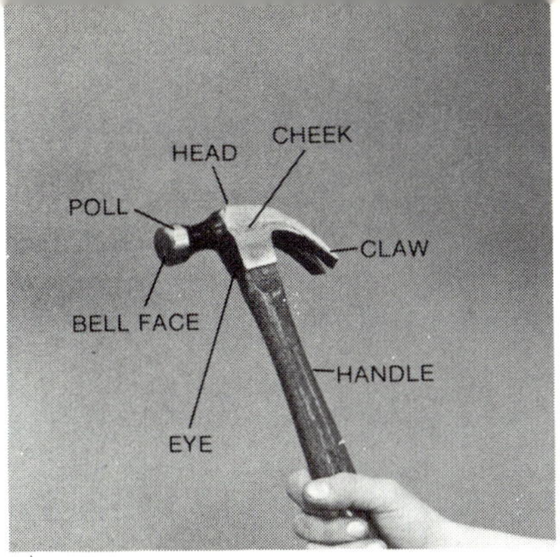

NOMENCLATURE for a nail hammer.

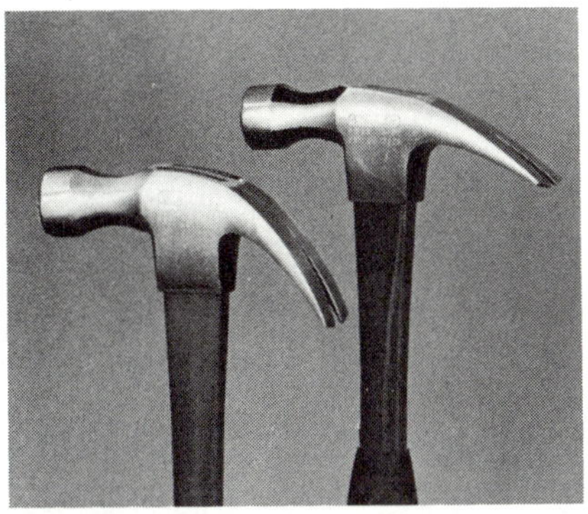

NAIL HAMMER heads come in two patterns—curved claw (left) and ripping.

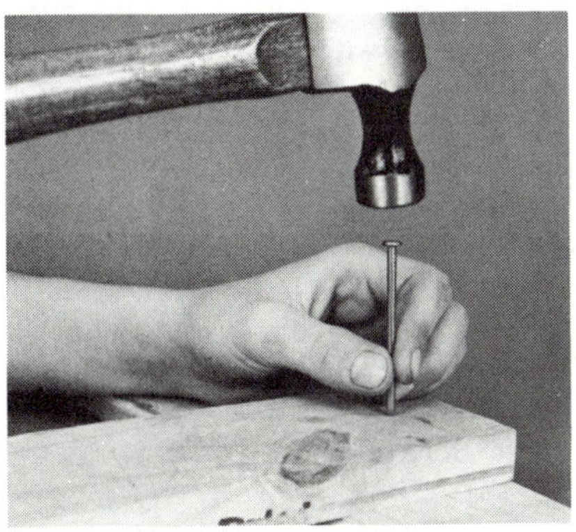

TO START a nail, hold it between thumb and finger, apply several light taps.

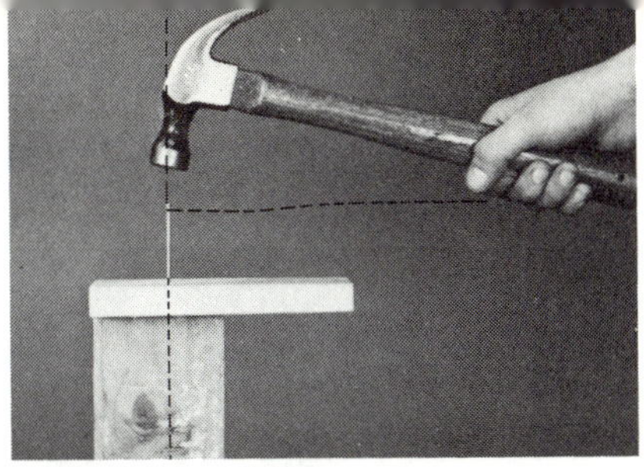

NOTE NAIL AXIS when driving. Hold handle on same plain as nailhead.

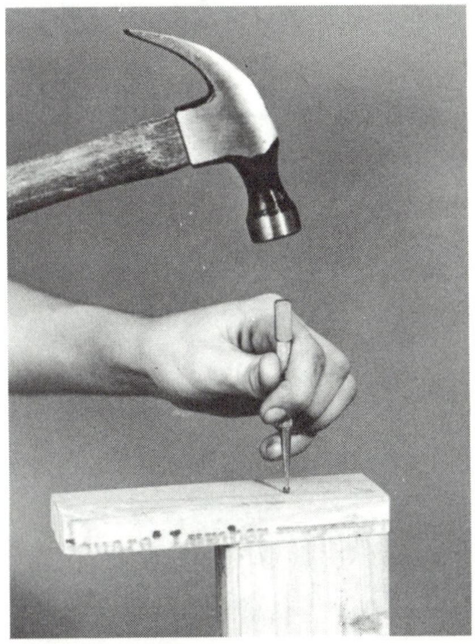

STOP DRIVING finishing nail when head is just above surface; use nail-set.

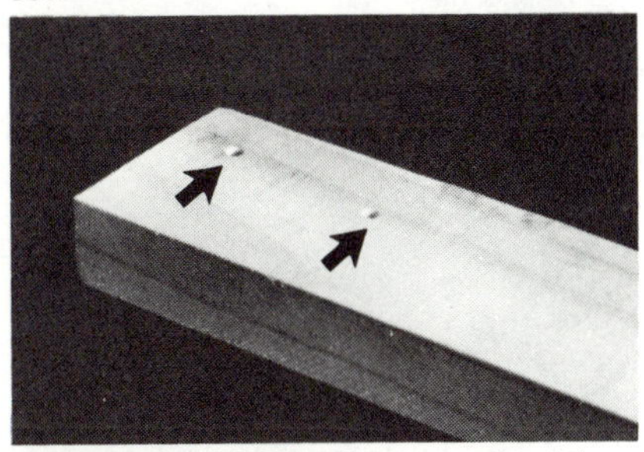

PROPERLY USED nailset countersinks nails without marring workpiece.

TO GAIN leverage when pulling nails and to protect work, use scrap block.

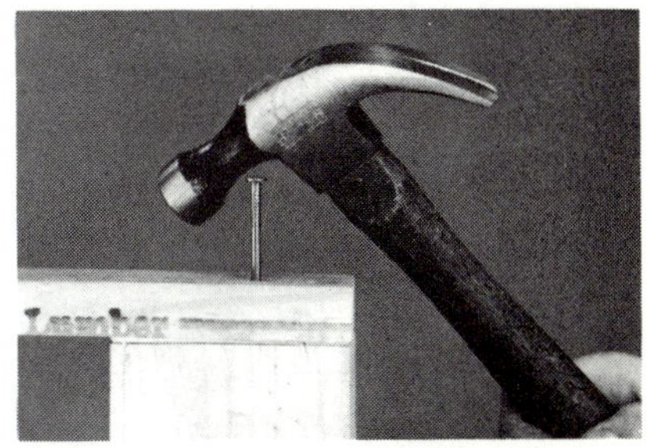

NEVER USE a hammer's cheek to drive a nail; you may chip the cheek.

How to use a claw hammer

■ WITHOUT DOUBT the ordinary "nail hammer" is the most frequently used tool in the home, yet many homeowners know little about using it. Study the photos above and you may learn a few things about hammers you never knew.

In addition, consider the following:

• Always use the right-size hammer for the job. For most chores, a 16-ouncer is just about right. A 13-oz. hammer is fine for bench work, cabinet making and the like. For house framing, use a heavy 20-oz. hammer.

• Never use one hammer to strike another because there is a high risk of breakage and possible injury.

• If a hammer shows excessive wear or mushrooming (misshapen head), toss it out.

• Your best choice for a first-hammer purchase is a curved claw, 16-oz. hammer with bell face. The latter means there is a slight convex surface on the hammer face that makes contact with the workpiece. The result is that dents and marks are less likely to occur.

• Don't try to save money by buying a cheap hammer. If treated with respect, most hammers will last a lifetime. Invest in a good one.

SEE ALSO

Caddies, tool . . . Calipers . . . Clamps . . . Combination squares . . . Micrometers . . . Nails . . . Screwdrivers . . . Sharpening, tool . . . Toolboxes . . . Tools, hand

Anyone can make pottery

By PENELOPE ANGELL

■ THE SIMPLE METHOD used to make this decorative pot is one you can learn in an afternoon: On various textured fabrics you roll clay into slabs, cut them to shape and combine the pieces.

The clay should be moist as you work. Knead it until smooth and free of air bubbles when cut in half. Smooth seams with a moist sponge. Each time you seam pieces together, set the work aside for an hour or two until the clay stiffens slightly but is still moist enough to seam with the next section. Cover the completed piece with a plastic bag several days so it dries slowly. Remove the bag and air the clay several more days until it's dry to the touch, then fire it.

When you fire the kiln, rest it on fireproof bricks or concrete floor. After firing, *don't open until it is cool* (at least six hours with the kiln shown). The pot needs two firings in the kiln shown—a bisque firing for 1½ to 2 hours at about 1873° and a glaze firing of 2½ to 3 hours at 2174°.

Gradually cover the kiln as it heats. This may take 45 minutes. The correct

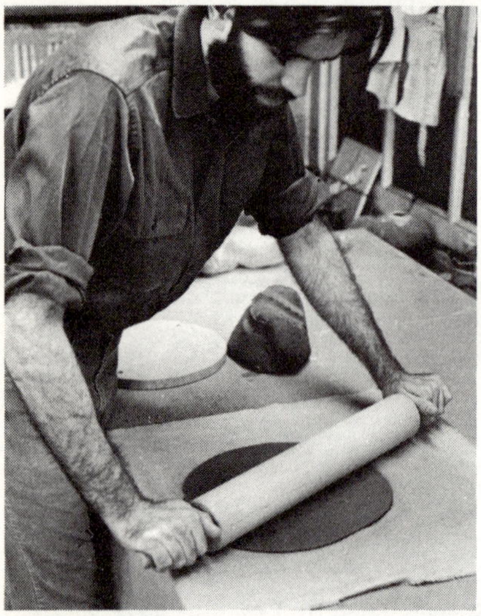

1. This pot is an excellent first project. Roll clay to a ¼-in.-thick slab somewhat like rolling pie crust.

2. Use any round object with a 6½-in. diameter as a template to cut a circle for bottom of the pot.

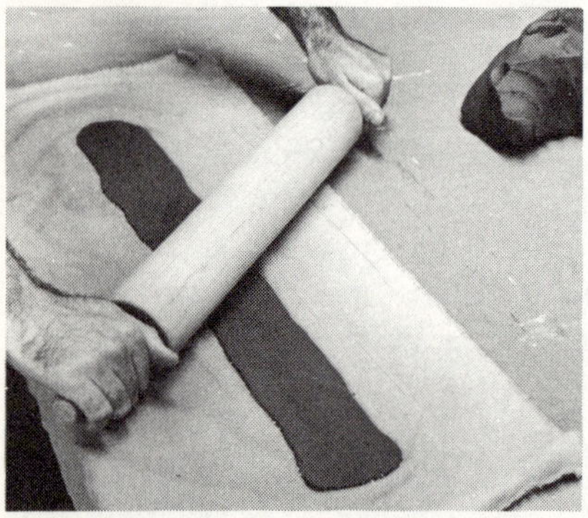

3. Hand shape a 1½-in.-dia. clay coil. Sprinkle grog (or sand) on canvas to give the clay texture and roll it flat.

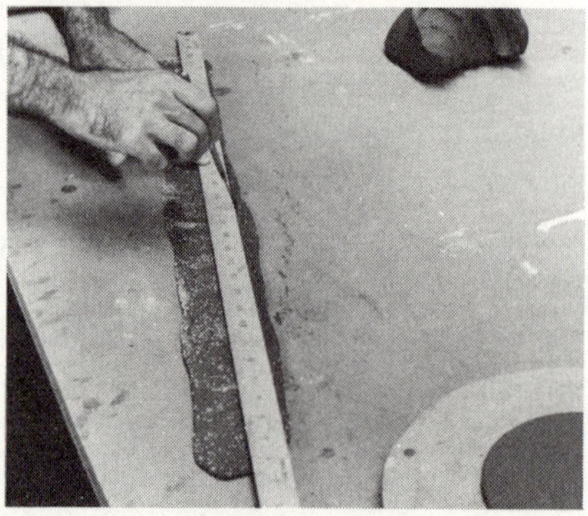

4. Trim the slab edges straight to a 2½-in. width. This slab wraps around pot bottom to begin forming sides.

MATERIALS AND TOOLS LIST

- 3 lbs. moist, de-aired stoneware clay (clay with air pockets can explode in the kiln).
- Vinegar (to help pieces adhere).
- Red iron oxide colorant; pin tool to cut clay.
- Commercially prepared glaze, compatible with firing temperature of clay, to waterproof pot.
- Grog (fired and ground clay) or sand for texture.
- Rolling pin, textured fabrics, fork (to score clay).
- Workboard (to turn piece when it's wet).
- Small paintbrush (to apply vinegar).
- 6½-in.-dia. and 3½-in.-dia. templates to use as cutting guides; e.g., pail or jar.
- Small kiln with firing cones. Make sure you follow the instructions carefully.
- (If pottery supplies aren't available locally, write: Eagle Ceramics, 11264 Wilkins Ave., Rockville, MD 20852.)

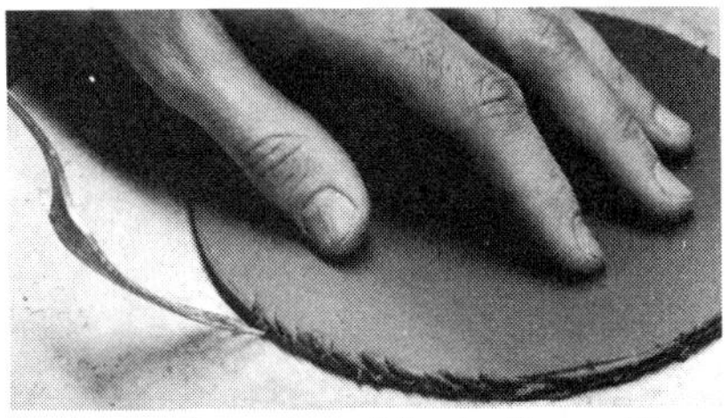

5. Score the edge of the bottom with a fork to aid adherence. As you work, score all points where slabs meet.

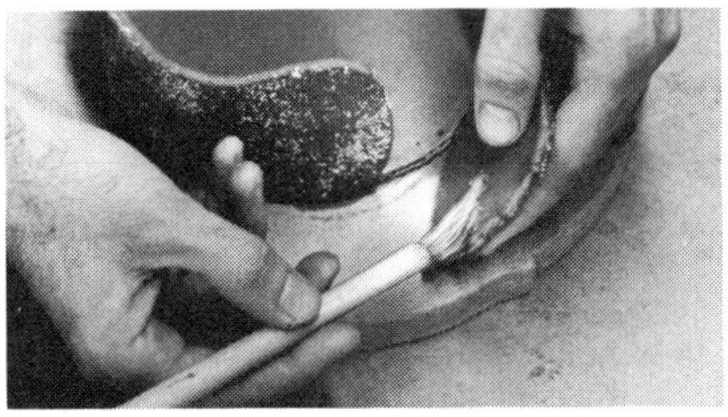

6. Also aid adherence by brushing pure vinegar on all seam edges. Wrap slab around pot bottom, overlap ends, seam.

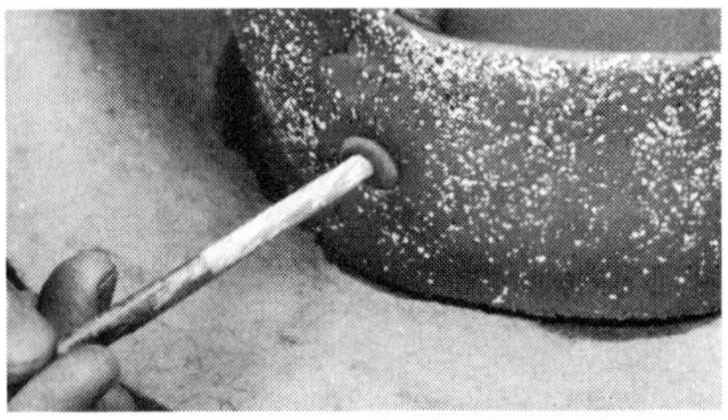

7. After seams are pinched together, press a decorative clay button on the side seam. Let dry an hour or two.

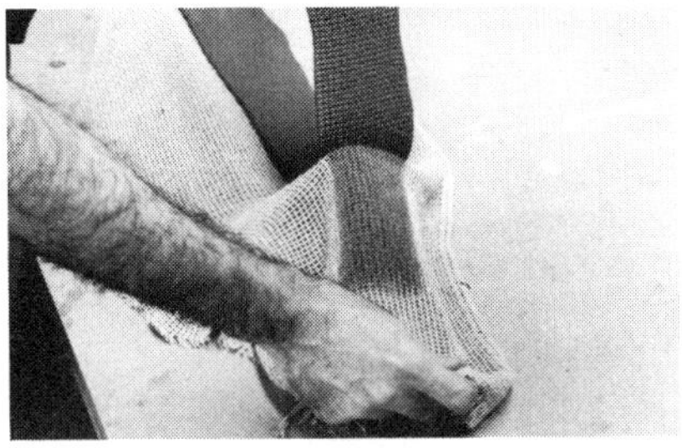

8. Shape a ¾-in.-diameter coil, roll it on a fabric to get texture, and peel it off. Trim to 1¼-in. width.

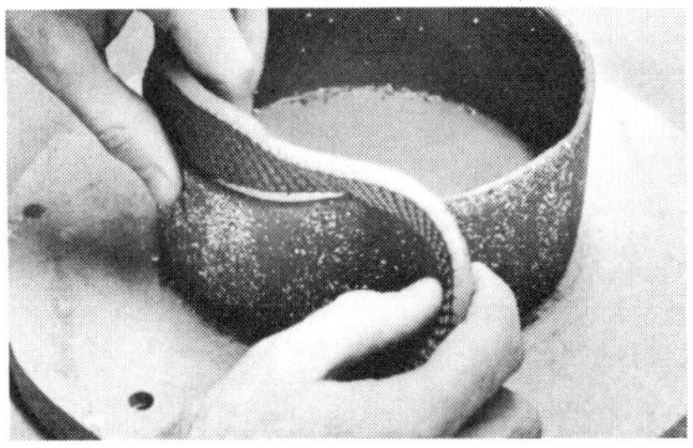

9. Score pot at seam, brush vinegar on all seam edges. Wrap slab around pot bottom, overlap ends, seam.

10. After rolling top slab on fabric for texture, peel off slab. Place pot upside down on slab; cut top.

11. After top of pot is treated and seamed, cut top opening using a 3½-in.-dia. template; let pot dry.

12. Roll a ½-in.-dia. clay coil to use as the neck of the pot. Flatten it, then trim to 1-in. width and attach.

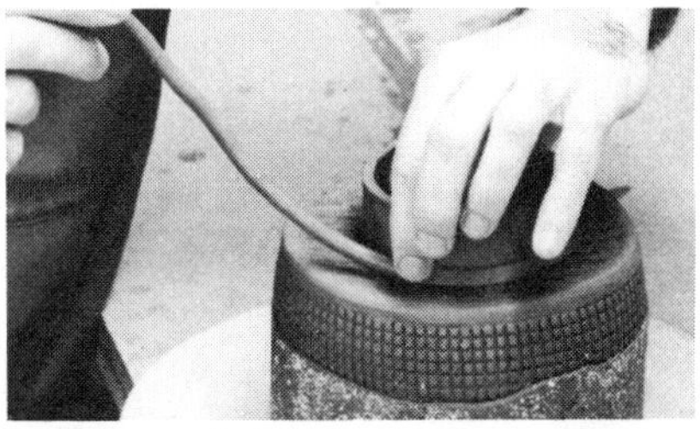

13. Use a pin tool to prick decorative holes in pot neck. Then flatten pencil-sized coil around neck seam.

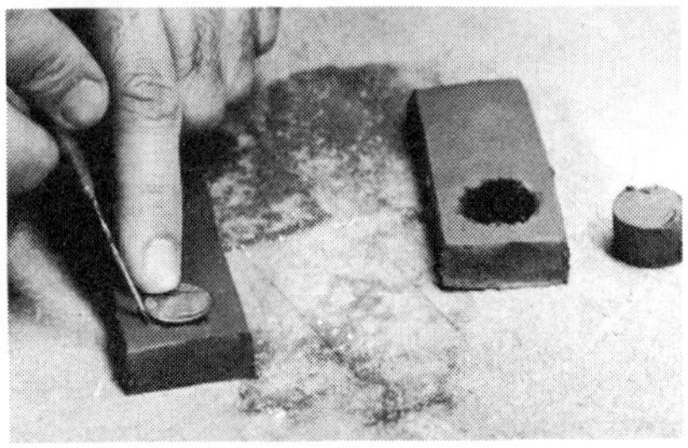

14. Shape two ⅜ x 1 x 3-in. handle supports. Cut handle holes. Score, apply vinegar and attach supports.

15. Roll handle coil, place it through the support holes and add a pea-sized handle stop near each end.

16. Place dry pot and a cone in kiln. Be sure cone is visible in kiln window. Kiln is from Eagle Ceramics.

firing temperature is reached when a 1-in.-high cone, placed on a pad of clay inside the kiln, droops over. Use a No. 06 cone for bisque firing and a No. 6 for glaze firing. A melting cone is a sign to turn off the heat and cool.

After bisque firing, sponge on a red iron oxide wash (one rounded teaspoon to one cup water) to darken the recessed area. Rub it off after two minutes. Pour a coat of glaze in the pot to waterproof it; glaze-fire.

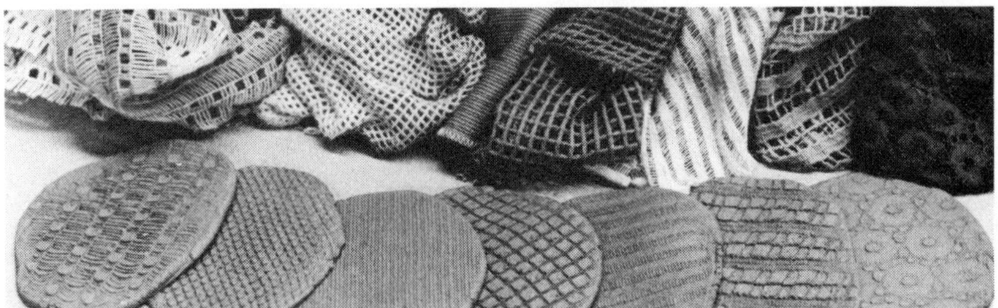

EACH CLAY SAMPLE was rolled on the fabric behind it to acquire a texture. Experiment with materials—try grasses and leaves—to get desirable, complementing patterns.

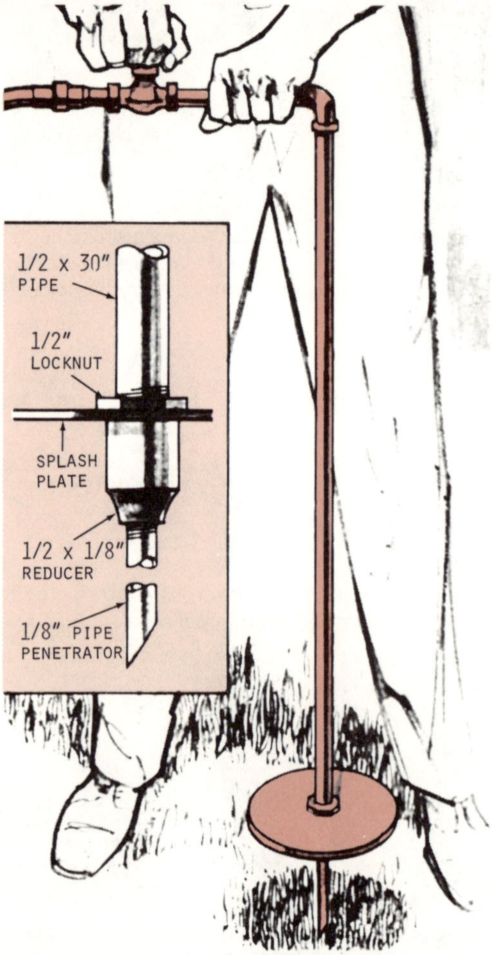

DEEP WATERING of lawns, shrubs and trees is no problem if you make a penetrator pipe to attach to your hose, like that shown above. Hydraulic action does the digging. When set, reduce the flow to a trickle.

A SPOUT OPENING cut in the protective seal of a new jar of instant coffee makes it easy to pour coffee into a measuring spoon and prevents anyone from dipping a wet spoon into the jar when making a second cup.

A SAWHORSE SHELF cut from a scrap piece of hardboard or plywood and attached with wood screws provides a place to put a can of paint, tools or any other necessities. Sand plywood edges to prevent splinters.

A LOW-COST SPLASHBOARD for a laundry-room counter is just a baseboard molding installed with oval-head screws and cup washers. The lower edge does a fine job of hiding unequal spacing between the counter and the wall.

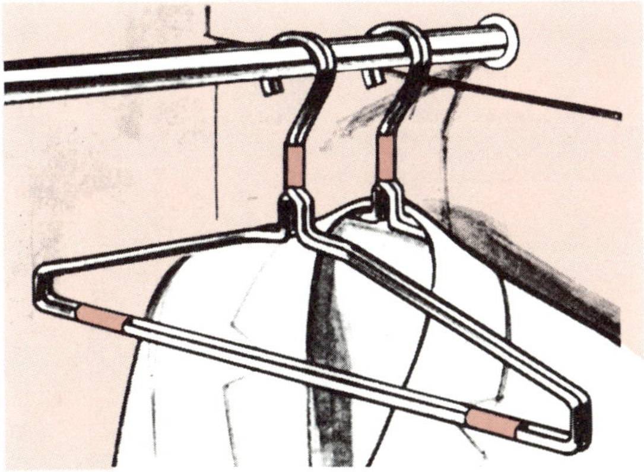

YOU CAN MAKE heavy-duty coat hangers out of light wire hangers simply by taping two or three of them together. Secure them at the top and at the ends of the crossbars so the tape won't snag on clothes.

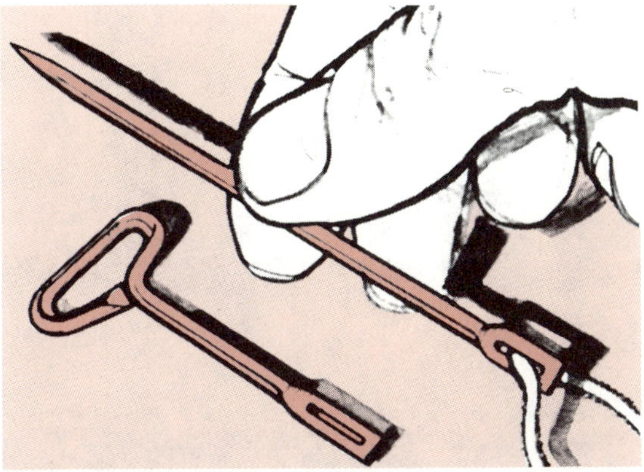

A COARSE NEEDLE for sewing burlap or other heavy fabrics is a converted key-type can opener. Just straighten the handle and file the end to a sharp point. The slot in the other end then becomes the eye.

A SAFE WAY TO STORE a stepladder is to drive a pair of screw eyes into the edge of the top piece and install a corresponding pair of L-hooks on the wall. A ladder hung this way can't be knocked over.

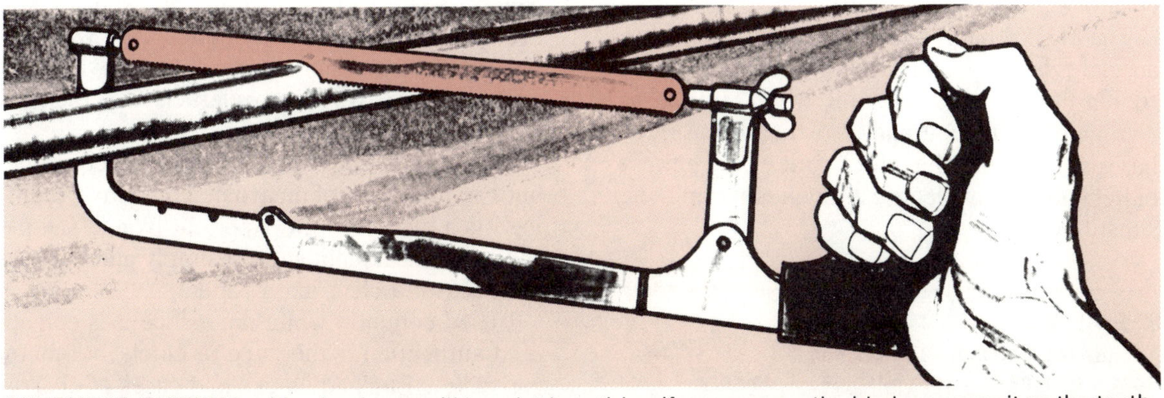

OVERHEAD CUTTING with a hacksaw will be a lot less tiring if you remove the blade, reverse it so the teeth face downward, then reassemble it around the pipe and make the cut. This lets gravity help with the work.

Build a Connecticut shelf clock

By FRANK L. GREENWALD

A fine example of Colonial design, its simple lines will blend well with either contemporary or early American furnishings

■ AS A PROJECT, this clock has just about everything to recommend it to the home craftsman. The styling is authentic, construction is simple and the cost is surprisingly low.

The clock I built, shown above, is fitted with an eight-day short-pendulum movement and a roman-numeral dial. If you would prefer to eliminate the ticking and also the necessity of having to wind the clock once a week, a battery-powered electric movement could be substituted.

SEE ALSO
Antique reproductions . . . Clamps . . . Gossip benches . . . Hutch tables . . . Joinery . . . Shaving cabinets . . . Stools . . . Weather instruments . . . Wood finishes

The original Connecticut shelf clocks (or "mirror clocks," as they were sometimes called) were made with a variety of different door panels. Some had a small mirror, while others used hand-painted scenes. When they were fitted with pendulum movements, however, a small oval area was always left clear so the pendulum action could be seen.

I wanted the effect of a hand-painted scene, but I'm not much of an artist. Thus, my "painting" is a piece of wall paper cut from a sample roll at the local paint store. I simply glued this to the back of a clear glass panel.

I used common white pine since it is considered authentic for this type of clock, but many early New England clocks had cases of cherry, mahogany and walnut.

The sides and top of the case require a piece of

wood ¾-in. thick, 4 in. wide and approximately 30 in. long. I ran the front and rear rabbets along the sides of the piece before cutting it up into specific lengths. I even found it best to first sand it, using No. 80 grit paper and then No. 220.

The sides are joined to the top piece by a joint called a rabbet-miter which you'll find makes a strong joint and simplifies the job of clamping. To cut such a joint you first set the blade on your table saw 5/16 in. high. Then you set the fence so it's ¾ in. from the outside of the blade. Make the cut across the end of both side pieces first, then shift the fence so you can make a second cut halfway from the end of the pieces. The area between the cuts is cleaned out with two or three passes. Now set the fence 7/16 in. from the outside of the blade and make a cut across both ends of the top piece. With this done, set the blade at 45° and miter each end. The miter cut should just reach the root of the first cut. Finally, make similar miter cuts at the upper ends of the side pieces. You can now trim the side pieces to 9¾ in.

The next step is to glue the miter joints and clamp them. A temporary spreader piece across the bottom of the assembly will assure square corners. It's best to use just a scrap at the bottom now so that any variation in width at the top caused by clamping can be compensated for by cutting the final bottom piece. Fasten the latter with glue and 6d finishing nails.

Next, rip a 20-in.-long piece for the three base pieces. I used my molding head to round the top edge, but you can also form it with a hand plane and sandpaper. The strip is cut into three pieces and mitered to fit around three sides of the case at the bottom. In doing so, the important thing to remember is that the inner face of the front piece must extend the full width of the clock case. The side pieces of the base were left extra long for final trimming after the miters are checked for a good fit. I drove small brads into the case at the bottom and cut the heads off so they'd impale the base and prevent shifting when gluing and clamping it.

Screwing the hardboard back to the case completes the job. Use ½-in. No. 6 oval or flathead crews to fasten it in the rabbets.

Simple butt joints are used to make the door. I rabbetted the members for the two pieces of glass and then glued the door together. After the glue dried, I ran saw kerfs in the joints at the corners and inserted splines. Fit the door to the case so there is 1/32-in. clearance at top and bot-

THE CLOCK MOVEMENT is a standard eight-day short-pendulum type which has a roman-numeral dial.

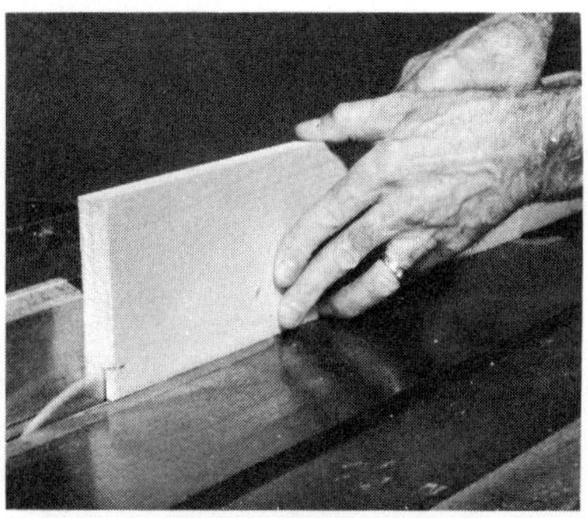

CUT BOTH RABBETS in one 30-in. board. Then cut the sides and top to length from this board.

THE RABBET MITER used to join the sides and top is begun by making a 5/16-inch cut ¾ inch from the end.

A SECOND CUT more than halfway to the end is then made and the area between the cuts is cleaned.

A MITER CUT at 45° should just reach the first cut. Sides are cut to length.

THE SIDES AND TOP are glued together after miter cuts have been made.

tom and 1/16-in. at the sides. The hinges are mortised into the edge of the door but not into the case. Use only one screw in each leaf for a trial fit. Then you can make an adjustment, if necessary.

Fasten the glass in the upper section of the door temporarily with a couple of brads. Then cut 3 and 6-in. squares of 1/8-in. hardboard. Locate the holes for the hand shaft and key stem in the 6-in. piece by using the dial plate as a pattern. Now center the 3-in. square and glue it to the rear face of the 6-in. square. This double thickness is needed since the threaded bushings supplied with most movements are designed for 1/4-in. panels.

For best visibility, the clock hands should be located as close as possible to the glass. Here is how I located the movement:

First I fastened the movement to the 6-in. square and measured the projection of the minute-hand shaft. Then I added 5/32-in. to the dimension, closed the door and measured in to locate the support cleats which are attached to each side of the case. I fastened the cleats only

GLUE AND NAIL the mitered joints with 6d finishing nails. I blunted the nail points to avoid splitting.

BRAD POINTS keep the base pieces from shifting when gluing. Drive them part way, then cut off the heads.

TIGHTEN THE CLAMPS slowly and evenly so as not to force the mitered corners out of line; apply as shown.

THE BACK OF THE CASE fits flush in rabbets previously cut in the top and sides. The back laps the bottom.

AFTER GLUING the butt corners of the door frame, 1/8-in. splines are inserted, glued and trimmed flush.

HINGE MORTISES are cut in the frame only. Make approximately 1/16-in. deep to assure proper clearance.

THE MOVEMENT is mounted on the dial backing plate, then used to determine the location of the support.

A MAGNETIC CATCH, stripped of its frame, is fastened to the case with a screw through the center hole.

A STRIP OF PAPER is used to check minimum clearance between the minute-hand shaft and the glass.

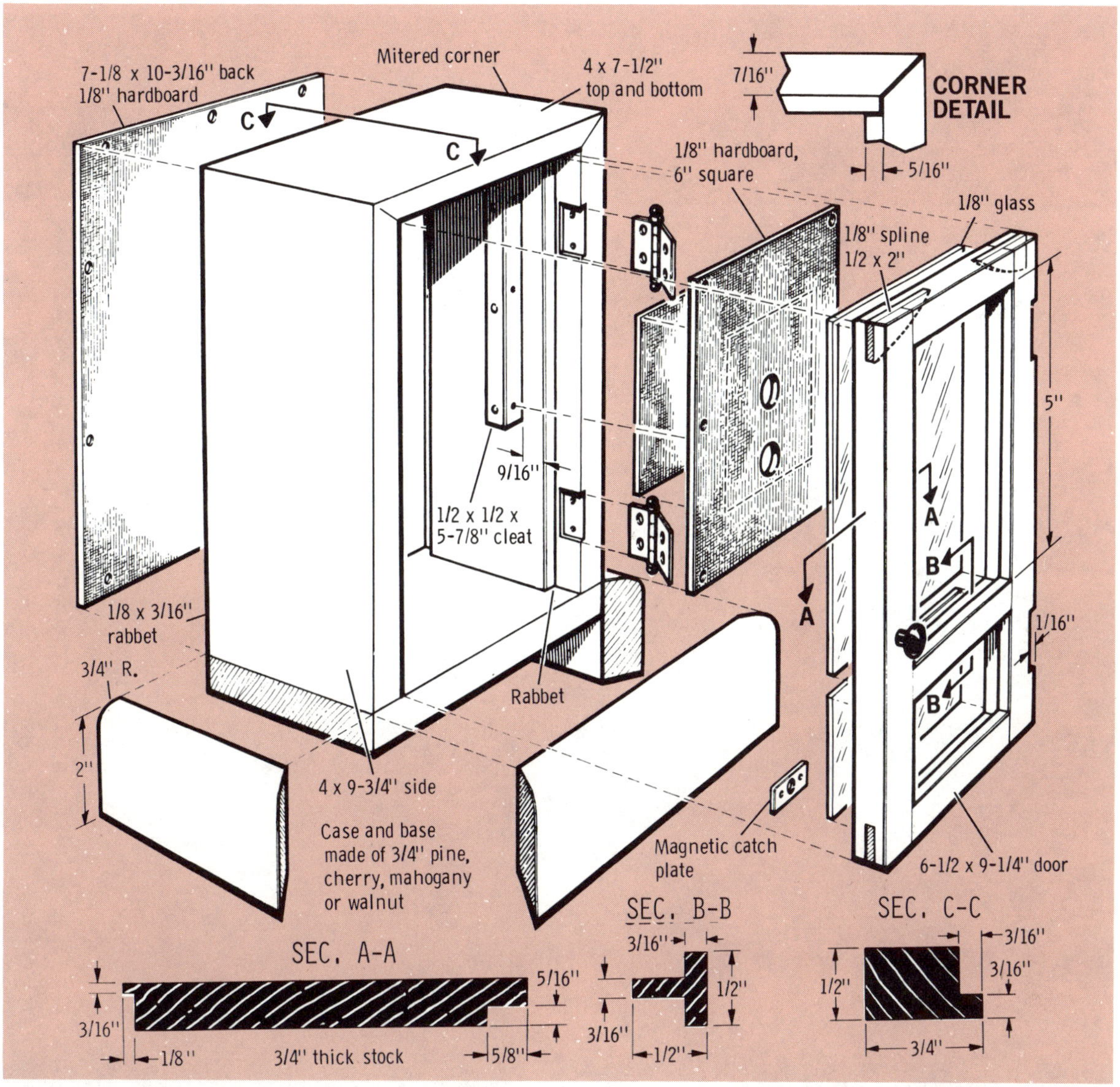

temporarily, placed the movement in position with the case on its back and checked the clearance between the glass and the shaft. Finally I removed the cleats, applied glue and fastened them permanently.

I used a magnetic catch to hold the door shut, after stripping off the metal frame and using just the magnet and the two pole plates.

If you'd like to finish your clock as I did, brush on pigmented wiping stain, a 50/50 mixture of walnut and French provincial. Let stand until it starts to flatten, then wipe with a cloth. Let dry 24 hours. Next apply a coat of color glaze (Martin Senour sable No. 457). Wipe off with a cloth, leaving traces in the corners, nicks and scratches. Let dry 24 to 48 hours. Follow with two coats of sanding sealer, letting them dry an hour or so between coats. Now sand *lightly* with 6/0 garnet paper and dust thoroughly. Next brush on four coats of lacquer, allowing 30 minutes between coats. Let dry 24 hours.

Wet-sand with soapy water and No. 400 wet-or-dry paper on a felt or rubber block. Use light pressure and inspect the surface frequently by wiping. Stop sanding when the surface has an even satin finish and clean up with a dry cloth.

Fasten the dial backing plate to the support cleats with ½-in. No. 4 flathead screws, drop the dial plate into position and install the movement with the bushings furnished. Always remember to remove the pendulum before moving the clock.

If you choose a hand-wound movement for your clock, as I did, you may want to put a small hook on the back of the case. Use it to keep the key from getting lost between windings.

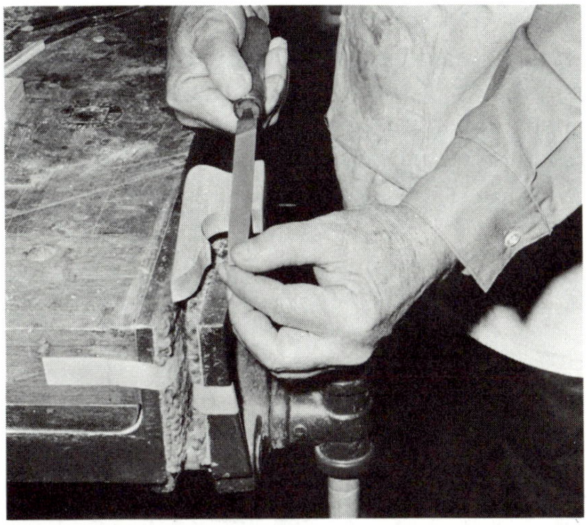

THE BRACKET FOOT is assembled, then shaped to contour with a rasp and file.

FEET ARE ATTACHED to the base frame with screws and glue. Position the feet with the long arms at the front.

Build this handsome hall clock

This family heirloom is easier to build than it looks. It's specially designed to blend with any decor. The project combines basic woodworking techniques with some fine Old World craftsmanship

By W. CLYDE LAMMEY

GREAT GRANDFATHER referred to his timekeeper in the hall as a "tall" clock, never as a "grandfather" clock. Both terms referred to the case, of course. Some early cases were huge and ornate—up to nine feet high and two feet or more wide. Our version is scaled to suit today's tastes; it's a clock that blends with any decor.

Though the case pictured is sometimes called a three-quarter case, it is more commonly known as "grandmother" size. Such cases usually varied from about 50 to 72 in. (or slightly more) in height with other details in proportion. Our version is 17⅜ in. wide and about 77 in. high overall.

The movement features visible weights with polished brass shells and chains. It chimes the quarter hours and strikes the hour on rods. The "moon" dial (ordered separately) will keep track of the moon phases, provided it is correctly adjusted and the clock runs constantly. Movement and dial (Model U-10) were purchased from Craft Products, Elmhurst, Il. 60126.

Woods to use are your choice. The case pictured was made from selected curly maple. Mahogany or black cherry are also good choices. The wood was ordered from Craftsman Wood Service, 2727 S. Mary St., Chicago, Il. 60608.

Actually, the clock enclosure is simply three boxes stacked one atop the other. The parts are built using simple construction techniques. Bracket feet, for example, *look* difficult to make, but aren't. The two parts are bandsawed to rough shape and ends are spline-mitered as detailed. After joining with glue, the triangular filler piece is added and each foot rasped to rough shape.

Next, you make the base frames. The lower one has a plywood panel framed in; the upper one is an open frame to allow the weights to pass through. If you don't have a molding knife of the proper size for shaping the frames, do this by hand (or this could be the project that justifies treating yourself to a molding head and cutter set). If you do the frame moldings by hand, duplicate the bead (right angle) portion of the shape by ripping a ¼-in. groove about ⅛ in. deep. Then, using a hand plane, round the edge to

SEE ALSO

Adhesives . . . Bench saws . . . Finishes, wood . . . Gifts, Christmas . . . Joinery . . . Marquetry . . . Moldings . . . Planters . . . Screws . . . Table saws

shape. Grooves in the mitered corners for the splines are stopped just before cutting through into the molded edges.

The front member of the three-sided base will require edge-gluing two or more pieces to obtain the necessary width. Select stock so that the boards are well matched for attractive grain design. Mitered corners are splined. Notice that mitered cuts come to a blunt point. You leave about $^1/_{32}$ in. as a bearing against the ripping fence then sand to a corner after joining.

Photos show how the waist, or column, is

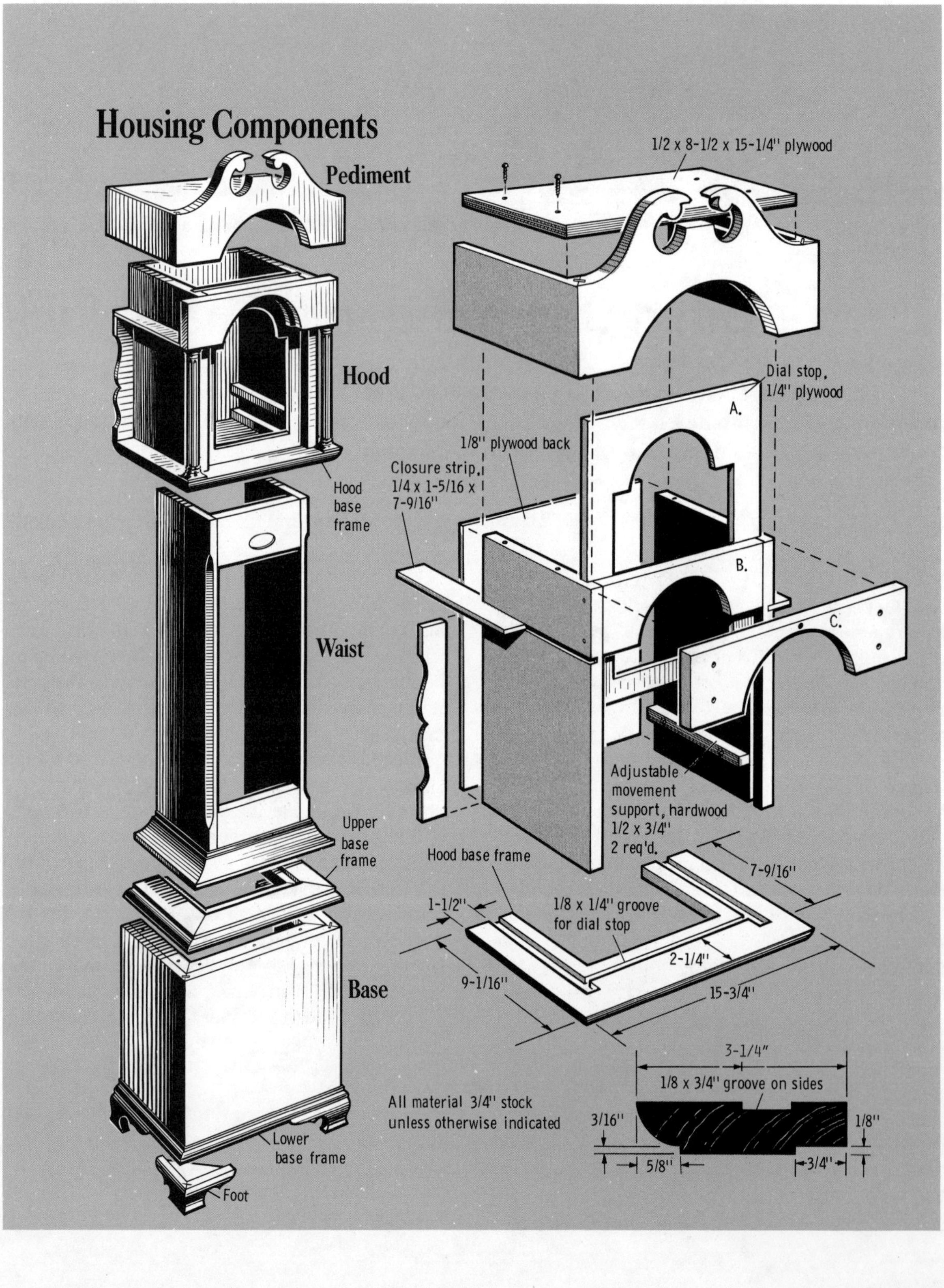

assembled. The inlaid eagle is a marquetry assembled from several woods, also sold by Craftsman Wood Service. It should be inlaid carefully to obtain as perfect a fit as possible. The depth of the recess receiving it should insure that the marquetry, when glued in, is slightly above the wood surface; it is then sanded perfectly flush. The joinery at top and bottom is by means of simple grooves and tenons, and must be done accurately to insure a neat fit. Cross members and base miter joints are glue-blocked. Each joint, further strengthened with a ¼-in.

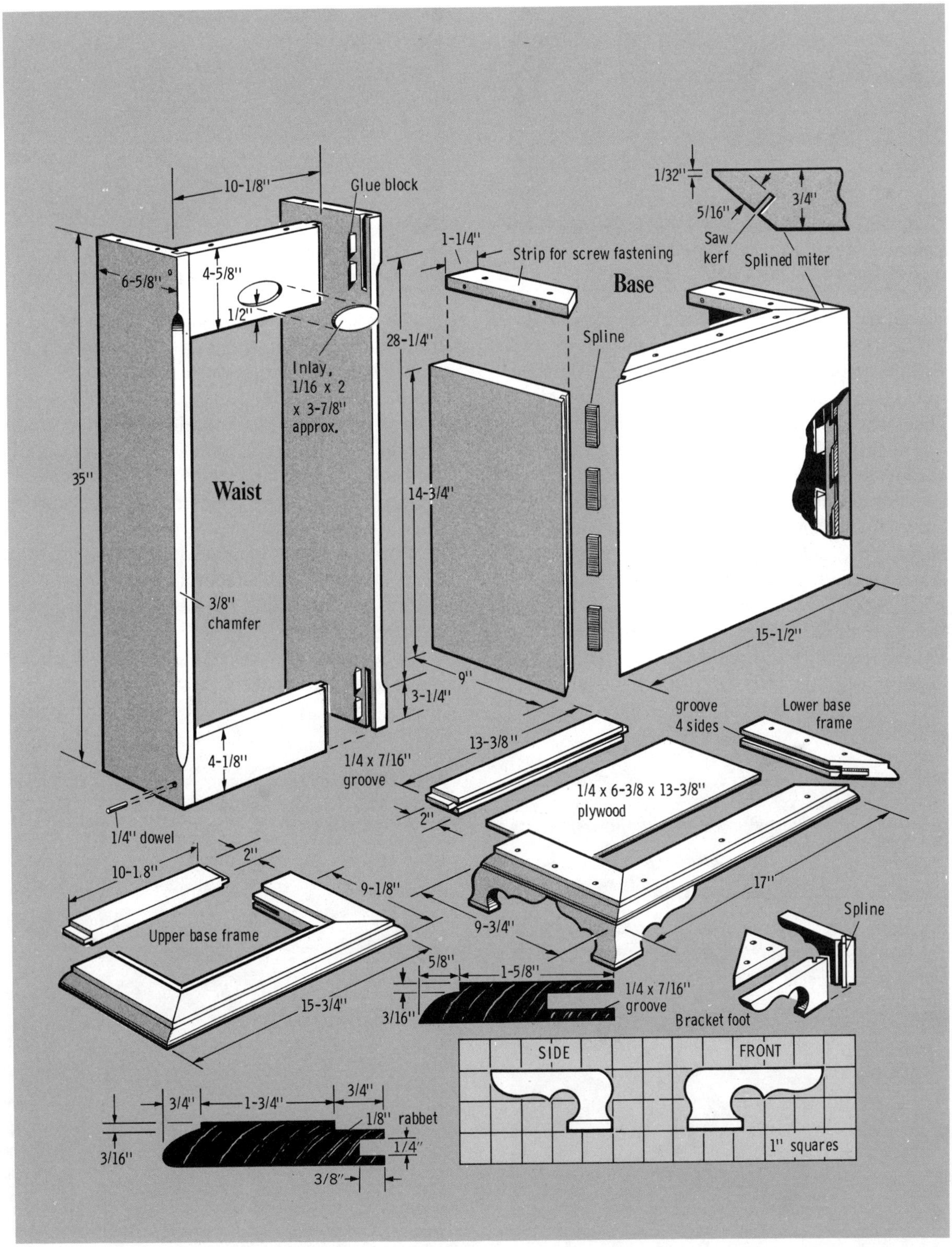

SCREW-FASTENING STRIPS are glued and screwed inside the the base, flush with the top edge.

THE LOWER BASE FRAME is attached to the base with screws only in a preliminary nonglue trial assembly.

dowel, will be concealed later by cove molding.

Use 1½-in. No. 4 flathead screws to assemble. Be sure that the base is properly located on the lower frame and make a nonglue test assembly to check for fit.

The strips for screw fastening are attached to the inside of the box, flush with the top. The top frame of the base is then attached with screws.

Next, turn the assembly upside down and install the bracket feet. To make sure the case will stand level when assembled, shim a piece of ¾-in. plywood level on your workbench, and place the assembled base on it. Then check the "stand" of the base with a level. If it is even slightly wobbly, remove stock from alternate feet with a rasp until the base stands perfectly level and firm on all four feet.

THE BASE is completed when the upper frame is attached with screws.

The waist now can be joined to the base in a trial fitting, leaving the joints dry. This dry run makes it easier and more workmanlike to disassemble the parts for finishing. It's also best to sand individual parts smooth as they are cut to size, and to "soften" (round) all corners slightly as you sand. Finishing stains and varnishes have a tendency to draw away from a sharp corner, thus leaving it unfinished.

With the basic housing built, you are now ready to start on the decorative ornamentation. Happily, construction is a lot easier than appearance indicates.

Since there are several checks you should make before you cut the parts for the hood, you should have the dial and clock movement on hand.

THE WAIST drops into place in the edge rabbets that are ploughed in the frame parts before assembling.

THE UPPER BASE FRAME is simply a hollow frame permitting weights to fall their required distance.

THE MOLDED EDGE of the upper base frame is fully rounded with a block plane, then sanded.

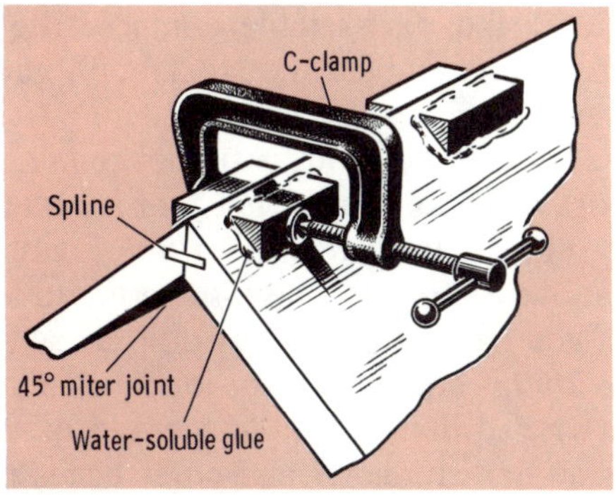

CLAMPING SPLINED MITERS. Triangular blocks are glued near the edges of the pieces to be joined. When the glue has dried, the joint is spread with glue and drawn tight with C-clamps. After the glue in the joint has dried, the blocks are cut off the workpiece with a chisel. Use sandpaper to thoroughly remove any glue that is left before finishing the sides.

SCREWS DRIVEN UP through the upper base frame hold the waist securely. Use nine equally spaced screws.

MATERIALS LIST

No. Reqd.	Size*	Use
		HARDWOOD
Base		
1	¾x2¼x40″	Bracket feet
1	¾x4x55″	Base frame (lower)
2	¾x9x15″	Base sides
2	¾x8x15″	Base front
Waist (column)		
2	¾x7x36″	Sides
1	¾x5x10½″	Top rail
1	¾x4½x10½″	lower rail
Hood		
1	¾x3½x36″	Hood base frame
2	¾x8x17″	Sides
1	¾x5x11½″	Inner arch (B)
1	¾x5x15″	Spacer (C)
1	¾x9x16	Pediment front
2	¾x5x9½″	Pediment sides
Cove Molding		
1	¾x2½x84″	Upper and lower
Arched Door		
2	⅝x1½x12″	Stiles
1	⅝x1½x11½″	Bottom rail
1	⅝x5½x11½″	Top (arched) rail
Waist Door		
2	¾x1½x27″	Stiles
1	¾x1½x10″	Bottom rail
1	¾x5x8″	Top rail
Miscellaneous Hardwood		
2	¼x1½x12¼″	Scrolled ornaments
2	¼x1½x8″	Closure strips
2	½x1x6″	Movement seat cleats
1	⅜x¾x12″	Retaining strip
2	¾x12″ dowel	Pilaster
		PLYWOOD
1	½x9x16″	Hood top
1	½x11x14″	Chime-rod bracket support
1	½x6x11½″	Movement seat
1	¼x12x17″	Hood dial stop (A)
1	¼x7x14″	Base
1	⅛x24x48″	Backing
1	⅛x12x36″	Backing

HARDWARE

2 each brass capitals and bases for pilaster; 1 pediment ornament with 2″ ball; 1 brass pull, ⅜″; 1 brass pull, ⅝″; 1 pr. 1½″ loose-pin hinges; 22-ga. brass for arched door hinges; clock movement and dial.

MISCELLANEOUS

1 2x3⅞″ marquetry inlay (eagle); 1 arched glass panel to suit hood door; 1 rectangular glass panel to suit waist door; assorted flat and roundhead screws; white glue, stain, lacquer, sandpaper.

*Pieces are listed slightly oversize in width and length to allow for finish trimming.

First make a test stand. Cut a piece of ½-in. plywood about 16 in. wide and 48 in. long. Fasten two pieces of plywood about 46 in. long and 6 in. wide to it at right angles. (Space the strips the same distance apart as the sides of the waist you have made.) Add a base so that the assembly will stand firmly when upright. Next, make the movement seat and chime-rod support. After assembling the two parts, screw the movement and chime assembly in place. Position it on the improvised test stand and add pendulum weights and dial.

With the movement in place, note the position and dimensions of parts A, B and C. Here, reference is made especially to the radii which determine the arch of these parts. Arched dials are generally held to close limits, but there *could* be some slight variations. *CAUTION: Don't take the dimensions given on the drawings literally.* Don't cut stock until you've made sure parts cut to these dimensions will accept *your* dial correctly. Check the radius of your dial arch to make doubly sure. This applies not only to the radii of parts A, B and C (the pediment has the same arch as part C) but also determines the radius of the arched door.

assembling the hood

With all dimensions carefully checked, you can start making the hood parts. Begin with the top waist frame. Again, all miter joints are splined. The sides of the hood drop into the dadoes in the frame and are fastened with screws driven from the underside. It's a good idea to omit cutting the grooves for the closure strips at this stage. It's far more accurate if done when the pediment is assembled; you can check location and width of the strips at one time. When cutting the curved parts, allow a little extra so you can sand-finish the rough-sawn edges. Chances are, you will also have to sand the outer edges of the dial stop (part A) so it will slip easily into its mating grooves.

The location of the movement support strips will normally be about 2½ in., measured from the top of the frame to the bottom face of the movement seat. Elongate the screw holes to provide an up-and-down adjustment of about ⅜-in.

Select your best stock for the pediment front. Miter and join it to the pediment sides with special care. Notice that the pediment half pattern shows a center-ornament seat of ½-in thickness. If you use an ornament with a 2-in. ball and spire as pictured, you should reduce this thickness to ⅜-in. or less.

Fasten the pediment over the hood temporarily, then locate and mark the position of the grooves in the hood sides for the closure strips. Disassemble, cut the grooves and reassemble with glue in all joints. (Note: No glue is used in the grooves taking the closure strips or the dial stop.)

Next, stand the case on a level surface and slide the movement into place. Check the position of the dial in relation to the stop. Raise or lower the movement by adjusting the movement supports up or down as required. You should see all the curved lines on the moon arch inside the arched portion of the stop and there should be about 3/16 to ¼ in. between the outer edges of the spandrels and the stop at the sides; a little more at top and bottom.

This done, remove the movement (handle it carefully) and disassemble joints of the base which were assembled dry. Next, apply glue and reassemble permanently.

The hood and waist door frames require careful workmanship. The arched door is a bit tricky since rabbets are cut on both inner and outer edges; one to take the glass, the other to form a lip. If you have a router, buy a ¼-in. rabbeting bit. With this equipment, the job takes minutes. Otherwise, drill a row of adjacent ⅛ or 3/16-in. holes around the inner and outer edges of the arch and then chip out the waste with a sharp, narrow chisel. Rabbets on the straight parts can be run easily on the table saw.

the arched door

The four corner joints are splined miters, but the two members of the arch are joined with a dowel. The hinges for the arched door are of necessity something special. Both are of flat brass, but the upper hinge is offset. Though not common in old clocks, an offset hinge was used here to give the door arch a more symmetrical appearance when closed. After assembling and placing the door, the hinges may need light filing to obtain clearance for smooth opening and closing of the door.

The lower rail on the waist door is splinemitered to the stiles but the upper arched rail is dowel-joined. Just how you make this joint depends on whether the corners are rounded or molded. With a router and a ⅛-in. bead cutter bit, you can run the molding all the way to the upper ends of the stiles, then turn the rail on end and cut a saw kerf the depth of the molding on both ends. To form the cope, undercut with a

THE HOOD BASE FRAME is attached to the partially assembled hood to check for a precise, neat fit.

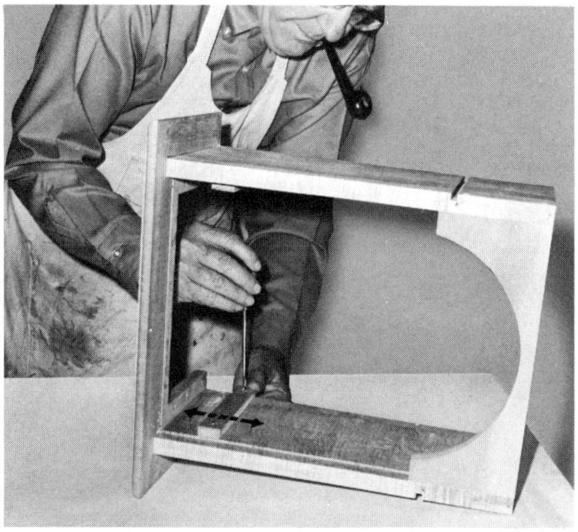

SCREW HOLES in the movement-support strips are elongated, providing an adjustment to locate the clock.

THE DIAL STOP (part A) must slide easily into position behind part B. Check the arch radius carefully.

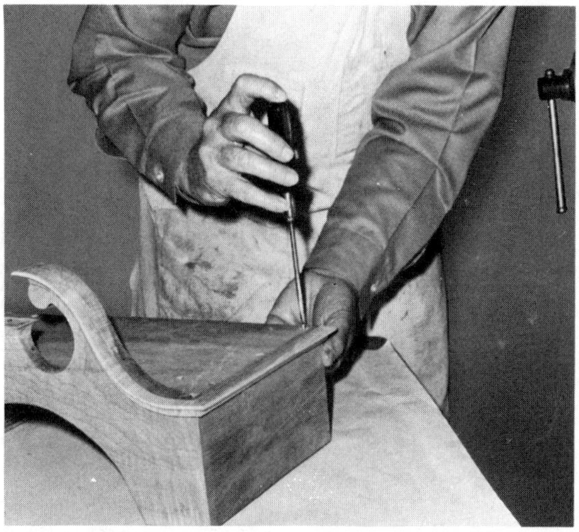

USE SCREWS to fasten the top. Moldings along the sides are mitered to mate with curved moldings at the front.

THE FULLY-ASSEMBLED PEDIMENT is slipped over the hood, then fastened with screws through the top.

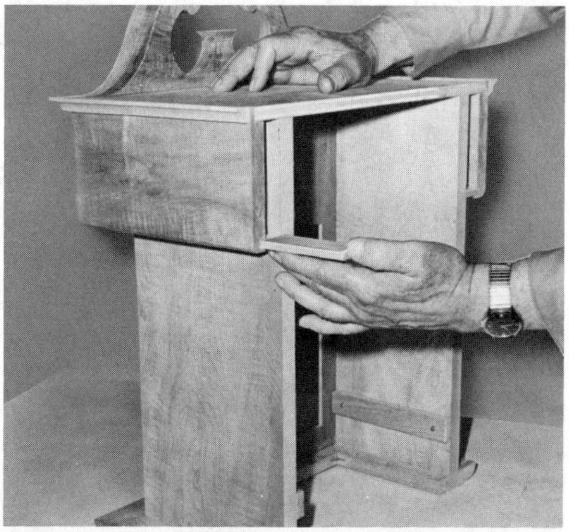

THE CLOSURE STRIPS slide in and close the openings between the pediment and hood. The hood is now fixed.

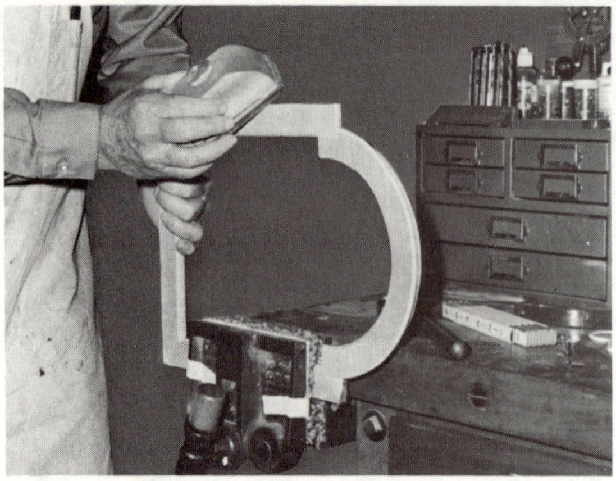

OUTSIDE CORNERS of the arched door are slightly rounded. The bottom edge is neither rabbeted or rounded.

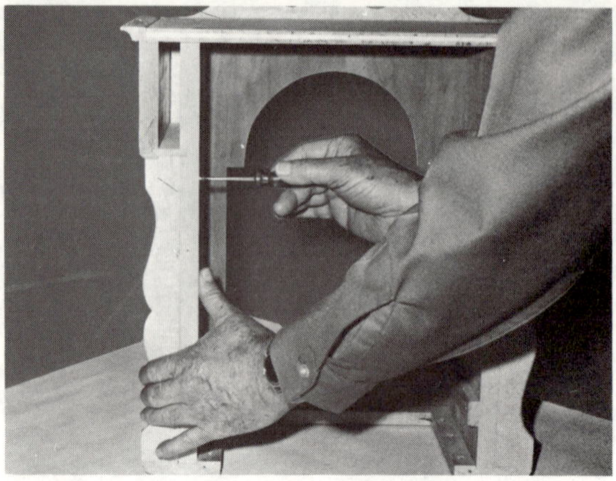

SCROLLED ORNAMENTS are attached with screws through the hood sides and notched to butt on the closure strips.

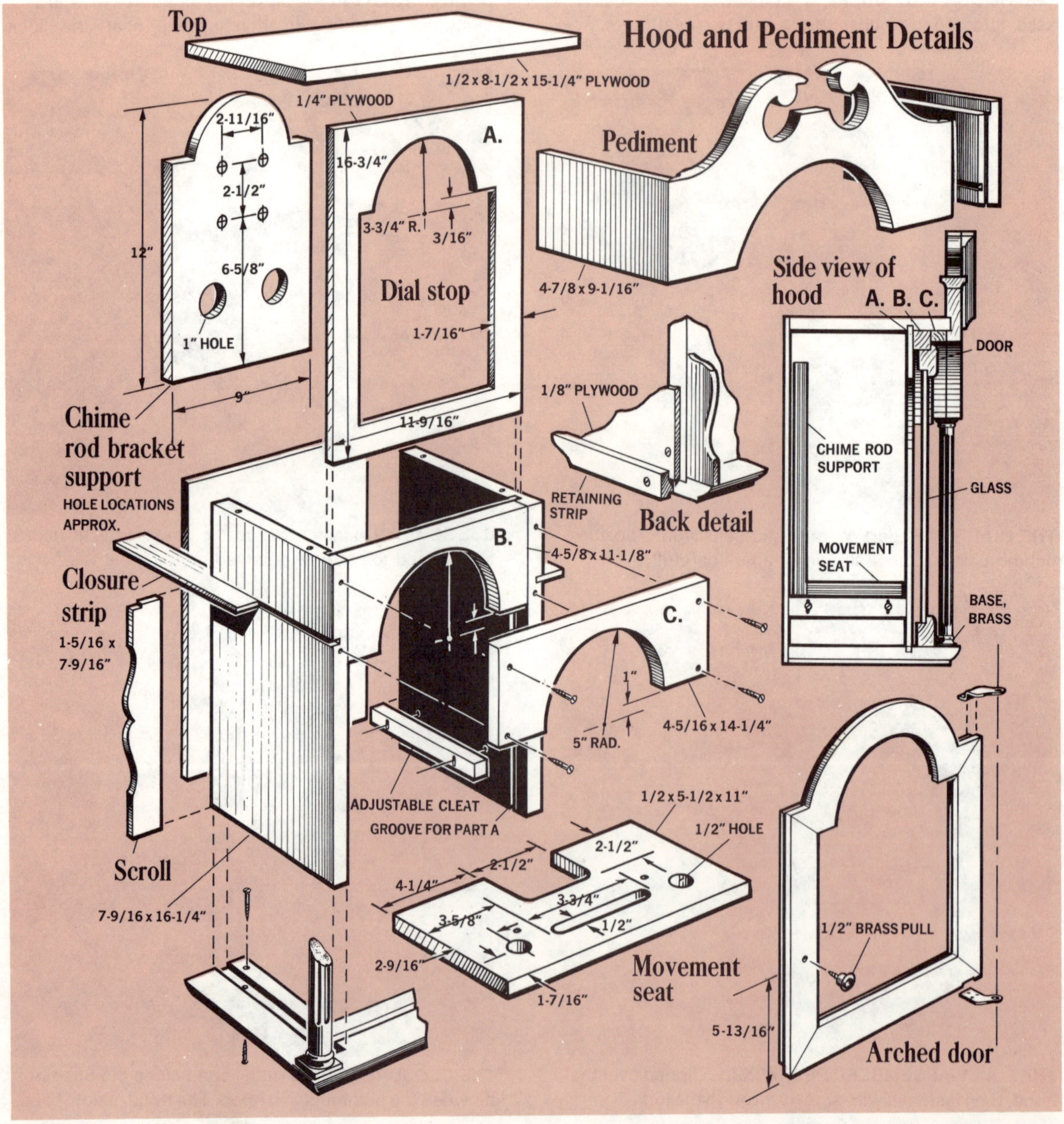

HINGING THE ARCHED DOOR and fitting the columns finishes the dry assembly. The door should swing without binding.

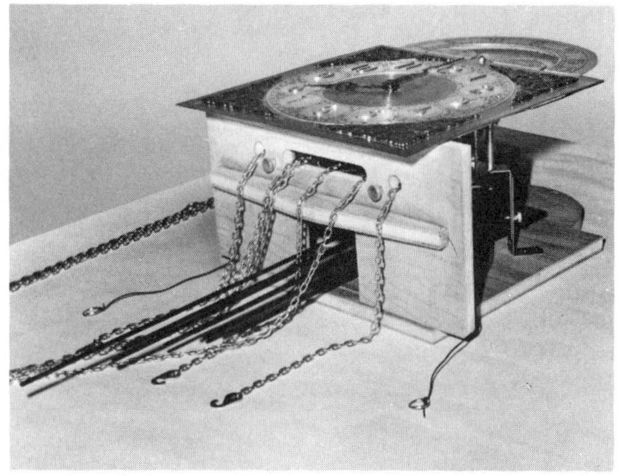

A STIFFENER, across the bottom of the seat, is optional. Notice that the movement is not attached to the case.

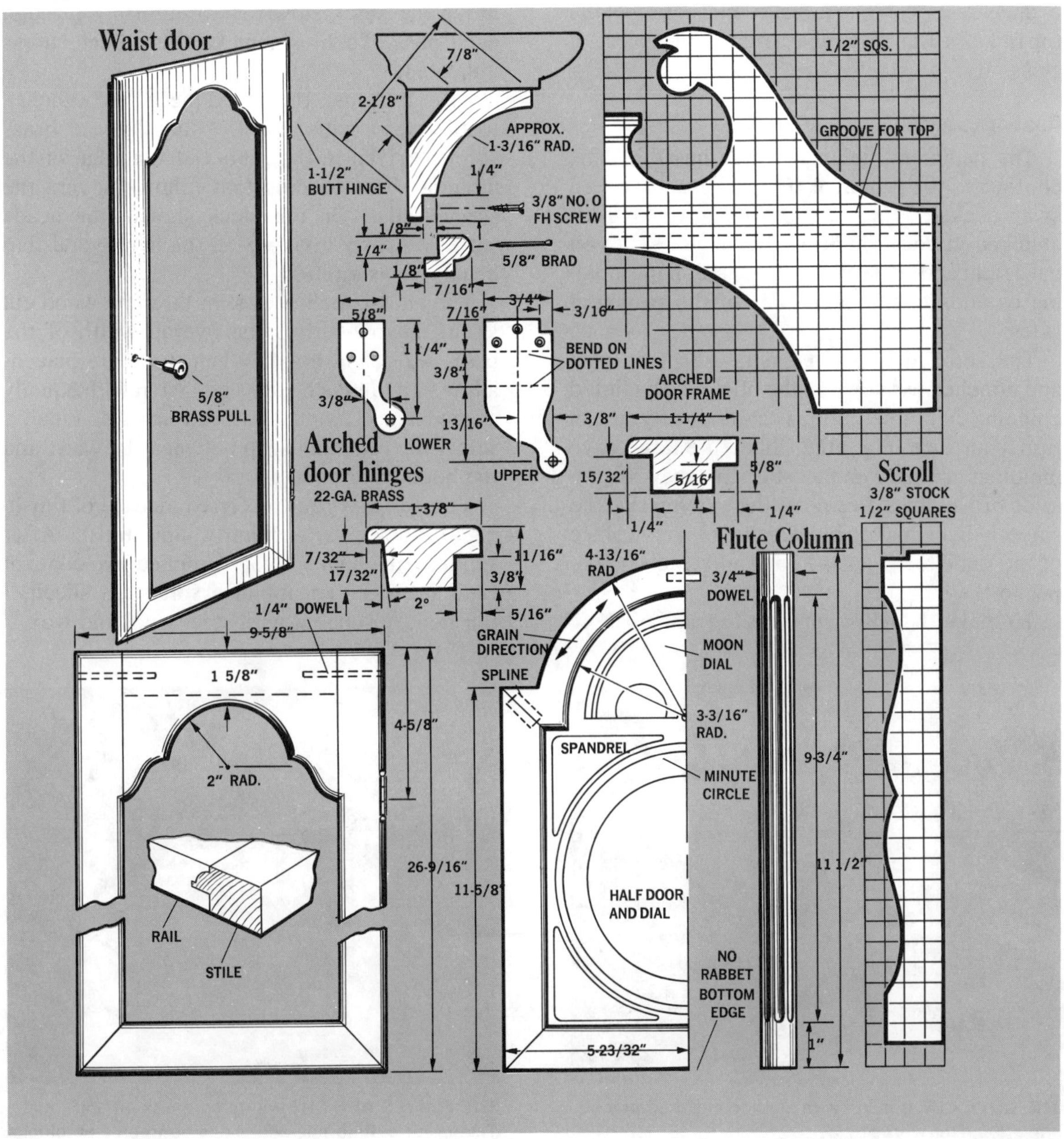

continued

PEDIMENT MOLDINGS of ⅝-in. stock are (1) cut using a bandsaw, (2) shaped with a cove bit chucked in the router, and (3) separated from the stock. The curve is reversed to make the other half of the pediment.

round file (or carver's gouge) to fit the rail's molded shape.

Since it is easier to do, and a straight-cut piece of glass costs less than a curved piece, rabbet the top rail ⅜ x 3-in. to receive a rectangular piece of glass.

final ornamentation

The pediment molding, which has the same contour as the pediment risers (correctly called swan necks), is quickly cut using a cove bit chucked in your router as shown. Be sure you cut a right and left section. The same shape molding extends to the back ends of the pediment sides.

The scrolled side ornaments are made next and attached as shown in the photos. The fluted columns can be set in brass capitals or you can turn your own in a lathe. Since the large cove moldings are made on the table saw, they require a lot of sanding to remove the saw marks. To smooth them, make a block having a convex face of the same radius as the cove and glue sandpaper to the face.

To make the miter cuts, tilt the saw blade to 30° and set the miter gauge to 54¾°. Run the cuts with the material right side up and flat on the table. Use a sharp, 6-in. combination blade and move the stock slowly and uniformly through each pass. To finish, make the rabbet cut as indicated.

After mitering, the coved pieces are attached to the waist with No. 0, ⅜-in. flathead brass screws driven in the rabbet at top edge of the molding. The beading that follows covers the screwheads. (On the clock shown, the heads were so nearly invisible on the light wood that beading was omitted.)

The back panels are ⅛-in. birch plywood cut ½ in. narrower than the overall width of the base, waist and hood. When these are placed, allow ¼ in. at each edge and fasten with equally spaced No. 1, ⅜-in. flathead screws. Finally, screw the retaining strip between the waist and the hood back panels.

You can use your preferred method of finishing. I stuck to a standard maple finish. After staining to a honey color, I applied two coats of clear lacquer. To obtain a soft satin sheen, I finished by rubbing with steel wool and wax.

THE COVE CUT is made with a guide clamped at a 52° angle. Feed the work slowly,

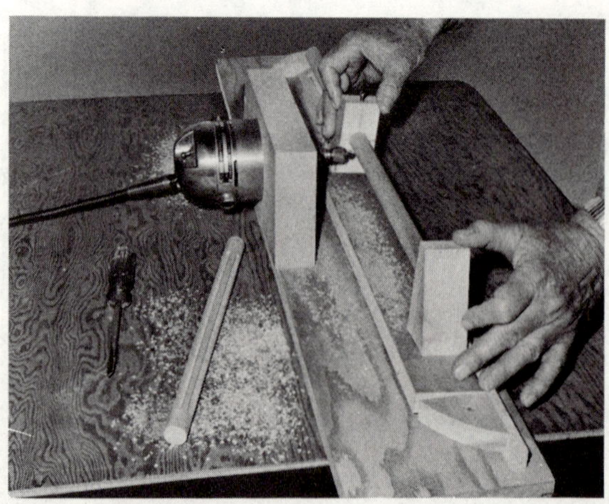

THE FLUTES ARE CUT with a core-box bit and router. The jig for cutting tilts and slides between stop blocks.

Removing pencil marks

My Junior marked several boards of hardwood I'd recently bought for a do-it-yourself project. I tried sanding lightly but this only spreads the marks. I think a soft-lead pencil was used but I'm not sure whether it was a lead pencil, china pencil or black crayon. What to do?—L.O., Wash.

If the marks were made by a lead or china pencil or even a crayon, then sanding won't do. If you think they are lead-pencil marks, try an ordinary eraser first. If that doesn't work, rub marks lightly with a cloth dipped in alcohol (substitute fine steel wool for cloth if the wood is open-grained such as oak). Wipe up any excess alcohol immediately. If you suspect that the marks were made by crayon or china pencil, try using turpentine.

Kitchen-cabinet door bumpers

I have steel cabinets in my kitchen and the rubber door bumpers have deteriorated. Several are missing. Are replacements available, or is there a substitute?—E.R., Kans.

The cabinet manufacturer can probably supply new bumpers, but you can make them yourself. From a small piece of 1/8-in. sheet cork cut pieces about 1/2 or 3/4-in. square. Remove the old bumpers and cement these replacements in their places.

Gold rush

I always have trouble applying gold paint to wood. Even though I spray the stuff from a pressurized can, it never looks quite right–can't get a smooth surface and the grain shows right through several coatings. Just what does one do to get a smooth, uniform finish?—M.O., Fla.

Gold paint, one of the so-called metallic paints, is quite sensitive to the surface over which it is applied. It will "reproduce" the surface in just about every small detail. I've always had fair success applying ordinary gold paints over an enamel coating. If the wood is open grained, apply a filler and sand the surface smooth. Then apply at least two coats of enamel, allowing ample drying time between each. Smooth the surface of the enamel with fine steel wool. This gives a surface that's smooth yet with sufficient "tooth" to hold the gold paint. Finally, although gold paint can be applied with a fine, soft brush, spraying gives a more uniform coating and a more realistic appearance of gold leaf, which most gold paints are intended to simulate.

Some newer types of gold paints contain special vehicles which are, in effect, self-leveling. They give very good results when applied as directed. However, in the end it's the surface you prepare that really determines the quality of the finish you get. A common rule, but one especially true when applied to metallic paints.

Tile over wide flooring

I've purchased an old home. The rooms upstairs are floored with wide boards that are rather rough. Some are cupped, with cracks and openings between boards. I'm thinking of laying tile in all the upstairs rooms and the hallway. My problem is to prepare these old floors. Can you help with suggestions?—E.L., Md.

First of all, it will be necessary to level the old flooring. Usually this can be done by nailing along the edges of the boards, but if not, the flooring will have to be sanded in order to provide a flat surface for overlayment. Any depressions at wear points should be overfilled with wood putty and sanded. Also any chance knotholes, splits or other defects should be filled in with a wood putty or otherwise repaired. In any event the old floor should be strengthened by new nailing. (Baseboards should be removed, of course.)

You have a choice of 1/4-in. plywood or hardboard of the same thickness for underlayment. In most cases, tempered hardboard is the better choice for laying over an old floor, although plywood is acceptable. In any case, the underlayment must be nailed solidly; otherwise, squeaks may develop in time. Try to plan and cut the pieces of the underlayment so that you do not end up with a narrow strip at the walls or in a doorway. Also be sure the underlayment is nailed down uniformly with no offsets at the joints.

Haunted house?

I live in a fairly new ranch home and when the wind blows hard from the northwest, I sometimes hear an alarming buzzing or whistling sound, loud enough to awaken me from a sound sleep. I've traced it to the front door but nothing I've done, even shifting the striker, has stopped it. All windows and doors are weatherstripped so they should be tight. Can you tell what's wrong?—D.W., Iowa.

It's probably the weatherstripping, likely at some point just above or below the lock. Drive a few extra nails at both of these points and you'll no doubt sleep more soundly.

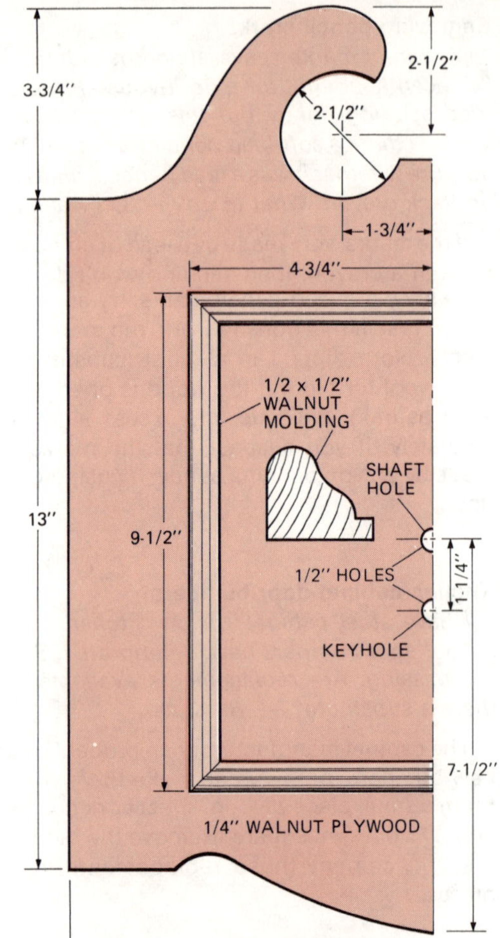

HALF PATTERN OF FRONT

6-7/8"

An 'heirloom' wall clock

IF THERE IS SOMEONE on your gift list who would like a fine clock, he'll be delighted with this handsome wall model—especially when he knows you made it. Its elegant, etched dial and spun-brass pendulum contrast beautifully with its walnut case.

Other than the ¼-in. veneer-faced plywood, you'll probably find most of the wood in your scrap box. In the case of the three-sided frame, only the side members need to be walnut since the top piece is not exposed. The two split pilasters are produced from a single square turning by gluing two pieces of wood together with paper between. Once turned, the two halves are easily pried apart with a knife blade down the paper joint. Use a fine-tooth blade to jigsaw the plywood parts and carefully sand the edges. If you have a router, you can run your own molding, or make use of a suitable stock picture-frame molding.

Gaston Wood Finishes, Box 1246, Bloomington, Ind. 47401, sells the eight-day windup movement, dial and brass finial. You also can buy a kit of partially cut wood parts, including preturned pilasters.

SEE ALSO

Adhesives . . . Comb boxes . . . Gifts, Christmas . . . Moldings . . . Plywood . . . Routers . . . Sanding . . . Wood lathe techniques

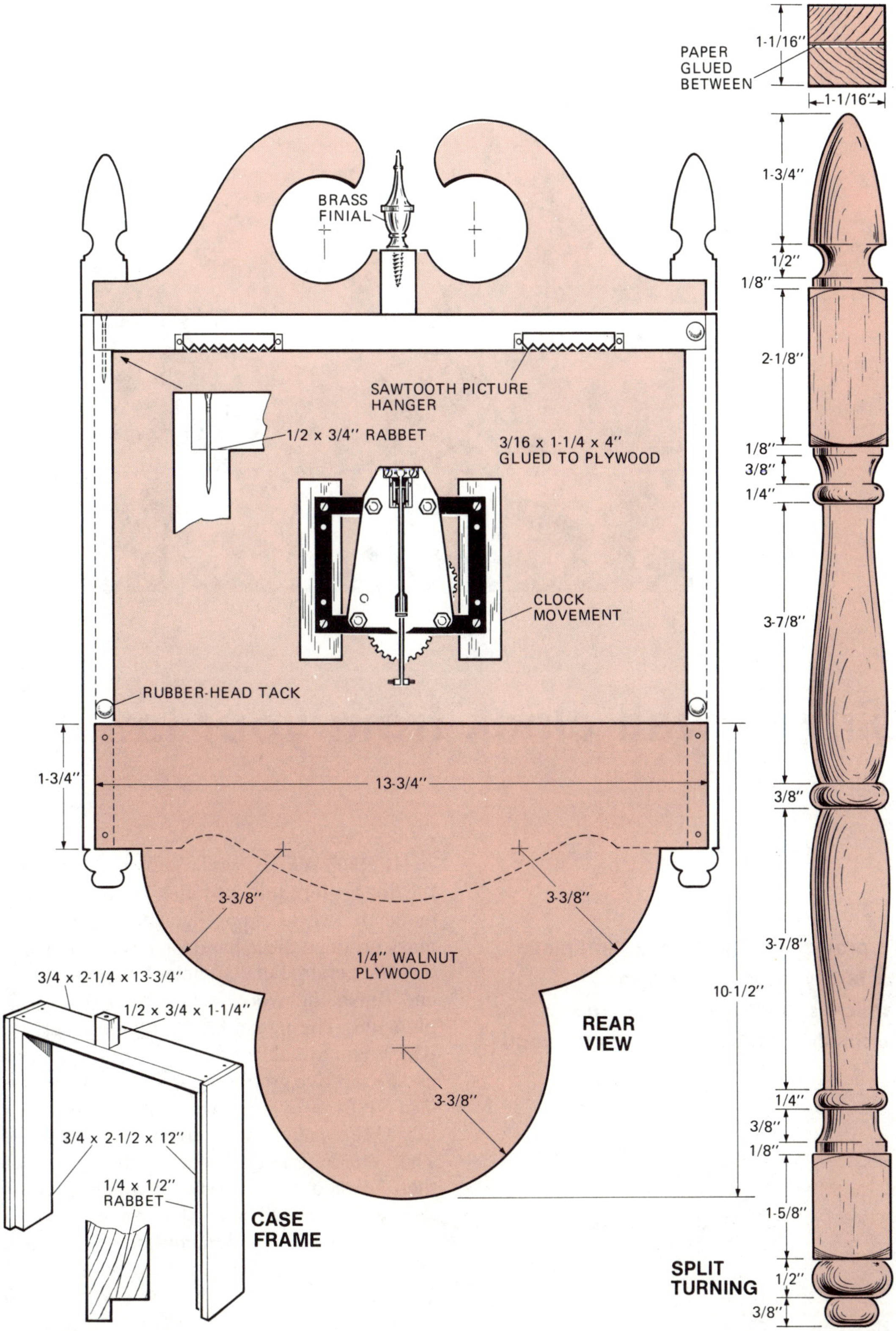
PAPER
GLUED
BETWEEN
1-1/16"
1-1/16"
1-3/4"
1/2"
1/8"
2-1/8"
1/8"
3/8"
1/4"
3-7/8"
3/8"
3-7/8"
10-1/2"
1/4"
3/8"
1/8"
1-5/8"
1/2"
3/8"
SPLIT
TURNING
BRASS
FINIAL
SAWTOOTH PICTURE
HANGER
1/2 x 3/4" RABBET
3/16 x 1-1/4 x 4"
GLUED TO PLYWOOD
CLOCK
MOVEMENT
RUBBER-HEAD TACK
1-3/4"
13-3/4"
3-3/8"
3-3/8"
1/4" WALNUT
PLYWOOD
REAR
VIEW
3-3/8"
3/4 x 2-1/4 x 13-3/4"
1/2 x 3/4 x 1-1/4"
3/4 x 2-1/2 x 12"
1/4 x 1/2"
RABBET
CASE
FRAME

A simple wall clock from your lathe

To provide this handsome timepiece for your den or family room, you buy the ceramic dial and clock works, then make and finish the face from fancy plywood

SEE ALSO

Adhesives . . . Discs, wood . . . Fasteners . . . Gifts, Christmas . . . Plywood . . . Sanding . . . Wood finishes . . . Wood-lathe techniques

■ HERE'S A GIFT you can literally turn out by the dozen. It requires a lathe, but once you have made the workholding jig, you can practically mass produce these handsome wall clocks. You buy the ceramic dial and clock works and make and finish the wooden face from fancy ¼-in. plywood. The jig serves as a large faceplate to which you attach the work for turning a recess and decorative grooves. It consists of an 11¼-in. disc cut from ¾-in. plywood and fitted with four ¼ x 1¼-in. roundhead stovebolts and wingnuts. The bolts automatically center the work, while their heads clamp it to the jig which is mounted on the lathe by a regular faceplace.

The work is cut octagon-shape before it is attached to the jig. If you plan to make more than one clock, each piece should be identical to fit the jig.

Gaston Wood Finishes, Box 1246, Bloomington, IN, sells the ceramic dial and clock. You have a choice of six dial designs and a battery or electric movement.

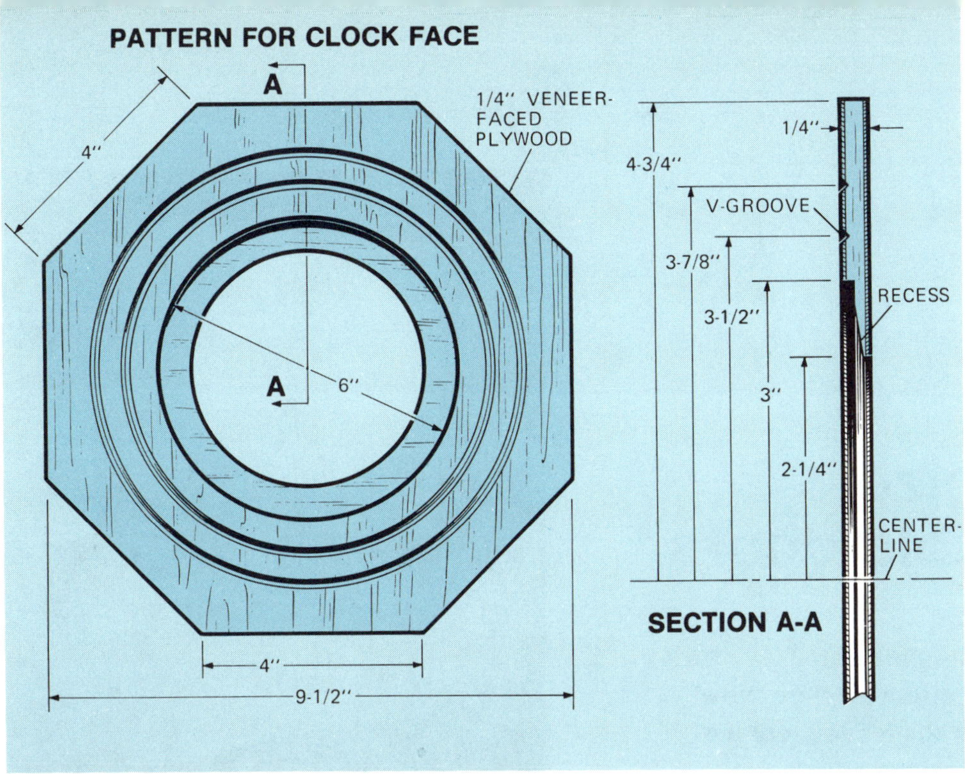

WINGNUTS ON BOLTS make it easy to clamp the work to face side of the plywood disc. Faceplate fastens disc.

BOLT HEADS grip the edge of the work, holding it as you turn dial recess and decorative grooves in the face.

CONTACT CEMENT is used to glue 6-in. ceramic dial in the turned recess. Apply adhesive to dial and recess.

TWO WOOD CLEATS, ¾ x 1 x 6 in., are glued to the back of the facing to gain clearance for the clock.

Modernize with bifold doors

Sliding closet doors are dated and inefficient. Now folding-door kits let you replace them with good-looking bifolds in less than a day

By WAYNE C. LECKEY

SEE ALSO

**Bookcases . . . Doors . . . Hinges . . .
Home improvement . . . Remodeling . . . Shelves . . .
Shoe drawers . . . Sliding glass doors . . .
Storage ideas**

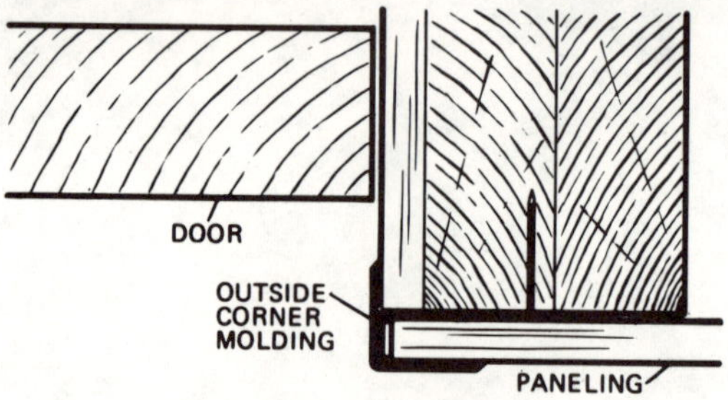

CONVENTIONAL WOOD bifolds (top) are smart-looking, even when used with metal molding trim.

■ WHEN FITTED WITH sliding doors, a closet is never more than half open. The doors always block half the opening, so that you have to keep sliding the doors back and forth to find what you want.

It's easy to get rid of these dated, unattractive and inefficient doors by replacing them with modern bifolds. Such doors make the whole closet immediately accessible, they glide open effortlessly and they're good looking. In addition, they simply lift out whenever you want.

You can find bifold doors in almost any lumberyard or building-supply store. They are offered in a choice of many decorator styles; in plastic, wood and metal; finished and unfinished, and in sizes to fit any standard-width closet or door opening.

Some are just plain louvered panels, others have fancy carved inserts to add to their good looks. Still others are molded in one piece, completely finished, ready to hang.

Bifold doors come in kits complete with mounting hardware, including the overhead track, jamb brackets, top pivot stud, guide wheel, snugger, aligners, brass pulls, screws and a wrench, plus full instructions. In most all cases the door panels come factory-hinged (in a few you'll have to add the hinges), with pivoting studs already in place in the top and bottom edges of the panels.

You can buy these doors in two-panel units to fit nominal closet openings of 24, 30 and 36 in., and in four-panel units to fit 48, 60 and 72-in. openings. All doors (whatever the make) come 80 in. tall to fit the standard opening height of 81¾ in. Where the closet opening is of an odd

THE WHOLE CLOSET is instantly opened (left) with bifolds—a real convenience compared to sliding doors.

MOLDED NYLON bifold doors (below) come factory-finished, ready to hang. A four-panel set sells for about $80.

width, you are faced with the work of remodeling it to accommodate stock doors. In cases where the opening might be as little as 1/4 in. too narrow, you can get by without remodeling the opening by trimming 1/4 in. from the aluminum track and countersinking the jamb brackets 1/8 in.

Plastic vs wood. There are good things to be said about both kinds of doors. DuPont turns out attractive bifold doors which consist of molded nylon facings attached to tubular steel frames. They're heavier than wood bifolds and they cost more but, because the facings are molded in one piece, you don't have to worry about joints opening up, shrinking or swelling. They come factory-painted, which saves time and paint, and they can be washed with soap and water. While doors are built to last a lifetime, the louvers in the molded facings are simulated and, for this reason, will not let air circulate through a closet. Also, such doors are suitable only for closets (as opposed to doorways) since the molded facings are attached only to one side of the steel frames.

With conventional, louvered wood doors, air circulation in a closet is no problem because even if the lower sections of the doors have solid panels, the upper sections have spaced slats. Wood doors also allow trimming if they're a bit too wide for the opening to be used. But you do have to paint them, which can be a time-consuming job. A spray gun makes good sense when it comes to this, if you have one.

The actual installation of the doors is fairly simple. After you have purchased doors to fit the opening, you begin by installing the overhead track by screwing it to the head jamb. Using a plumb line, you next screw two jamb brackets to

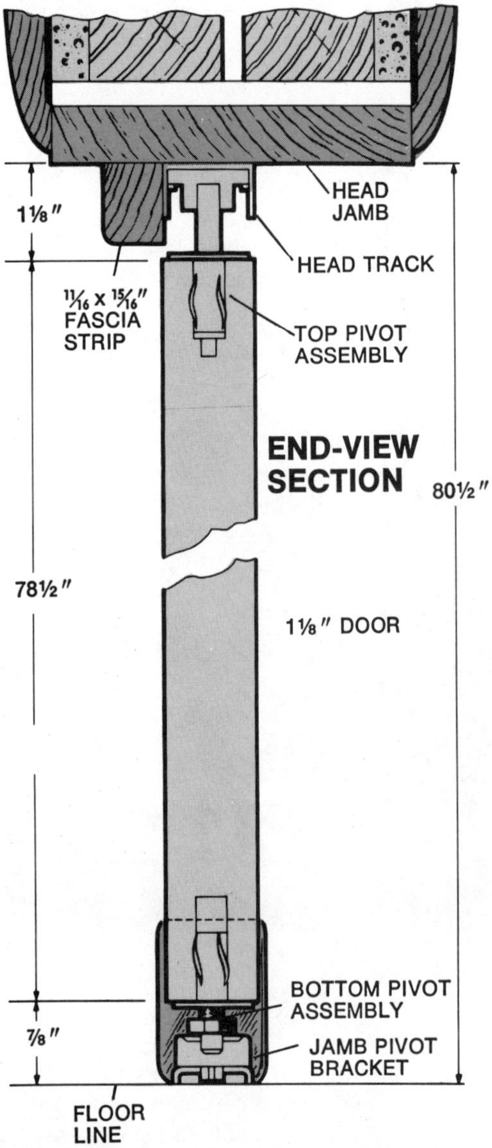

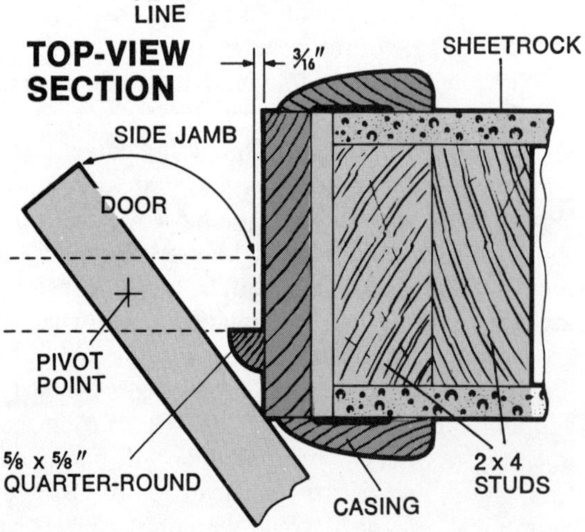

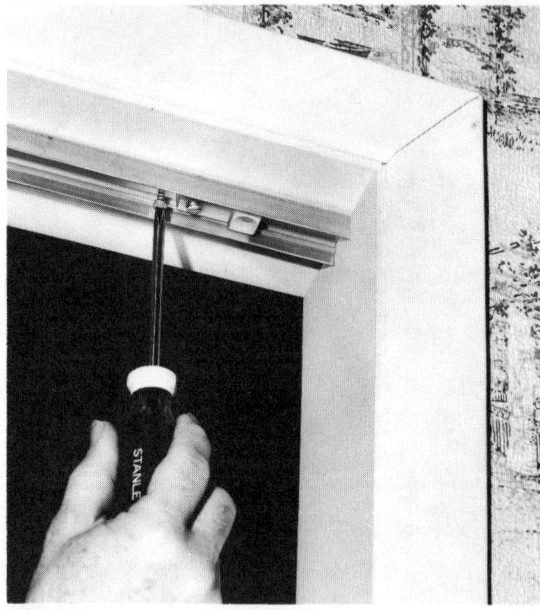

FIRST STEP: Install the track by screwing it to the door-opening header 1½ in. in from the edge.

the floor immediately below the overhead track. The doors are then lifted and fitted into both the overhead track and the jamb pivot bracket. Finally, the aligners are installed on the back of the doors. These help the doors mate properly when they are closed, so they meet snugly.

PRIVACY, plus air, is obtainable with bifolds. Here's a two-panel unit in a 30-in. doorway.

SECOND STEP: Attach the two jamb brackets at the floor and on a plumb line with the overhead track.

THIRD STEP: After lifting the doors into the tracks and brackets, add aligners to rear sides.

THESE SMART-LOOKING bifolds have bottom panels decorated with expanded polyurethane carvings combined with open slats at the top.

A SHALLOW CLOSET such as this will hold a multitude of items. This one is used as a hobby closet to store games, sports gear, movie equipment. The roomy shelves, however, will be found handy for storing just about anything.

LOUVERED BIFOLD DOORS give instant access to shallow closets and are most attractive. Pivoting on pins and sliding on overhead track, the doors glide open with little effort. They come full-louvered, as shown, or partially paneled.

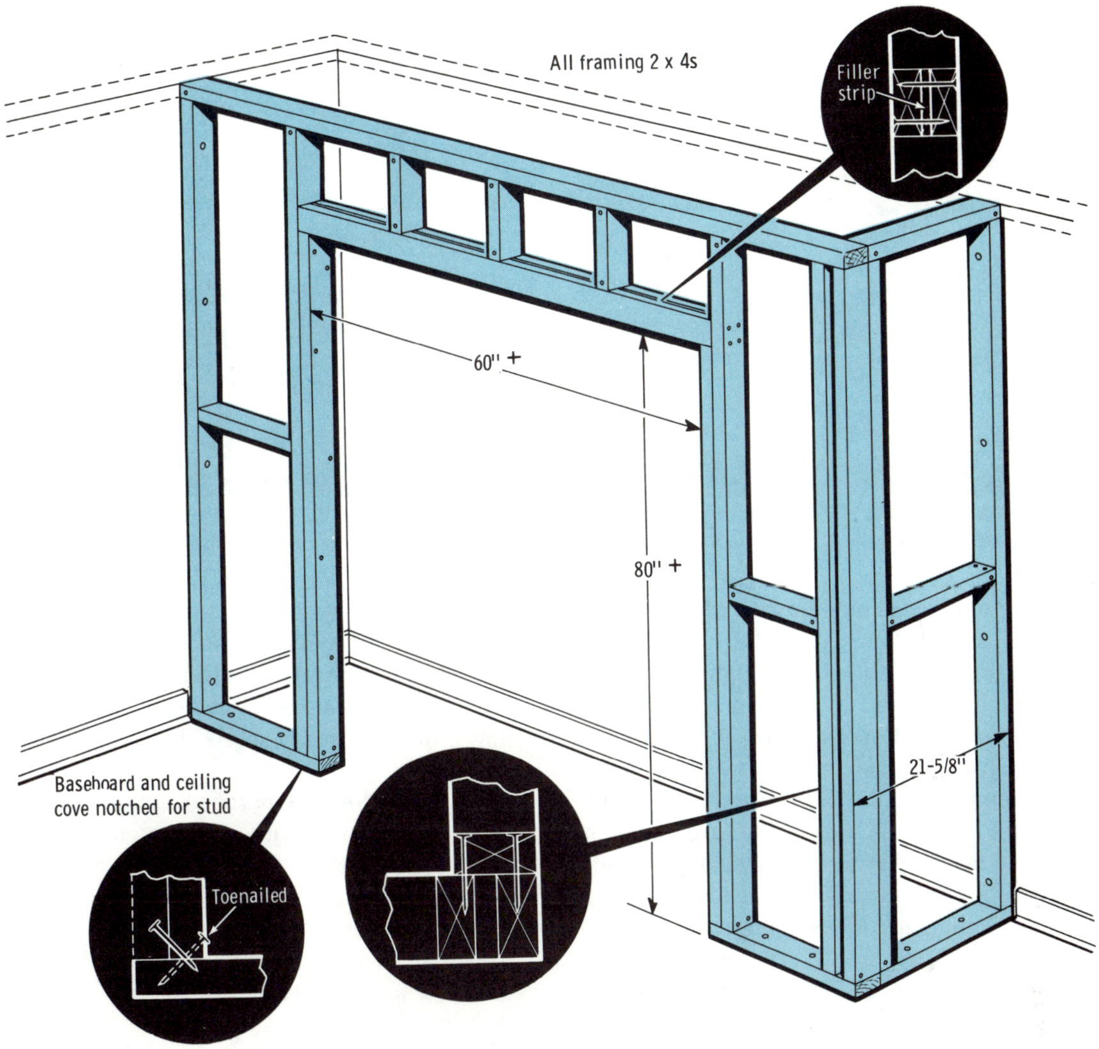

With as little as 20 in. borrowed from the corner of a room, you can go a long way toward relieving the storage problem at your house in a single weekend of basic carpentry

Build in an extra closet

By WAYNE C. LECKEY

■ FEW HOMEOWNERS can boast of having too many closets. More often it's a case of not having enough. The solution, of course, is to add another.

While the thought of building an extra closet could cause the less experienced home remodeler to turn and run, it's not the major job it sounds. Actually, a good share of the task is rough work, particularly the framing. As to where to put it, most times there's a corner that will let you rob it of 20 in. or so without it being missed a bit. And as for it looking like a "sore thumb," you can see in the photos on page 792 that such a closet adds considerable eye appeal.

The length and depth you make the closet is up to you. I made it shallow so it would accept six 16-in. shelves, 8 ft. long. While the overall size can vary to suit your needs, the size given for the

SEE ALSO

Bookcases . . . Fasteners . . . Hardboard . . . Paneling, hardboard . . . Plasterboard . . . Remodeling . . . Room dividers . . . Shelves . . . Storage ideas . . . Storage walls . . . Tile, floor

SLOTTED STANDARDS, 5 ft. long, are screwed to the studs in the back wall of the closet for solid support.

TABS ON the brackets hook in slots of the standards and a tap of a hammer or mallet locks them in place.

rough door opening should be maintained if you use standard-size 15-in. bifold doors. Here the actual width and height of the rough opening is determined beforehand by the way the opening is to be trimmed. For example, if ¼-in. prefinished hardboard paneling is to be used, the rough opening is made ½ in. greater than the finished width of 60 in., and ¼ in. greater than the finished height of 80 in. If, on the other hand, you plan to face the walls with plasterboard and trim the opening in the conventional manner with ¾-in. jambs and casings, the rough opening would have to measure 61½ in. wide and 80¾ in. high.

You can't go astray by following the drawing shown on page 775. Your very first step after plotting the closet's size on the floor, is to cut out 4-in. sections of the existing baseboard so the framing will butt tight where it joins the wall. When this is done, 2x4 plates are nailed to both the floor and ceiling, fastening the ceiling ones first so they can be used in locating the floor plates directly below. A plumb line dropped from the top plates will spot the exact position of the floor plates quickly.

Whether you have anything to which to nail the ceiling plates depends on the direction the ceiling joists run. If they cross the top plate at right angles, you're in luck. If they don't, a few toggle bolts will do the trick. The same holds true in fastening the vertical framing members to the walls. Chances are they won't fall directly on a stud for nailing.

Once the top and bottom plates are in place, it's now a case of cutting the 2x4 studs to wedge between. The three-piece corner post is preassembled in the manner shown in the circular detail and then nailed in place as a unit. All studs are toe-nailed, and those framing the door opening are doubled up in the manner shown. Keep in mind that the studs should be placed 16 in. on centers.

I used prefinished hardboard paneling to cover the studs since I wanted to match the paneling which was already there. If you do likewise, the detailed drawings show how matching metal molding is used to add a neat trim to the hardboard around the door opening and to both inside and outside corners.

In using hardboard (and the same procedure is followed in using plywood paneling), you first line the door opening with strips of paneling ripped 3½ in. wide. These are cemented with special mastic directly to the studs and headers. Next, outside corner molding is applied around the outer edges of the opening, front and back, by nailing through the flange part of the molding. Note that it's mitered at the corners and nailed every 4 in.

From here on you apply the paneling to the studs and cut it to fit into the grooves of the molding. When you reach the corner, the same molding is applied in the same manner, first hooking it over the paneling, then nailing through the flange and inserting the succeeding piece in the molding as you continue around the corner. Inside corners are trimmed similarly but with molding of a different shape.

If you plan to use plasterboard, study the drawings below. Procedure differs in that the door opening is lined with ¾-in. jambs, ripped 4⅝ in. wide, and centered so they project ½ in.

HARDBOARD TREATMENT

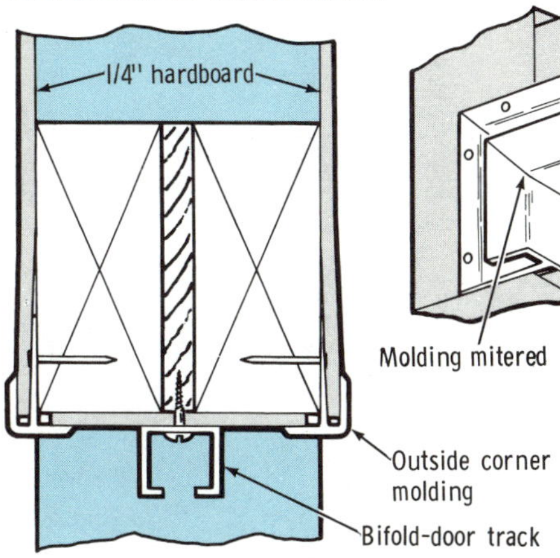

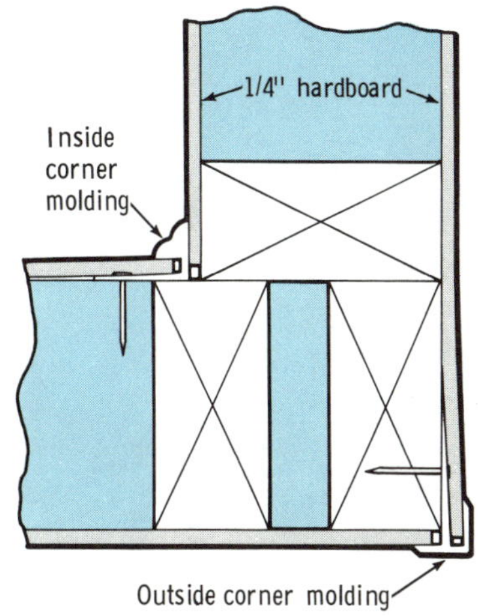

each side. The ½-in. plasterboard is cut to butt against the shoulders formed by the overhanging jambs, after which regular door casing is applied to cover the joint and add a finished trim. Regular plasterboard nails are used to fasten the ½-in. sheets, spacing them 8 in. apart.

Where the plasterboard laps at an outside corner, the corner is reinforced with a strip of regular metal plaster beading. The nails which hold it, plus those holding the plasterboard, are later covered with joint compound. Just how you do this, as well as tape joints, is explained in the article "How to work with plasterboard" on page 2180.

Louvered bifold doors are ideal for shallow closets. They open wide for full access, help ventilate the closet and are good-looking. Two pairs of 15-in. doors will fit a 60-in. opening perfectly. They come complete with hardware and full instructions for hanging. Some even come ready-hinged and primed.

Completion of your closet requires adding matching baseboard along the floor and molding at the ceiling, and, of course, either papering or painting the walls if you used plasterboard.

Popular standards and brackets provide the easiest way to add shelves to your closet. Being fully adjustable, you can place the boards wherever you want them, and add as many as you want. Solid support is assured by locating the standards over studs. Where this can't be done, plastic screw anchors or fiber plugs should be used in plastered walls.

I used ½-in. plywood for the six shelves and supported each one with five brackets. The trick in getting the 8-ft.-long shelves in place is to first put all six boards on the floor of the closet (resting them on edge) and then raise them one at a time as each of the five brackets is hooked in the standards. The brackets shown are of the heavy-duty type which features a plastic clip that's used for screwing the shelves to them.

PLASTERBOARD TREATMENT

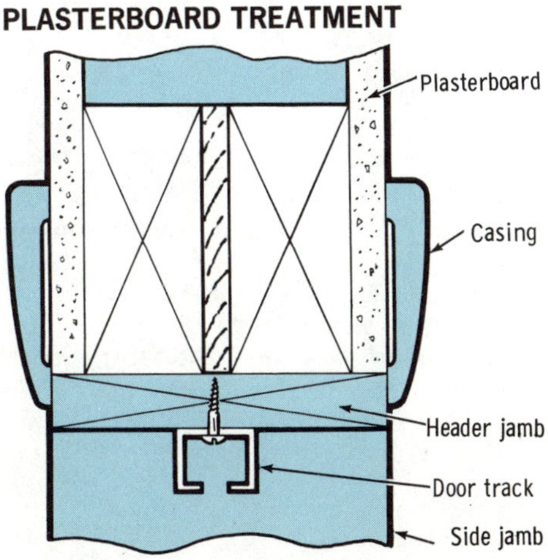

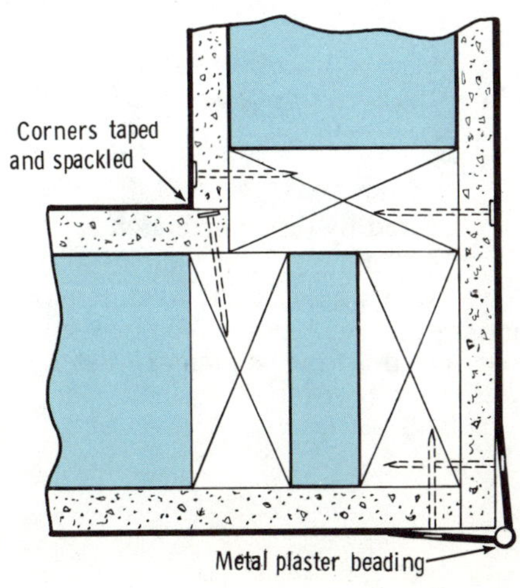

TWO INEXPENSIVE metal towel racks can be fastened vertically to open studding in a garage or workshop to provide an easy-to-get-at storage rack for such miscellaneous shop "clutter" as dowels, molding, pipe and thin strips of stock. The racks also provide good storage for such nonworkshop items as mailing tubes and garden stakes.—*Victor Lamoy, Saranac Lake, NY.*

A DRILL PRESS can be used to punch neat, clean holes in paper, soft plastics or thin metal. Clamp a piece of scrap steel to the press table and drill a hole through it using a drill bit the size of the hole to be punched. Remove the bit; grind the shank end flat and square. Replace the drill in the chuck with the ground end aligned over the hole in the steel for punching.—*R. S. Hedin, Minneapolis, MN.*

A METAL STRIP with a hole drilled in it and bent 90° can be loosely screwed above a hook eye on a gate to prevent the hook from becoming unlatched in strong winds. The bracket swings away for unlatching the hook.—*Clarence Breitenfeldt, Marathon, WI.*

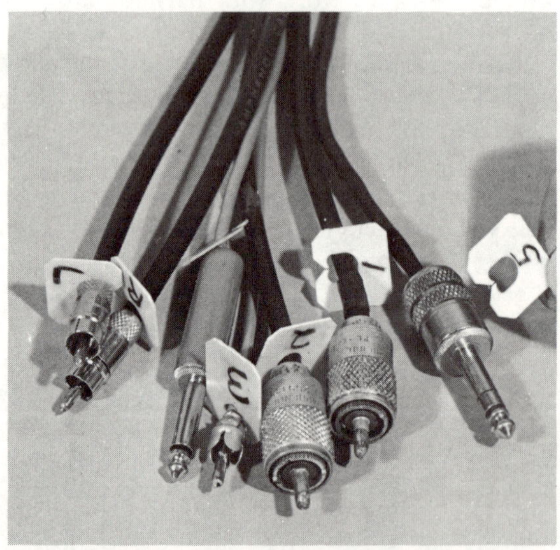

PLASTIC BAG fasteners commonly attached to bread wrappers can be used to identify immediately the right cable for different input sources for your hi-fi or stereo. Simply number each fastener and slip it around the cable.—*Ken Patterson, Regina, Sask.*

Make your closets work

■ IF YOU COMPILED a list of the 10 most common homeowner complaints, insufficient storage space, both for daily and seasonal use, would be sure to be high in the ratings. And, in most cases, the complaint is justified. Even new homes show a lack of thought in design and treatment of closet construction. However, since family needs vary, exactly how to get complete use of a closet depends upon what you need to store and for what length of time.

Three good ideas shown on these pages are all in the home of Mr. and Mrs. Albert O. Foster II of Wayzata, Minn. The bedroom closet, below, makes use of what previously was (and unfortunately in most homes is) wasted space. By

In most homes, closets have space going to waste. Here are ideas for closets for most every room in your house. By using sliding shelves, all those 'lazy' areas can be put to good use

SEE ALSO

Bookcases . . . Cabinet furniture . . .
Family rooms . . . Fasteners . . . Hi-fi centers . . .
Room dividers . . . Sewing centers . . . Shelves . . .
Shoe drawers . . . Storage walls

BEDROOM CLOSET has hanger space reduced and pull-out shelves to meet the needs of the user.

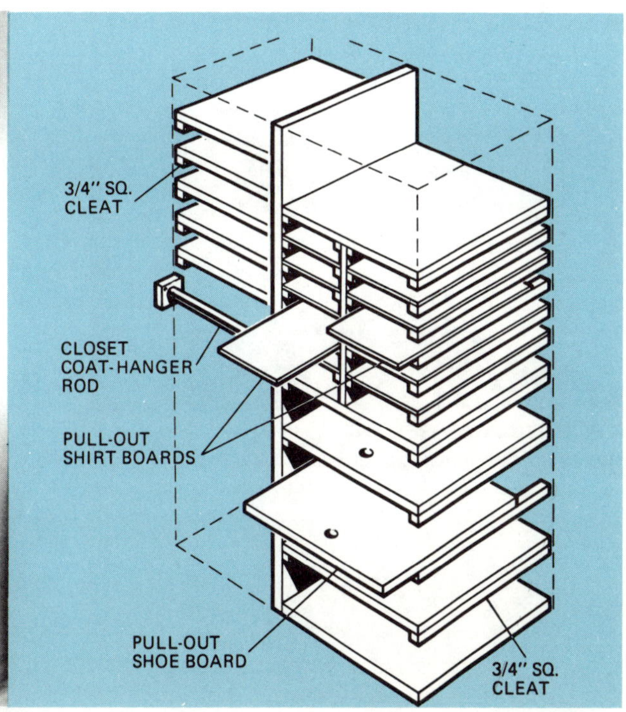

A PENINSULA CLOSET gives shelving on living-room side plus convenient hanging for coats in the foyer.

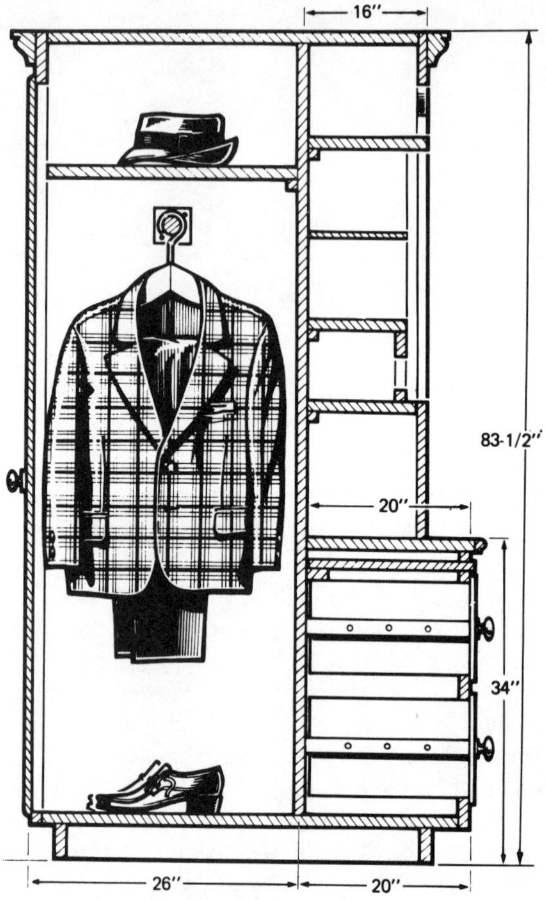

SECTION

putting down on paper the everyday items for which they needed out-of-sight storage space, the Fosters gained a functional closet. Built as shown in the sketch on page 779, the closet holds shirts, socks, and the like on handy sliding shelves. Extra shelves were installed above the clothes-hanger rod to handle seasonal items such as heavy clothing during the summer months.

The second, and most elaborate "closet" is the peninsula unit which was added to the living room. The project initially started as a simple wall to shield living-room users from icy winter blasts each time the front door was opened. Because the living room could afford the floor space and the Fosters were imaginative planners, what would have been wasted space was used in a most practical way.

The front side of the unit faces the foyer and provides convenient hanging space for outerwear. The back side, facing the living room, has the look of a hutch. It houses stereo equipment, books and art objects, and also has pull-out counters for additional storage.

The third storage change the Fosters made was to add a much-needed linen closet in the bath.

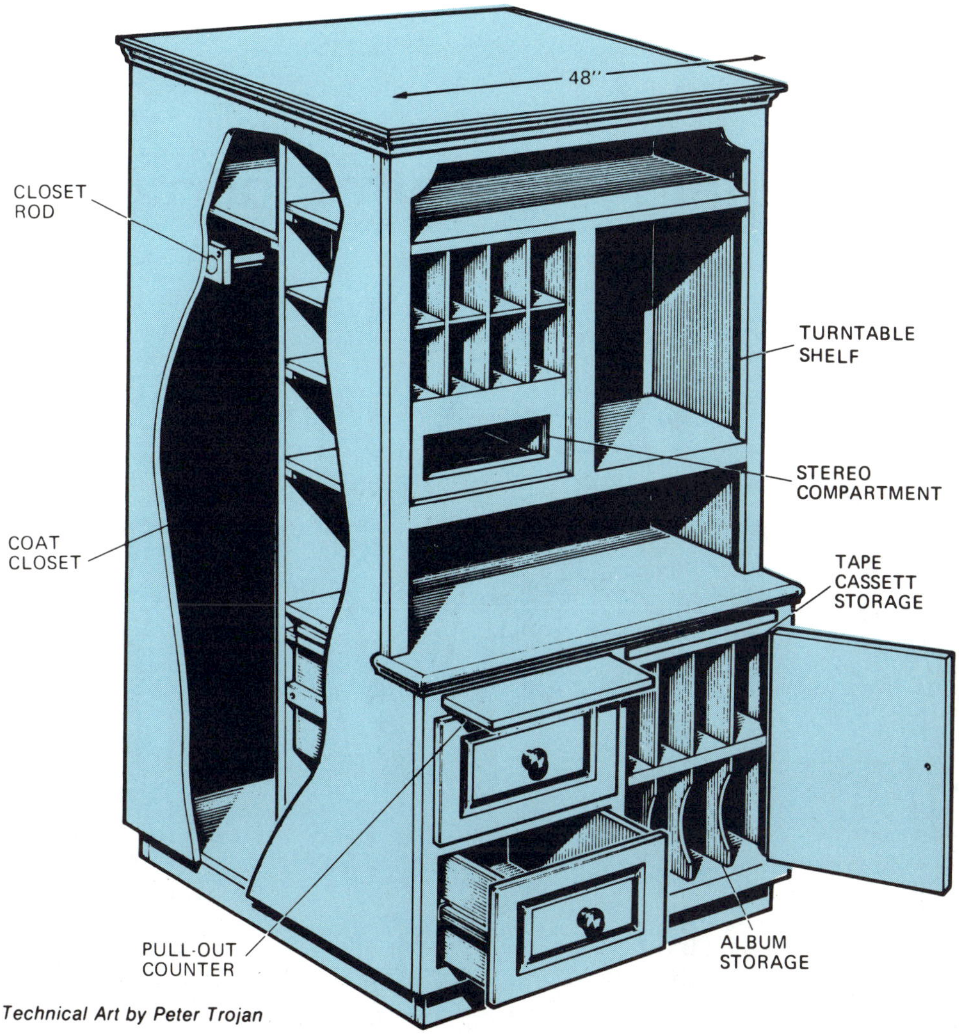

Technical Art by Peter Trojan

A TOWEL CLOSET convenient to the sink has louvered bypassing doors to insure adequate circulation of air.

Eight 15-in. open shelves are above the counter for towels and linens. Four cubes below are where two sons store boats and other kids' bathtub paraphernalia.

Other ideas you might consider: Even though they are 4 ft. or more wide, many closets in all rooms of the house, have a single door for access. Why not install bypassing doors to permit easy access to the full closet?

Also, if it's structurally practical, don't overlook the possibility of using 8-ft.-high bifolds. These let you add shelves above that can make seasonal storage a snap. If you put the tall bifolds in bedrooms, each family member can then store his own clothing in one handy place instead of using the attic or basement. In this way everyone's clothing will be close at hand when it's needed.

How to repair your coffee percolator

By MORT SCHULTZ

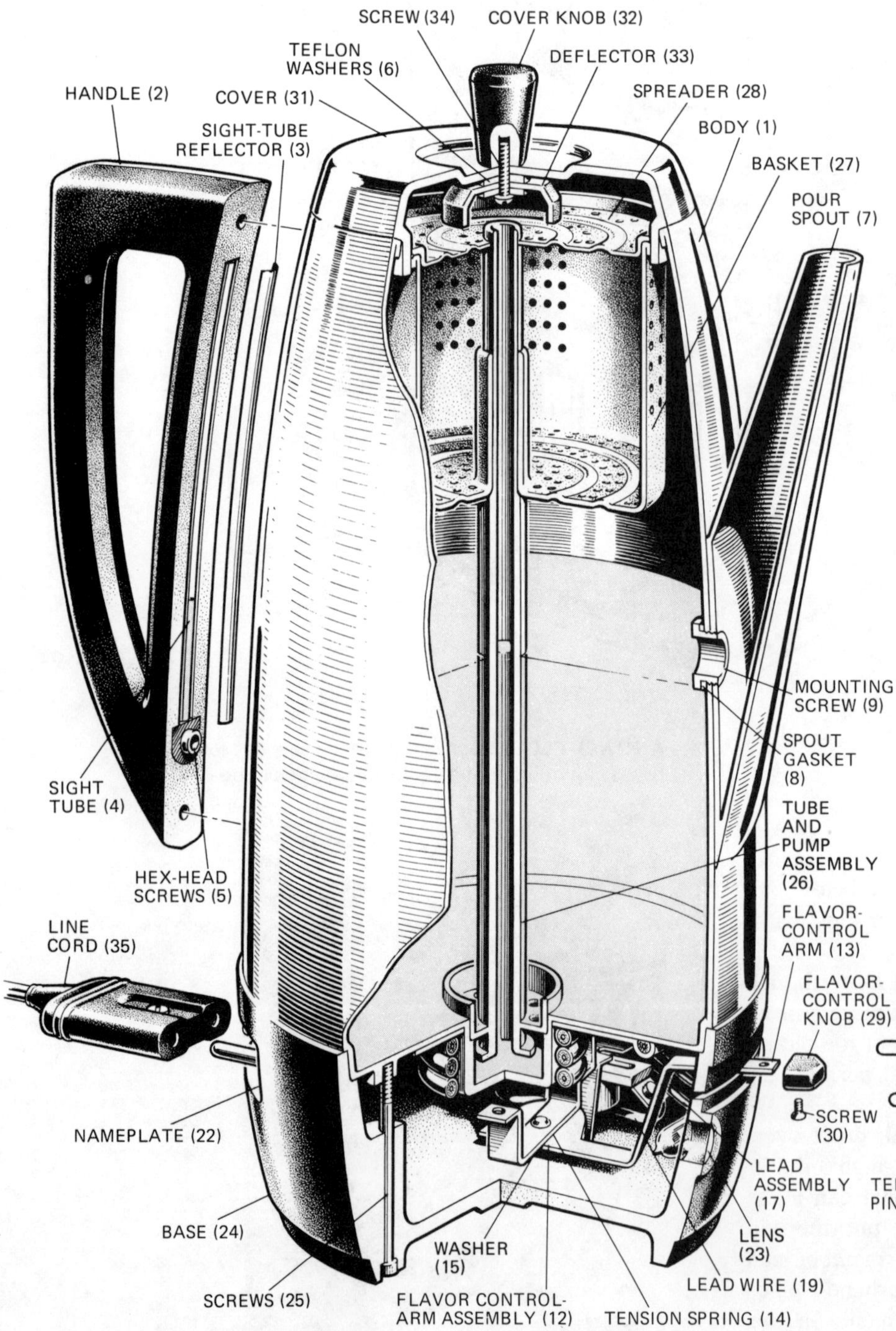

WIRING DIAGRAM

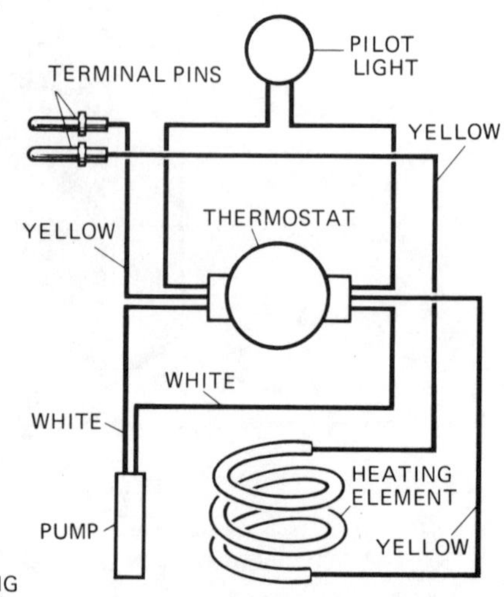

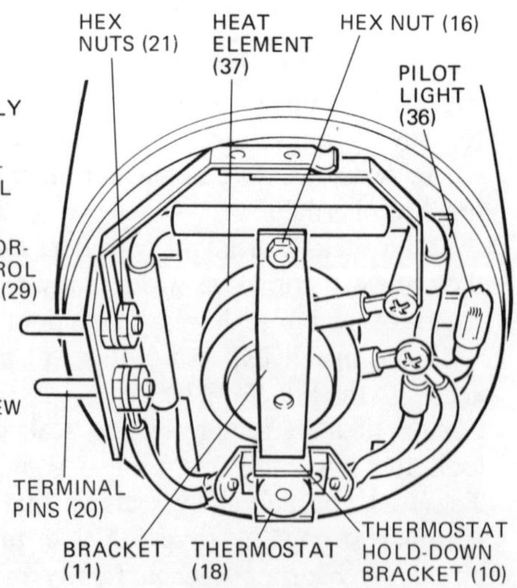

BOTTOM VIEW

GOT A PROBLEM with an electric coffee percolator? Consult the troubleshooting chart below to pinpoint possible causes. Then proceed to find the pertinent section below, which may be used as a guide in making repairs.

Replacement parts can usually be obtained from a dealer selling your make of appliance. If there is no dealer in your area, contact the manufacturer. His address is normally stamped on the bottom of the percolator's base.

In the instructions which follow, numbers in parentheses correspond to those on the main illustration for easy identification of parts.

Caution: Except for specific tests requiring power, be sure to disconnect the percolator before doing any work on it.

replacing the pour spout (7)

1. Remove the mounting screw (9) and spout gasket (8) holding the pour spout (7) to the percolator's body (1).

Coffee tastes bitter

POSSIBLE CAUSE	WHAT TO TRY
1. Residue and stains.	Periodically clean all coffeemaking parts and the inside of the percolator with a cleaner made for electric coffee percolators which is sold in hardware stores, home supply centers and supermarkets. Follow instructions on the package.

Water boils, but does not percolate

POSSIBLE CAUSES	WHAT TO TRY
1. Percolator tube and pump assembly not seated.	Make sure that the pump portion (base) of the percolator tube and pump assembly is seated in the heater well in the body.
2. Percolator tube and pump assembly is bent or pump portion is inoperative.	Replace the percolator tube and pump assembly.

Coffee is too weak or too strong

POSSIBLE CAUSE	WHAT TO TRY
1. Reduced percolating time.	Make certain the percolator is being filled with cold water—never with hot water. Hot water will reduce percolating time.
2. Slow percolating action.	See that the inside of the heater well in the body and the bottom of the percolator tube and pump assembly are free of coffee grounds and deposits that will slow percolating action.
3. Defective thermostat.	Test the unit by removing the percolator tube and the pump assembly and then filling the unit with cold water. Insert a thermometer and connect the percolator to an electrical outlet. The thermostat should open at 180° to 195° F., which is signified by the pilot coming on. If the thermostat should open sooner (or later), replace the thermostat.

Unit does not heat

POSSIBLE CAUSE	WHAT TO TRY
1. No voltage at the receptacle.	Check the receptacle with a table lamp or voltage tester.
2. Line cord has gone bad.	Replace any line cord that has frayed insulation. Check the cord for continuity. A bad cord should be replaced with one of the same size as that originally used by the percolator's manufacturer.
3. Badly corroded or burned terminals, pins.	Try cleaning the terminal pins with a small piece of sandpaper. If this doesn't work, replace the pins.
4. Defective thermostat.	Replace the thermostat.
5. Defective heating element.	Replace the heating element.

2. Replace the pour spout with a new one, making certain you install the spout gasket to prevent leakage around the spout.

Possible difference: Spouts of some coffee percolators are a molded part of the body and cannot be replaced.

replacing the handle (2) and sight tube (4)

1. From inside the body (1), remove the hex-head screws (5) and Teflon washers (6) holding the handle and sight-tube assembly.

2. Lift off the handle and sight-tube assembly and disassemble the handle (2), sight tube (4) and sight-tube reflector (3).

3. Replace the damaged part or parts and prepare for reassembly by placing sight-tube parts in correct sequence into the groove in the handle.

4. Place the entire assembly against the percolator's body, lining up the assembly with the screw holes.

5. Insert screws and washers and tighten the handle and sight-tube assembly to the body.

Caution: Make sure Teflon washers are used to prevent leakage around holes.

Possible differences:

1. Some units do not possess sight tubes.

2. Handles of some units are held by a screw at the top of the handle only. The bottom of the handle is released from its seat by inserting a screwdriver beneath the metal bracket-type clip and prying outward. To replace, press the bracket-type clip into place and insert the screw into the top part of the handle.

3. Handles of some other units cannot be replaced. The handle is a molded part of the body.

replacing the base (24)

1. Invert the percolator and remove the screw (30) holding the flavor-control knob (29). Remove the knob.

2. Remove the two screws (25) holding the base to the bottom of the percolator.

3. Slowly lift the base up, tipping it to the side slightly so the flavor control arm (13) slides through the slot in the side of the base, which is covered by the nameplate (22).

4. Take the pilot light from the lens (23).

5. Remove the hex nuts (21) securing leads to terminal pins (20). Damaged parts may now be replaced.

Possible differences:

1. Some percolators do not have a flavor-control knob.

2. Some percolators that do have a flavor-control knob do not have knobs held by screws. They are pressed on the flavor-control lever and are removed by pulling them off.

3. Bases of some percolators are held by a single screw that may or may not be slotted to accept a screwdriver. If not slotted, screws may be removed with pliers.

4. Bases of some percolators have gaskets between the base and the body that should be examined. If damaged, the gasket should be discarded and replaced with a new one. However, if the unit is an immersible percolator, treat the percolator as non-immersible once the base has been removed on the chance that the sealing qualities are destroyed. Nonimmersible means that the unit's base should not be submerged in water when the percolator is being washed.

replacing the thermostat (18)

1. Remove the base (24) as just described.

2. Disconnect the two leads at the thermostat (18).

3. Using a pair of needle-nose pliers, gently raise up on the top part of the thermostat's hold-down spring (not shown).

4. Slip the thermostat to the side, so the end of the spring slides through the groove in the thermostat.

5. Install a new thermostat by tipping the part so you can engage the groove in the thermostat with the hold-down spring.

Possible difference: Some units have the thermostat and leads riveted together. To disconnect the leads from the thermostat, you must grind off the rivet heads using a small hand grinder or file and tap out the rivet with a punch. You should use steel Pop rivets to reassemble leads to the thermostat.

replacing pilot light, heating element and lead assembly

1. Remove the base (24).

2. Disconnect the pilot light, heating element and lead assembly (17) from the terminal pins (20) and thermostat (18).

3. Using the wiring diagram shown in the main illustration, reconnect a new pilot light, heating element and lead assembly (17) to the thermostat (18) and terminal pins (20).

Possible differences:

1. Some percolators don't have pilot lights.

2. Heating elements of some percolators are molded into the base, and the base has to be replaced to replace the element.

3. Heating elements and pilot lights of other units may be replaced individually.

Blow it up big!

This simple setup lets you produce eye-catching close-ups of tiny objects with any 35-mm SLR camera

By ROSARIO CAPOTOSTO

SEE ALSO

Bookends . . . Candid photography . . . Copy photography . . . Darkrooms . . . Developing, photo . . . Dryers, photo . . . ID photos . . . Mountings, photo . . . Photography . . . Prints, photo

WANT TO STARTLE your audience the next time you put on a slide show? Try projecting some extreme close-ups of common household objects and ask your friends to guess what they are. Chances are they'll have a hard time identifying some of the strange-looking results you'll get.

Blown up several hundred times, the eye of a tiny sewing needle comes out so big you could put your head through it. Bristles in a toothbrush take on the appearance of logs the size of telephone poles. Some typical examples of such effects are shown at the bottom of this page.

All you need to produce sensational close-ups like these is a 35-mm single-lens-reflex camera and the homemade lens adapter shown here. The adapter is essentially a mammoth extension tube. It spaces the regular camera lens about 30 inches away from the film plane, enabling you to make enlargements 10 times actual size. When these are further blown up on a projection screen or in an enlarger, the results are macro-images of tremendous magnification. The adapter is

FAMILIAR OBJECTS look quite different when viewed in extreme close-ups like those at right. Left to right, a lady's nylon stocking, tip of a screw, teeth on a fine machinist's file and toothbrush.

simply a long, square box made of ¼-inch plywood or hardboard and some scraps of ¾-inch solid stock. The camera with its lens removed is mounted at one end of the box and the lens is inserted in the other end. The lens must be turned around and used backward—with its front facing the camera—because a rule of optics requires the elements to be reversed if the distance to the film plane is increased more than eight times the focal length. So size the opening in the end of the box to take the forward barrel of the lens rather than the rear threaded portion.

To join the hole in the camera body to the hole in the other end of the box, you need a short length of adapter tubing. This can be a standard extension tube sold to fit your camera or, for a less expensive dodge, a piece of 1½-inch-diameter drain tailpiece tubing. The latter is a common hardware-store plumbing item and has a flange that makes it easy to attach to most SLR cameras. All you need is an accessory screw-in adapter ring to match your camera (the Practica type shown here fits many SLRs). Clamp the flange of the tubing between the two parts of the adapter ring and screw the assembly into your camera body. Make the hole in the box a snug fit for whatever tubing you use.

Paint the inside of the box flat black to kill light reflections. A circular light baffle at the box's midpoint also helps to mask off glare. Objects to be photographed are placed in a movable stage made to straddle the base. The stage is slid back and forth to focus the image sharply in the viewfinder instead of focusing the lens itself. Objects too big to fit inside the stage can be stretched across the opening and taped in place.

always increase exposure

Exposures must be greatly increased because of the extreme distance between lens and camera. A magnification of 10 times requires an exposure increase of 100. Thus, if a light meter reading indicates an exposure of $\frac{1}{10}$th of a second at a given lens opening, the required exposure will be 100 times this or 10 seconds. Work with small lens openings for maximum depth of field and place the setup on a solid surface to avoid movement during the long exposures. Use lenses of at least 50 mm in focal length. An enlarging lens may give even better images than a regular camera lens.

INSIDE OF LENS TUBE is painted flat black to reduce glare that might degrade image clarity. Circular light baffle mounted at center also blocks reflections.

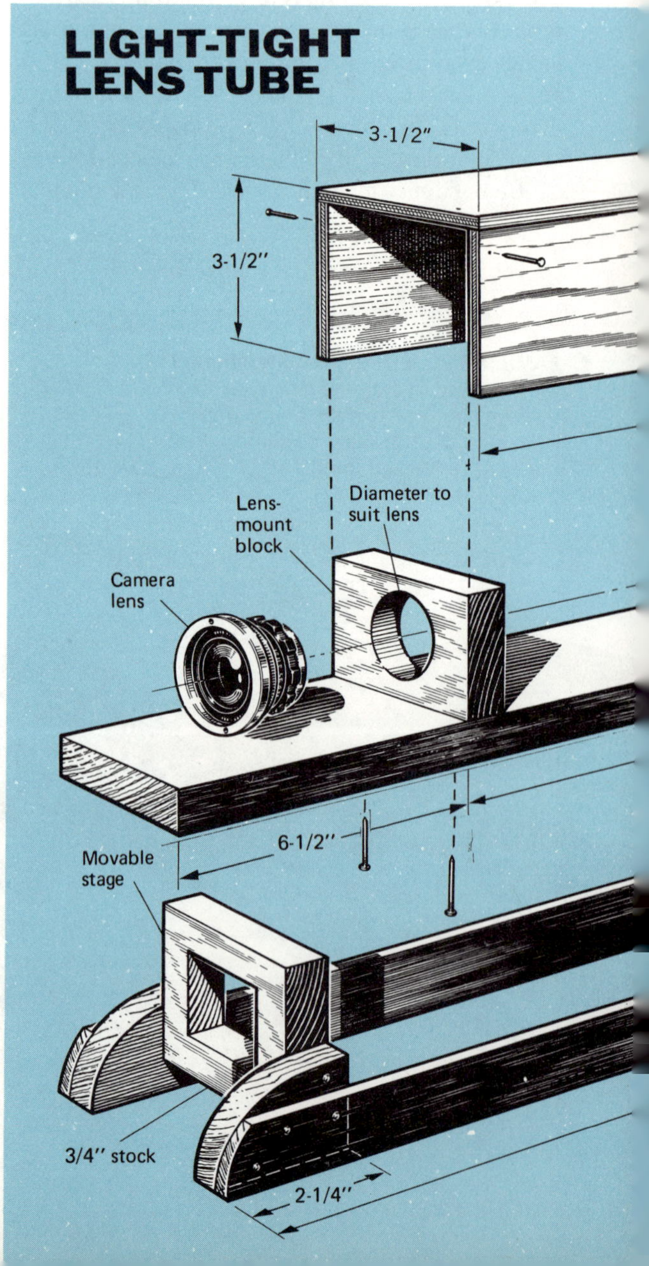

CAMERA BODY can be joined to box with extension tube or short length of plumbing drain clamped between the rings of a standard screw-in lens adapter.

LENS IS MOUNTED in hold at opposite end of box from camera. Remember to reverse lens so rear end faces camera. This is necessary because of long separation.

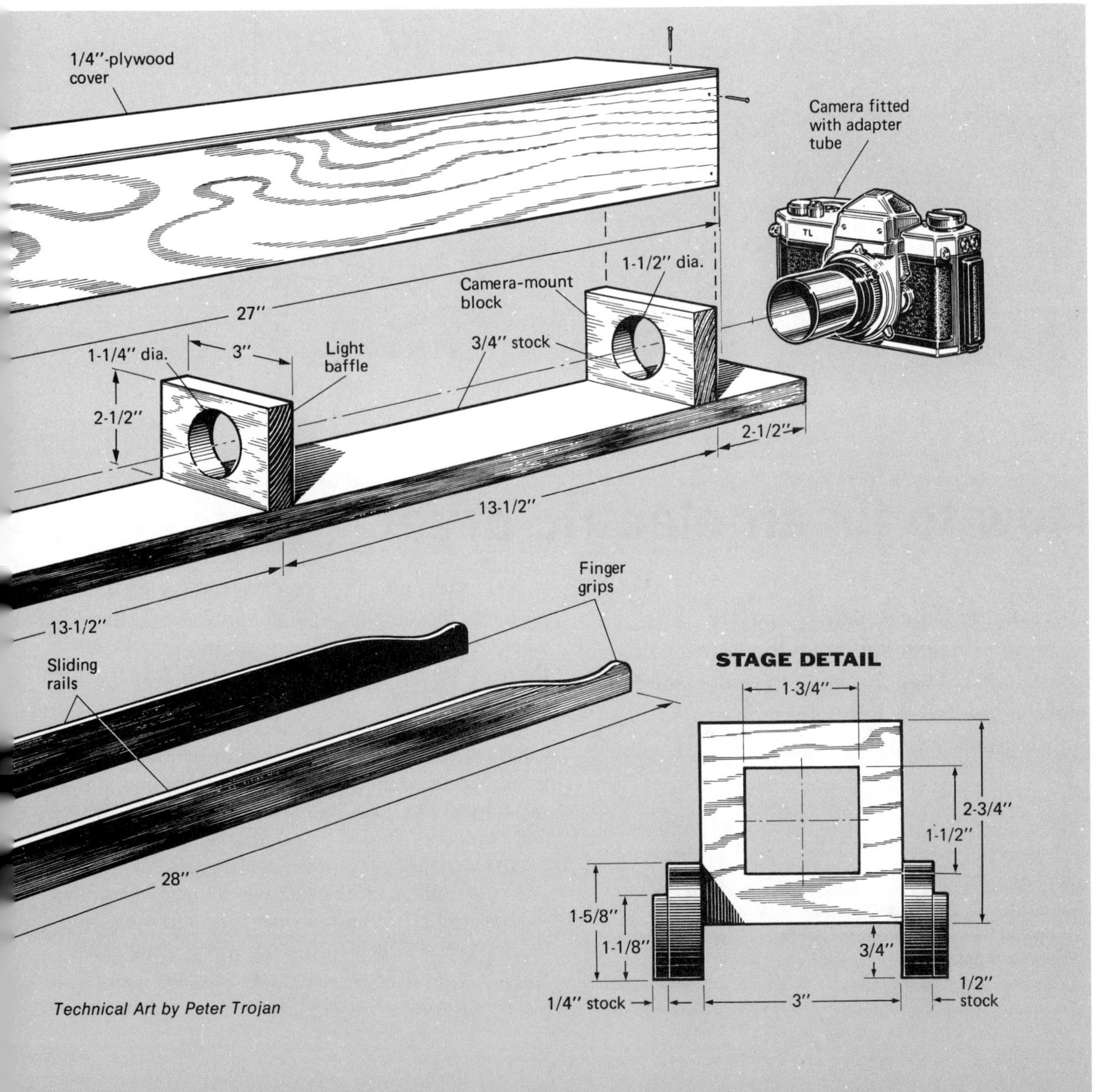

Technical Art by Peter Trojan

Typical dryer components

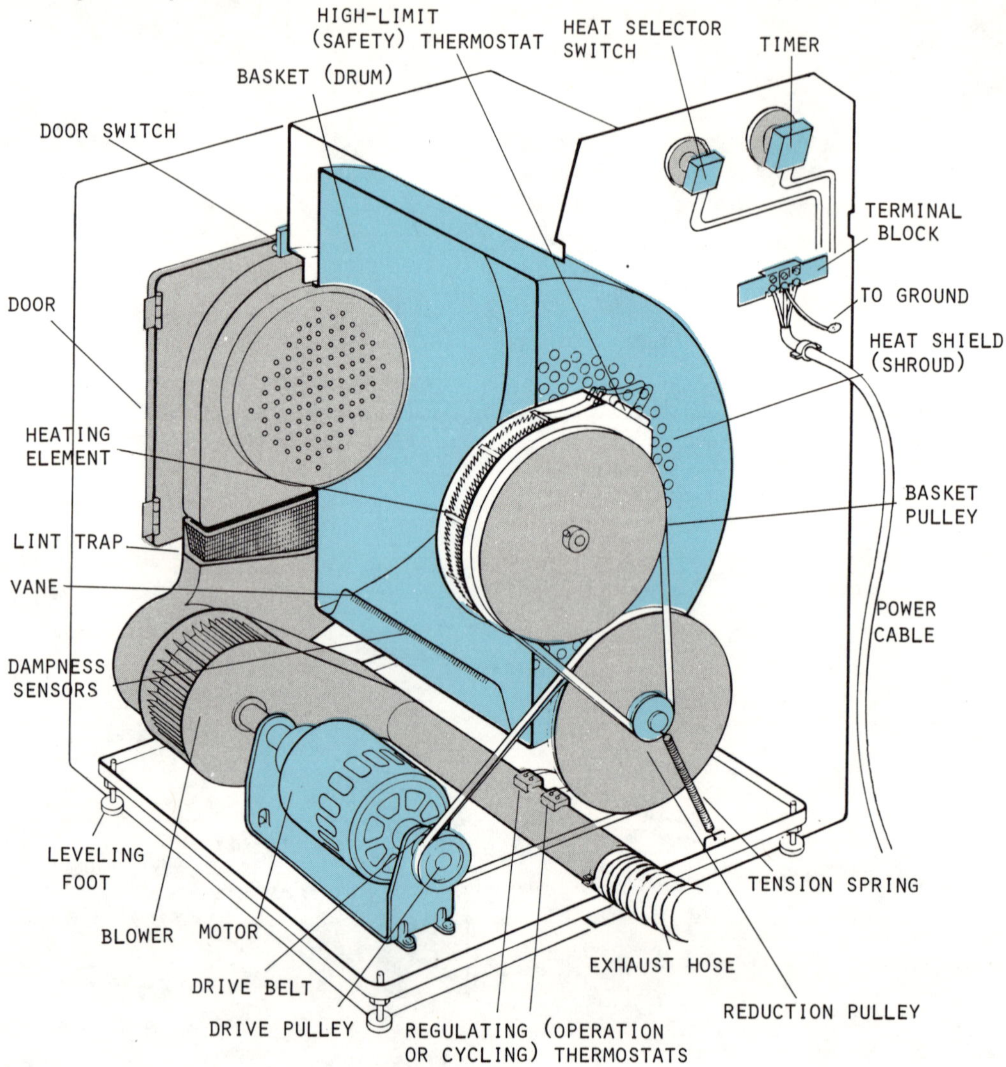

How to fix an electric dryer

All electric clothes dryers operate on the same principle and have the same basic components. They are easy to understand, especially if you follow the helpful charts and diagrams on these pages

SEE ALSO
Appliance repair . . . Appliances . . . Electrical wiring . . . Heaters, water . . . Irons . . . Washing machines

AN AUTOMATIC CLOTHES DRYER is probably the simplest of major appliances: Basically, its function is to pass hot air across and through wet clothes to evaporate moisture from them.

The major components of an electric dryer are a basket to hold the clothes, fan or blower to move the air, motor to turn both basket and fan, resistance-wire heating element to heat the air, and controls for motor and heating element.

An electric dryer is normally run on a 30-amp., 220-v. circuit, with the heating element operating on a full 220 v. and the motor on 110 v. Some dryers are designed to run on 110-v. circuits as well. But, while this is perfectly safe, the heating element is less efficient at the lower voltage and drying time is considerably longer.

Nearly all electric dryers work like this: Air at room temperature is drawn into the appliance at the bottom or through front or rear openings. It is passed to the heating element, heated and drawn into the clothes basket. In dryers with unshrouded baskets, hot air enters through holes at the rear of the basket; in dryers in which the basket is shrouded, hot air is drawn into the shroud and enters the basket through holes around its side. Passing over and through tumbling clothes in the basket, the hot air picks up moisture and lint (a result of normal wear) from them. When it leaves the basket at the front through ducting built into the door assembly, the air passes through a screen lint trap, usually just below the door. The air then is sucked into the blower, and forced through a duct to an exhaust hose that leads outdoors.

Motor and heating element are controlled by a timer, a heat-selector switch, two or more thermostats, a door switch and, in newer machines, an electronic dampness sensor. The thermostat located near the heating element, called a high-limit thermostat, is a safety device and will not trip if the machine is operating normally. One or more regulating thermostats govern the heating element in normal operation. In old dryers, these may be of the adjustable, capillary type (you should *not* attempt to adjust one of these). Simple bimetal thermostats are more common. Regulating thermostats are usually located in the door assembly or on the exhaust duct, one for each heat setting for which the dryer is designed.

A dryer with a permanent-press cycle may have a "cool-off" regulating thermostat to run the motor with heat off until clothes cool to about 115°F.

Operation of electronic dampness sensors is based on the fact that the electrical resistance of clothing increases as it dries. Damp clothes

TIMERS

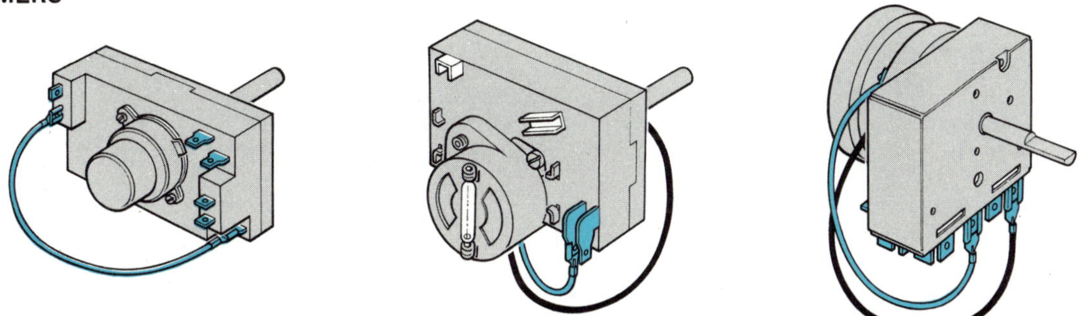

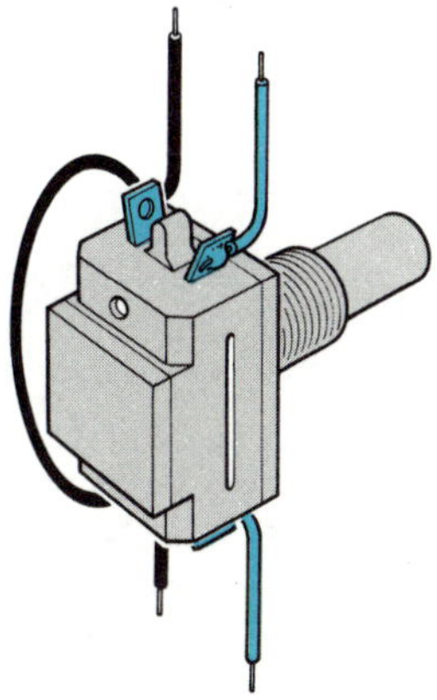

DOOR SWITCHES

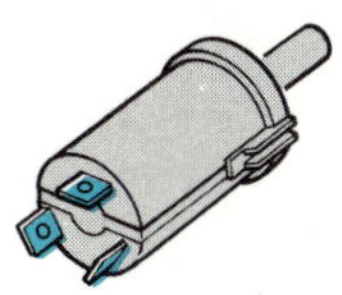

Motor does not start

POSSIBLE CAUSES	WHAT TO TRY
1. Line fuse blown.	Replace fuse (or reset circuit breaker).
2. Door open.	Close door tightly.
3. Timer defective.	Check the line voltage at timer. Turn timer on and place 115-v. test lamp across its terminals. If you get a reading, it indicates open contacts. Replace contacts or timer.
4. Door switch defective.	Remove wires from door switch, place continuity tester across terminals and press button. No reading indicates a defective switch. Replace.
5. Motor wiring loose or disconnected.	Tighten or reconnect loose or disconnected wires.
6. Centrifugal switch defective.	Refer to the manufacturer's schematic diagram for switch terminals on the motor; place continuity tester across terminals. If you get no reading, replace switch or motor.
7. Motor defective.	Direct-test motor with test jumper. If motor still fails to run, replace.

Motor hums

POSSIBLE CAUSES	WHAT TO TRY
1. Voltage too high or too low.	Check panel fuses or circuit breakers. Check voltage at dryer line or terminals. Any variation greater than 15 percent from normal can cause hum. Notify power company.
2. Centrifugal switch in motor stuck.	Remove both motor and switch. Grease shaft, clean the contacts and reassemble. If the switch still sticks, replace it.
3. Basket binding or idler wheel broken.	Check the basket while turning it by hand. Replace any worn or broken idler wheels. Check leveling of machine.
4. Motor defective.	Direct-test motor with test jumper. Replace it if it fails to operate properly.

MOTOR AND MOUNT

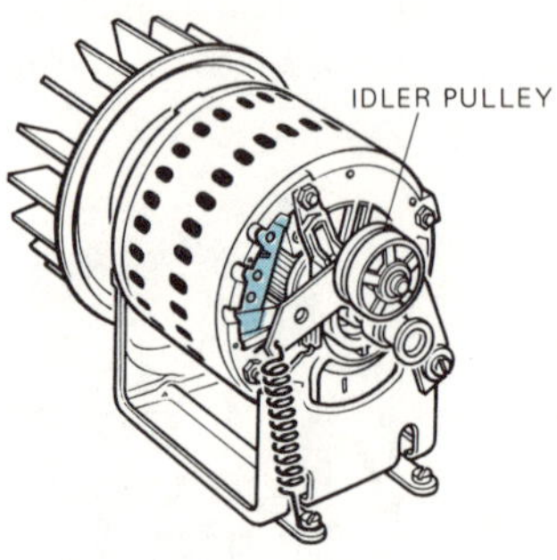

THERMOSTATS

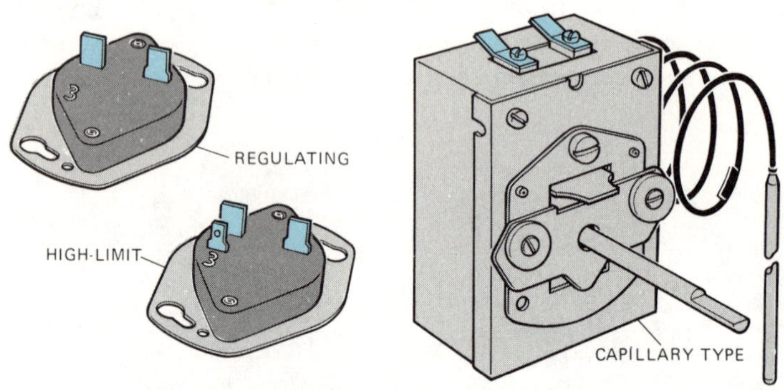

Motor hums, basket does not rotate

POSSIBLE CAUSES	WHAT TO TRY
1. Broken belt.	Remove back of dryer and replace any broken belts you find.
2. Loose pulley.	Check setscrews in all pulleys. If pulleys are slipping on their shafts, realign them first and then tighten setscrews.
3. Tension spring broken.	Replace broken tension spring.
4. Basket binding or idler wheel broken.	Check the basket while turning it by hand. Replace any worn or broken idler wheels. Check leveling of machine.

BASKET DRIVE WITH REDUCTION PULLEY

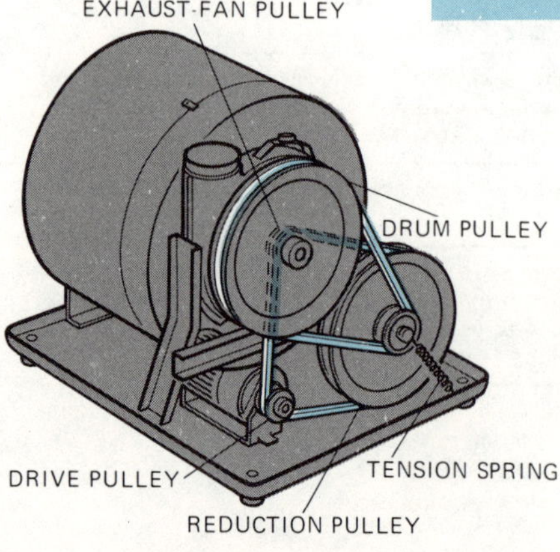

Noisy operation

POSSIBLE CAUSES	WHAT TO TRY
1. Loose fan.	Retighten fan-blade setscrew on motor shaft.
2. Loose objects caught in basket.	Remove all loose objects from basket.
3. Loose motor pulley.	Retighten motor-pulley setscrew.
4. Worn belt.	Replace any worn or frayed belts.
5. Basket binding.	Turn basket by hand to locate the point of binding. Check felt gaskets, wire harnesses and leveling of the unit.
6. Vibration.	Check for a loose fan blade, an out-of-balance fan blade, also for worn basket bearings and motor mounts. Tighten any loosened parts and replace worn parts.

QUICK corrective action—when the dryer runs noisily—is the best insurance against more serious damage to the dryer later.

Clothes dry slowly or not at all

POSSIBLE CAUSES	WHAT TO TRY
1. Drum overloaded.	Check size of load. Refer to the manufacturer's minimum and maximum standards.
2. Operating thermostat defective.	Place a thermometer in an exhaust duct, then record the temperatures at which the dryer heat is turned on and off. Check these figures against the manufacturer's specifications. If they should be out of the suggested range, replace the thermostat.
3. Lint trap clogged.	Clean lint trap thoroughly.
4. Heating element open.	Place a continuity tester across the heating-element terminals. If there is no reading, an open coil is indicated. Replace.
5. Exhaust hose clogged.	Clear exhaust hose.
6. Timer set too low.	Check your owner's operating manual; then increase the timer setting.
7. Blown panel fuse or tripped circuit breaker.	Check fuse or circuit breaker at the panel; then replace or reset it. If fuse or breaker should blow or trip again, then check for a short circuit in the heating element.
8. 110-v. operation.	If possible, change to 220-v. operation. Clothes takes 2½ to 3 times longer to dry on 110-v. line.
9. Clothes excessively wet when placed in the dryer.	See that clothes are spun-dry or wrung out—not dripping wet—before they are placed in dryer.

TOO OFTEN, slow drying will occur because the maker's instructions are not followed to the letter. The first step is to reread the operating instructions.

continued →

complete a circuit across sensor elements located on or near the basket vanes. By measuring their resistance in this circuit, the sensor determines whether or not a desired dryness has been reached, and shuts off the dryer when it has. Repair of these sophisticated electronic controls should also be turned over to a qualified serviceman.

A dryer basket may be driven by a belt that passes around it and also passes over a pulley on the motor shaft. Where the dryer is equipped with a shrouded basket, that basket is usually driven through two belts and a reduction pulley.

A dryer motor has two windings—one for starting and one for running. It is shifted from the former to the latter winding by a centrifugal switch. The motor terminals and their corresponding wires are usually coded with matching colors. Refer to the manufacturer's schematic diagram for correct terminals when you test your equipment.

The troubleshooting charts on these pages should help you correct most common electric dryer problems. Gas dryers are discussed in another article. When working on your electric dryer, or any other appliance, follow these safety precautions:

- Refer to your manufacturer's manual to locate components.
- Be sure that power is *turned off* before you handle components.
- Make all of your continuity tests with *power off*.
- When making tests with a 115-v. lamp, turn

DRYER ASSEMBLY

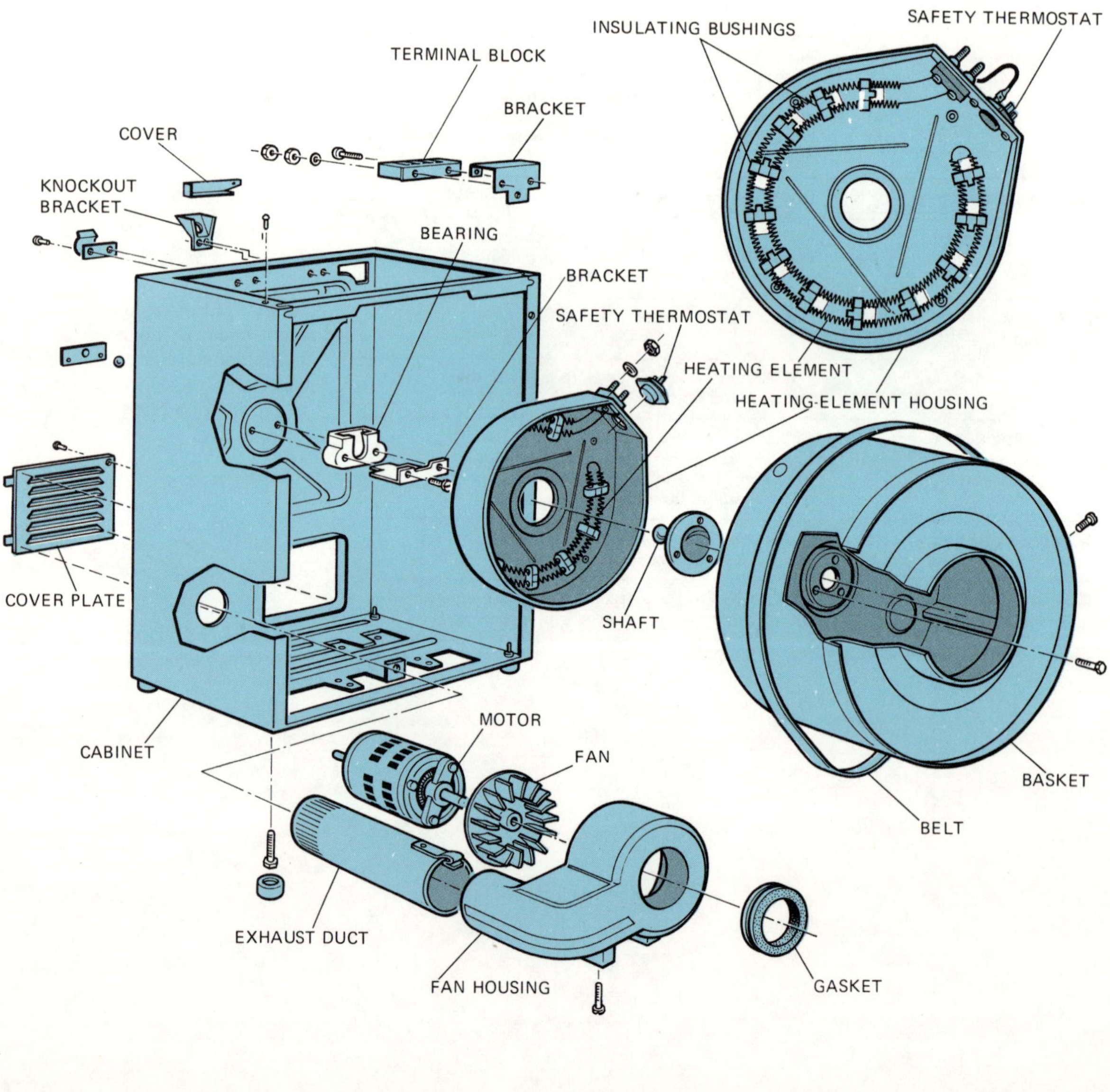

AIRFLOW PATTERN IN TYPICAL DRYER

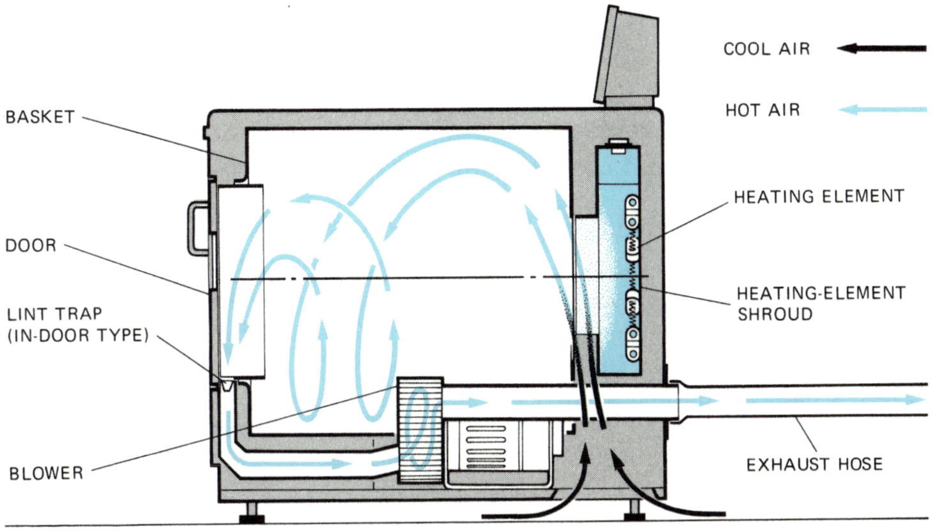

Dryer does not shut off

POSSIBLE CAUSES	WHAT TO TRY
1. Timer defective.	Check for a stuck timer or welded contact points. Replace.
2. Door switch defective.	Remove wires from the door-switch terminals; then place continuity tester across terminals. If there is a reading before the switch button is pressed, replace.
3. Operating thermostat defective.	Check thermostat against the manufacturer's specifications with a thermometer in the exhaust duct. If defective, replace.
4. Motor grounded.	Remove wires from motor terminals. Touch one lead of the continuity tester to a terminal and the other lead to the motor housing. If you get a reading on the tester, the motor is grounded. Replace.

power off first, connect the lamp, turn power on again, observe the result, then turn power off again and disconnect the lamp.

■ Make sure that the appliance is properly grounded, in accordance with your local electrical code.

■ Use replacement parts that meet factory specifications; those that are made by the manufacturer of the appliance are your best bet.

Extra tips: Before replacing an electrical part you believe to be faulty, make sure that the problem isn't caused by a loose connection. Tighten all connections after replacing an electrical part. Use new parts, not rebuilt ones, unless your appliance is so old that you can expect little further service from it.

How to fix a gas dryer

Many of the problems of gas-fueled clothes dryers are the same as those of electric dryers, except when it comes to the gas burner's controls and safety devices

A GAS CLOTHES DRYER, like an electric dryer, is designed to remove moisture from damp clothes by passing hot air over and through them. In place of a simple heating element, a gas dryer has a burner with complex controls and safety devices. While controls and ignition systems vary from one manufacturer to another, there are a few basic types and troubleshooting charts on the next five pages will tell you how to deal with the most common problems that may arise. Gas problems more complicated than those covered in the charts should be handled only by a qualified serviceman.

Many electrical and mechanical functions of a gas dryer are the same as those of an electric model and many of its problems are handled the same way—these are also covered in the charts. But the electronic dampness sensors found on many newer gas and electric dryers are delicate devices best left to the serviceman.

Typical gas dryer components

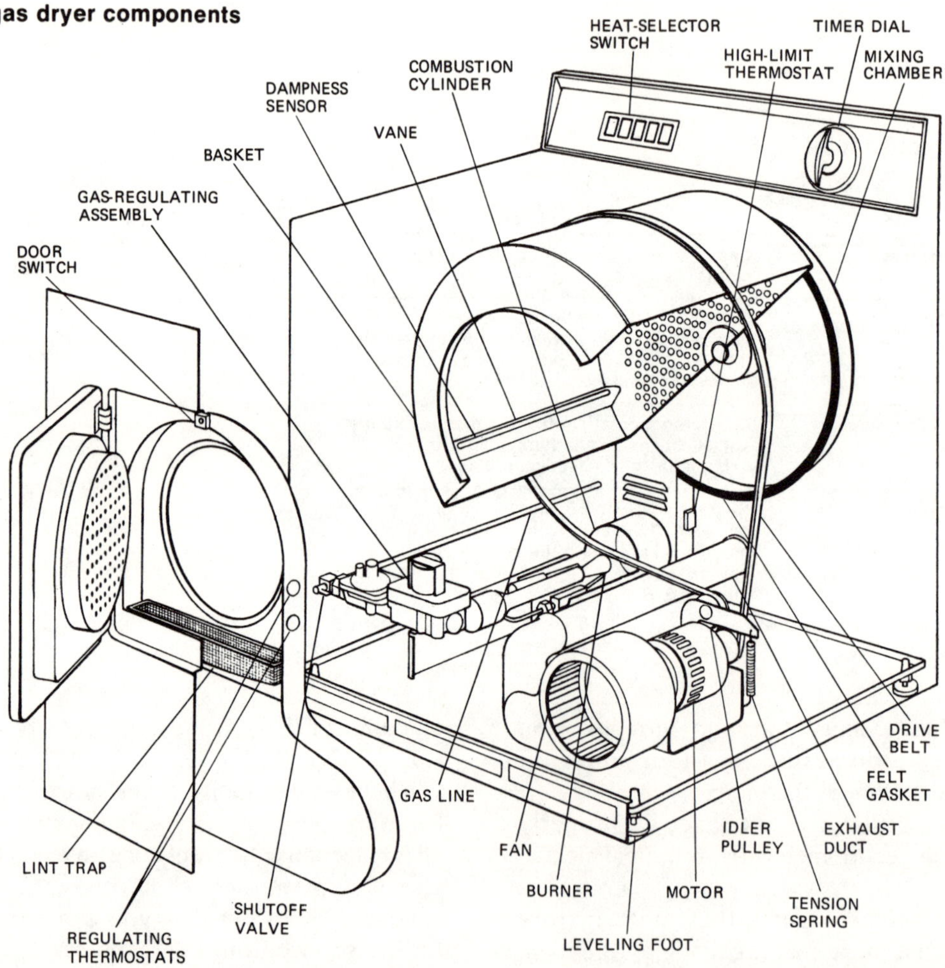

SEE ALSO

**Appliance repair . . . Appliances . . .
Heaters, water . . . Humidifiers . . . Irons . . .
Ranges . . . Washing machines**

Motor does not start

POSSIBLE CAUSES	WHAT TO TRY
1. Fuse blown.	Replace fuse (or reset circuit breaker).
2. Door open.	Close door tightly.
3. Timer defective.	Check the line voltage at timer. Turn timer on and place 115-v. test lamp across its terminals. If you get a reading, it indicates open contacts. Replace contacts or timer.
4. Door switch defective.	Remove wires from the door switch, then place continuity tester across the switch terminals and press button. No reading indicates a defective switch. Replace.
5. Motor wiring loose or disconnected.	Tighten or reconnect loose or disconnected wires.
6. Centrifugal switch defective.	Refer to the manufacturer's schematic diagram for switch terminals on the motor; place continuity tester across terminals. If you get no reading, replace switch or motor.
7. Motor defective.	Direct-test motor with test jumper. If motor still fails to run, replace.

DOOR SWITCH

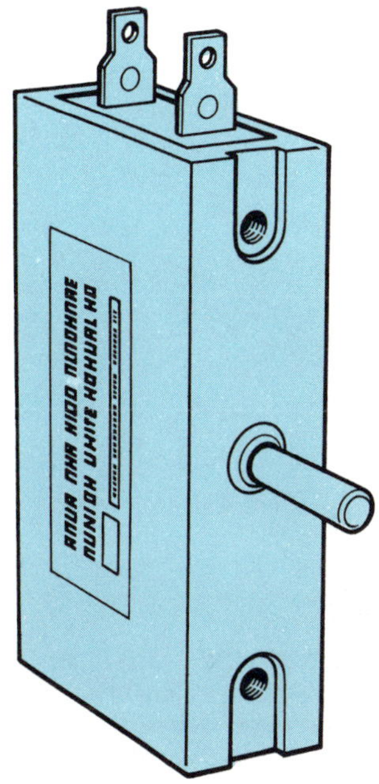

Motor hums

POSSIBLE CAUSES	WHAT TO TRY
1. Centrifugal switch in motor stuck.	Remove both motor and switch. Grease the shaft, clean the contacts and reassemble. If the switch still sticks, replace it.
2. Basket binding or idler wheel broken.	Check the basket while turning it by hand. Replace any worn or broken idler wheels. Check leveling of machine.
3. Motor defective.	Direct-test motor with test jumper. Replace motor if it fails to operate properly.

TIMER

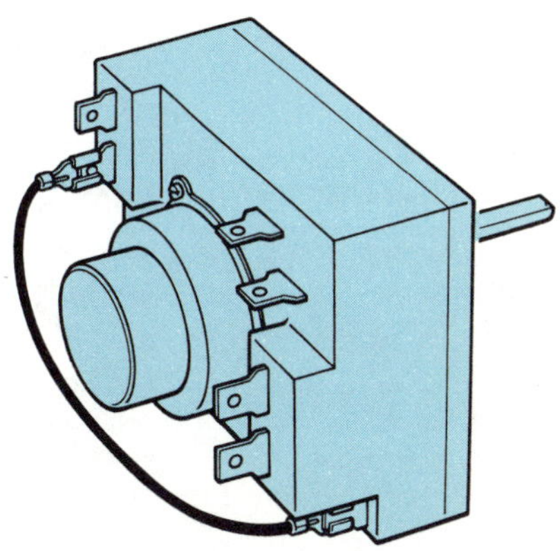

Motor runs, basket does not rotate

POSSIBLE CAUSES	WHAT TO TRY
1. Broken belt.	Remove back of dryer and replace any broken belts you find.
2. Loose pulley.	Check setscrews in all pulleys. If pulleys are slipping on their shafts, realign them first and then tighten setscrews.
3. Tension spring broken	Replace broken tension spring.
4. Basket binding or idler wheel broken.	Check the basket while turning it by hand. Replace any worn or broken idler wheels. Check leveling of machine.

TIMER

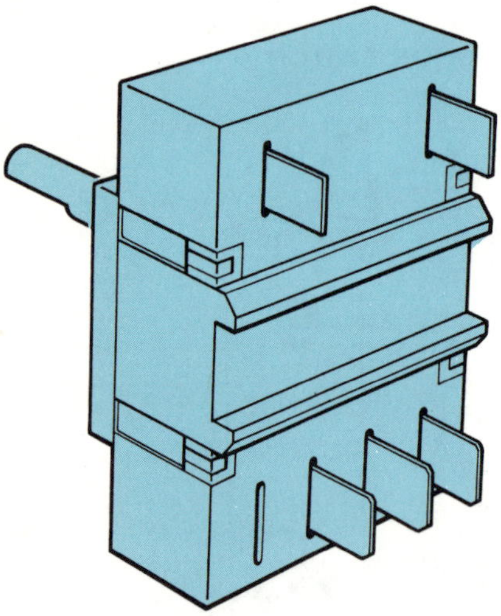

PATTERN OF AIRFLOW in most gas dryers is shown below—air is mixed with hot flue products behind basket, sucked through it and through lint trap to fan; then it's forced out through exhaust duct and hose. Below, right, is the type of basket-drive system generally found in the dryers that do not use the single-belt drive.

Noisy operation

POSSIBLE CAUSES	WHAT TO TRY
1. Loose fan.	Retighten fan-blade setscrew on motor shaft.
2. Loose objects caught in basket.	Remove all loose objects from basket.
3. Loose motor pulley.	Retighten motor-pulley setscrew.
4. Worn belt.	Replace any worn or frayed belts.
5. Basket binding.	Turn basket by hand to locate the point of binding. Check felt gaskets, wire harnesses and leveling of the unit.
6. Vibration.	Check for a loose fan blade, an out-of-balance fan blade, also for worn basket bearings and motor mounts. Tighten any loosened parts and replace worn parts.

Dryer does not shut off

POSSIBLE CAUSES	WHAT TO TRY
1. Timer defective.	Check for a stuck timer or welded contact points. Replace.
2. Door switch defective.	Remove wires from the door-switch terminals; then place continuity tester across terminals. If there is a reading before the switch button is pressed, replace switch.
3. Operating thermostat defective.	Check thermostat against the manufacturer's specifications with a thermometer in the exhaust duct. If defective, replace.
4. Motor grounded.	Remove wires from motor terminals. Touch one lead of the continuity tester to a terminal and the other lead to the motor housing. If you get a reading on the tester, the motor is grounded. Replace.

AIRFLOW IN DRYER

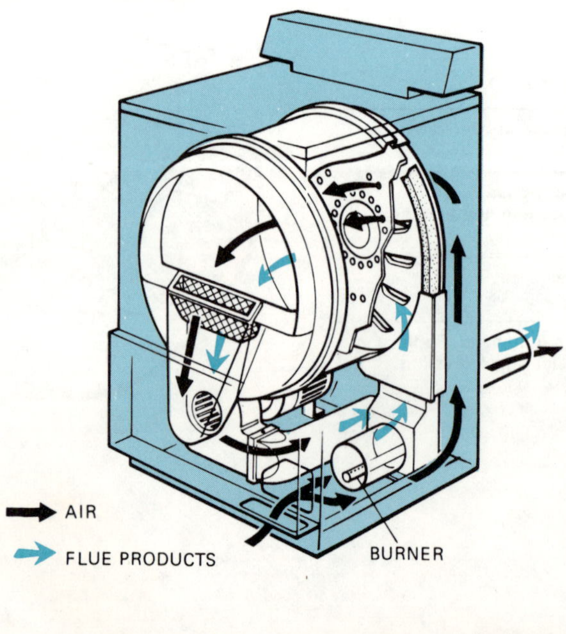

BASKET DRIVE WITH REDUCTION PULLEY

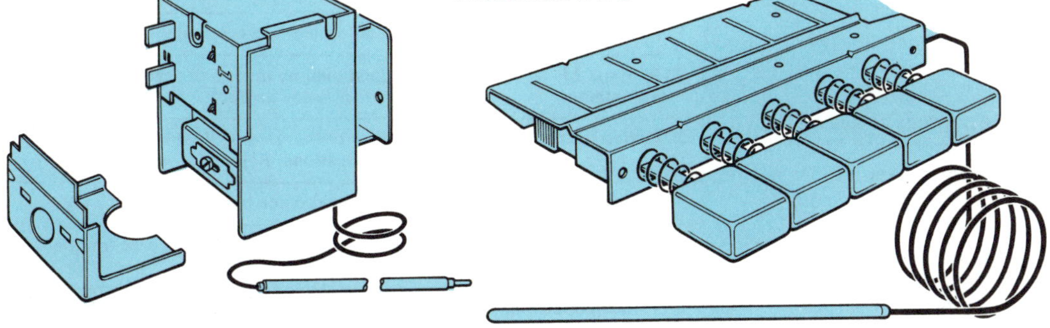

CAPILLARY THERMOSTATS

Clothes dry slowly or not at all

POSSIBLE CAUSES	WHAT TO TRY
1. Basket overloaded.	Check size of load. Refer to manufacturer's minimum and maximum standards.
2. Operating thermostat defective.	Check thermostat against the manufacturer's specifications with a thermostat in the exhaust duct. Replace thermostat if it does not operate at correct temperatures.
3. Lint trap clogged.	Clean lint trap thoroughly.
4. Exhaust hose clogged.	Clear exhaust hose.
5. Main burner orifice too small.	Check size of orifice (usually stamped on fitting) against manufacturer's specifications. Replace if incorrect.
6. Timer set too low.	Check owner's operating manual and increase the timer setting.
7. Ignition assembly defective.	Refer to following charts that cover pilot and ignition problems.

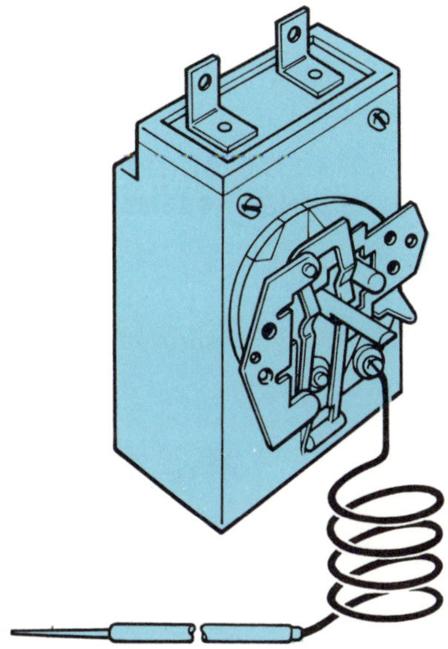

BIMETAL THERMOSTATS

Pilot will not light or goes out

POSSIBLE CAUSES	WHAT TO TRY
1. Loose connections in thermocouple circuit.	Check thermocouple fittings and tightness of screws on terminal leads.
2. Vent pipe off fan housing; draft blows pilot out.	Check position of the vent pipe (exhaust duct). Reposition it if necessary and secure it with a retaining clip.
3. Pilot burner or orifice dirty.	Check and clean pilot burner and orifice. Do not ream orifice.
4. Filter clogged.	Clean or replace pilot line filter.
5. Thermocouple defective.	Check thermocouple voltage with pilot on. Reading should be between 10 and 18 millivolts. Check against manufacturer's specifications.
6. Magnetic (Baso) valve defective.	Check thermocouple voltage as above. If okay, replace Baso valve.
7. Low gas pressure.	Pressure after regulator should be 2 to 3 ounces per square inch, or show a 3½-in. water column in a U-tube manometer, with the main burner operating. Check with gas company if low.

CAUTION: Be sure power is turned *off* before you handle components. Make all continuity tests with power *off*. When using a test lamp, keep power *off* while connecting and disconnecting the lamp. Use your manufacturer's manual to locate components, and use only replacement parts that meet his specifications.

Pilot burning high, low or erratically

POSSIBLE CAUSES	WHAT TO TRY
1. Orifice clogged.	Clean orifice—do not ream.
2. Pilot out of adjustment.	Adjust pilot by means of screw on Baso valve to raise or lower flame.
3. Orifice wrong size.	Check orifice size against the manufacturer's specifications. Replace if wrong.
4. Filter clogged.	Clean or replace pilot line filter.
5. Gas pressure too high or too low.	See "Low gas pressure" in preceding chart.
6. Yellow-tipped flame.	Open air shutter or use smaller orifice. Clean orifice—do not ream.
7. Orange flame.	Clean orifice, surrounding area—do not ream.

MANUAL-IGNITION BURNER ASSEMBLY

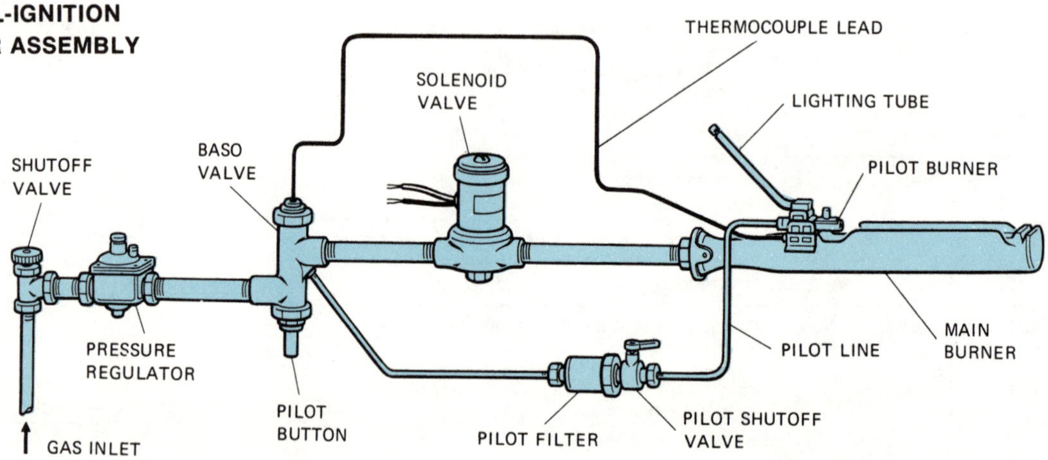

MANUAL-IGNITION BURNER

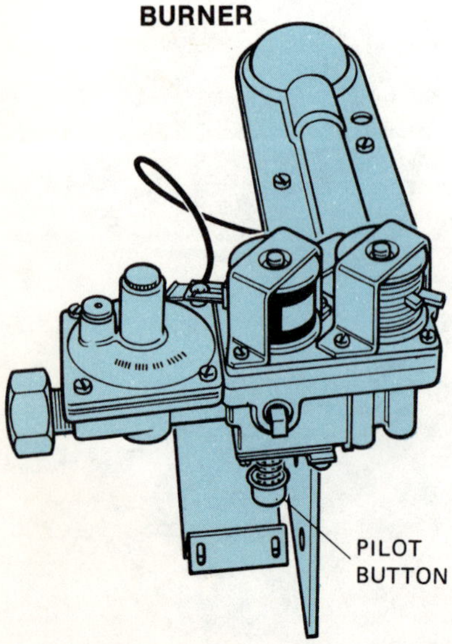

Pilot lights, main burner does not light

POSSIBLE CAUSES	WHAT TO TRY
1. Orifice plugged.	Clean main burner orifice.
2. Main solenoid coil defective.	Disconnect power and remove leads from solenoid coil. Place continuity tester across terminals. No reading indicates a defective or open solenoid. Replace.
3. Open circuit to main solenoid.	Disconnect power. Check continuity of circuit through pilot switch, door switch, thermostats and line fuse. Correct wherever circuit is open.
4. Timer defective.	Turn timer on. Check voltage at the solenoid with 115-v. test lamp. No voltage indicates a defective timer. Replace.
5. Valve closed.	Open valve in line to main burner.
6. Centrifugal switch in motor defective.	See "Centrifugal switch defective" in chart titled "Motor does not start".

Glow coil does not heat

POSSIBLE CAUSES	WHAT TO TRY
1. Broken or damaged coil.	Replace coil.
2. Leads broken or shorted to housing.	Replace broken leads; remove leads from shorted points. Check transformer secondary voltage.
3. Open circuit in transformer	Disconnect power and check transformer windings for continuity. If open, replace transformer.
4. Open circuit between timer and transformer.	Disconnect power; check continuity through warp-switch (bimetal) contacts, fuses, safety pilot contacts, timer contacts. Correct wherever open.

ELECTRIC-IGNITION ASSEMBLY

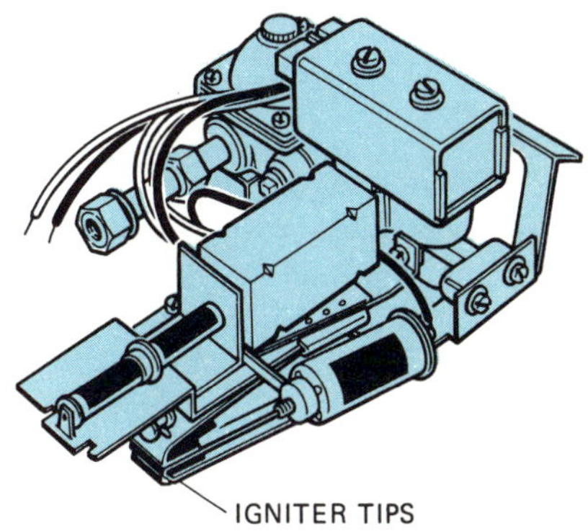

GLOW-COIL ASSEMBLY WITH PILOT

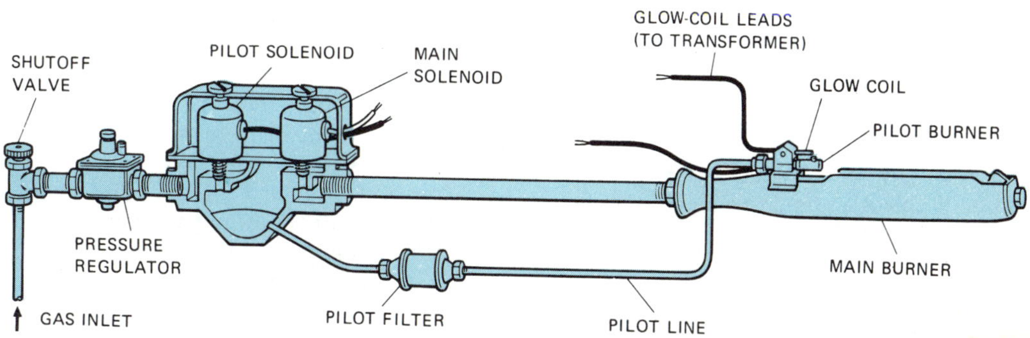

Glow coil heats, pilot does not ignite

POSSIBLE CAUSES	WHAT TO TRY
1. Orifice plugged.	Clean pilot orifice—do not ream.
2. Valve shut.	Open gas valve.
3. Pilot solenoid defective.	Disconnect power and solenoid leads. Test for continuity across terminals. No reading indicates a defective solenoid. Replace.
4. Vent pipe off fan housing causing draft across pilot.	Check position of the vent pipe (exhaust duct). Reposition it if necessary and secure it with a retaining clip.
5. Coil not hot enough.	Glow coil should be white hot. Refer to the following chart.

GLOW-COIL BURNER ASSEMBLY

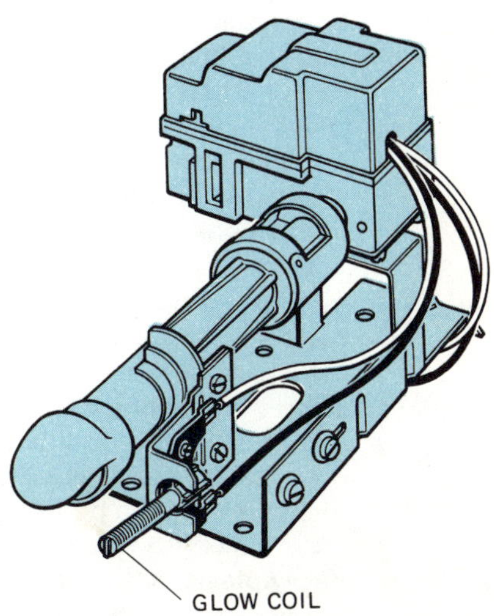

Glow coil not hot enough

POSSIBLE CAUSES	WHAT TO TRY
1. Loose connection or short circuit.	Check and tighten all connections in the circuit. Reposition leads to avoid shorting them to bracket or housing.
2. Low voltage.	Check the line voltage, then check the voltage on both sides of the transformer against the manufacturer's specifications. If low, replace the transformer.

Waiting game

Why do I have so much trouble taking off old finishes with a remover? I put the stuff on, but can't get the old finish off. After several applications, I still have to do a lot of scraping.—I.L., Ore.

Perhaps you don't wait long enough for the remover to "work," or you may be using a liquid remover on a vertical surface, where a paste-type should be used. Give it time—10, 15, 20 minutes or even more—to cut through the old finish. You'll find the washoff-type less messy.

Rare 'find' in attic

While cleaning the attic of an old home I recently occupied, I found an odd-looking hook, apparently a brass casting shaped like a dolphin with the tail and part of the body turned up to form the hook. What looks like a lagscrew extends about 3½ in. from the mouth. Can you tell what it is, and what it's for?—P.N., Me.

Judging from your description, you've made a rather rare find. I'm guessing it's what was known as a "jamb hook." The lagscrew end was turned into a hole in the mortar between bricks of a huge colonial fireplace to hold fire-tending tools.

Bugs in fireplace wood

I've been told that if I bring fireplace wood into the house I'll populate the place with bugs, that in time they'll eat up the furniture, and maybe the house itself. True, or false?—R.E., Mo.

Mostly false, if you're referring to the several pieces of wood you bring into the house in a carrier for the evening fire and not to the storing of a winter's supply of wood somewhere inside the house. True, you might bring in an occasional spider, a wood roach and even some wood borers. The latter won't riddle the furniture—they'll be done to a turn by the time the fire becomes ashes—and the spiders and roaches are objectionable only when they become sufficiently warmed to race for cover. Usually these stay put until you replenish the fire.

The bug to worry about is the carpenter ant. If he gets inside the house via the wood carrier there's almost sure to be trouble. Some homeowners spray their woodpile, piece by piece with a spray containing chlordane in a recommended mix, paying special attention to any cracks or crevices. It's wise to stack the winter supply some distance from the house. Lay down two "stringers," stack the wood on these over a piece of heavy plastic and then wrap the plastic up over the stack to keep the wood dry. Remove only what you'll need for one evening.

Old red paint

How do you mix the old red paints that were so often used on colonial furnishings? What are the ingredients? I want to finish a reproduction of an old blanket chest I've made.—A.F., Vt.

I've had fair success simply by thinning red paints of the color desired and using them as a stain, rather than a paint. The trick is to get the paint thinned to just the right consistency—not too watery. If it's too thin you generally get a splotchy coloring; if too thick you get an ordinary paint job. You'll have to determine the consistency by tests on small pieces of the same wood.

You can also use artist's reds, thinned so that they act as a stain, rather than a paint. At best it's a tricky business and I can't go along with the procedure all the way. Neither do I recommend that you try the old "recipes" as some of the materials are difficult, if not impossible to obtain. There are several old recipes and, just for the fun of it, here's one: It calls for 3 pounds of red oxide of iron, 2 quarts of skim milk, 8 ounces of fresh-slaked lime, 6 ounces of linseed oil, 2 ounces of white Burgundy pitch, all mixed with whiskey to a fairly thick liquid. The lime is slaked in water, exposed to the air for a time and then thinned with one-fourth of the skimmed milk. The pitch is dissolved in the oil before adding to the original mix a little at a time, then the rest of the milk and finally the iron oxide, stirring in the ingredients as you go. Presumably this makes a paint, not a stain, but according to the record such mixtures were used before ready-mixed paint was available.

Checking for termites

A neighbor and myself have reason to suspect the presence of termites in our houses. How can we check for sure?—George Desmond, Indianapolis.

Termites usually indicate their presence by tiny mud tunnels on masonry foundations, these tunnels extending from ground level or below up the walls to the wood framing. Tunnels can appear on masonry walls, inside or outside, in a crawl-space or on a basement wall. To discover them, one must make a foot-by-foot search, inside and out. There are other wood-boring insects—often mistaken for termites—that attack buildings. Powderpost beetles and carpenter ants are those most often found. They make small entry holes in exposed ends of rafters and especially in floor joists and the wood posts that support center beams in basements. Look for holes in the beams and wood dust below them, as an indication of their presence.

Performa - Maytag
Model: P4EZ000AYW Rev. 11
Serial: 11460253UH 5 KW

METRIC CONVERSION

Conversion factors can be carried so far they become impractical. In cases below where an entry is exact it is followed by an asterisk (*). Where considerable rounding off has taken place, the entry is followed by a + or a - sign.

CUSTOMARY TO METRIC

Linear Measure

inches	millimeters
1/16	1.5875*
1/8	3.2
3/16	4.8
1/4	6.35*
5/16	7.9
3/8	9.5
7/16	11.1
1/2	12.7*
9/16	14.3
5/8	15.9
11/16	17.5
3/4	19.05*
13/16	20.6
7/8	22.2
15/16	23.8
1	25.4*

inches	centimeters
1	2.54*
2	5.1
3	7.6
4	10.2
5	12.7*
6	15.2
7	17.8
8	20.3
9	22.9
10	25.4*
11	27.9
12	30.5

feet	centimeters	meters
1	30.48*	.3048*
2	61	.61
3	91	.91
4	122	1.22
5	152	1.52
6	183	1.83
7	213	2.13
8	244	2.44
9	274	2.74
10	305	3.05
50	1524*	15.24*
100	3048*	30.48*

1 yard =
.9144* meters
1 rod =
5.0292* meters
1 mile =
1.6 kilometers
1 nautical mile =
1.852* kilometers

Fluid Measure

(Milliliters [ml] and cubic centimeters [cc or cu cm] are equivalent, but it is customary to use milliliters for liquids.)

1 cu in = 16.39 ml
1 fl oz = 29.6 ml
1 cup = 237 ml
1 pint = 473 ml
1 quart = 946 ml
= .946 liters
1 gallon = 3785 ml
= 3.785 liters
Formula (exact):
fluid ounces × 29.573 529 562 5*
= milliliters

Weights

ounces	grams
1	28.3
2	56.7
3	85
4	113
5	142
6	170
7	198
8	227
9	255
10	283
11	312
12	340
13	369
14	397
15	425
16	454

Formula (exact):
ounces × 28.349 523 125* =
grams

pounds	kilograms
1	.45
2	.9
3	1.4
4	1.8
5	2.3
6	2.7
7	3.2
8	3.6
9	4.1
10	4.5

1 short ton (2000 lbs) =
907 kilograms (kg)
Formula (exact):
pounds × .453 592 37* =
kilograms

Volume

1 cu in = 16.39 cubic centimeters (cc)
1 cu ft = 28 316.7 cc
1 bushel = 35 239.1 cc
1 peck = 8 809.8 cc

Area

1 sq in = 6.45 sq cm
1 sq ft = 929 sq cm
= .093 sq meters
1 sq yd = .84 sq meters
1 acre = 4 046.9 sq meters
= .404 7 hectares
1 sq mile = 2 589 988 sq meters
= 259 hectares
= 2.589 9 sq kilometers

Kitchen Measure

1 teaspoon = 4.93 milliliters (ml)
1 Tablespoon = 14.79 milliliters (ml)

Miscellaneous

1 British thermal unit (Btu) (mean)
= 1 055.9 joules
1 calorie (mean) = 4.19 joules
1 horsepower = 745.7 watts
= .75 kilowatts
caliber (diameter of a firearm's bore in hundredths of an inch)
= .254 millimeters (mm)
1 atmosphere pressure = 101 325* pascals (newtons per sq meter)
1 pound per square inch (psi) = 6 895 pascals
1 pound per square foot = 47.9 pascals
1 knot = 1.85 kilometers per hour
25 miles per hour = 40.2 kilometers per hour
50 miles per hour = 80.5 kilometers per hour
75 miles per hour = 120.7 kilometers per hour